CLEARLY LOVE

Harris has provided the church with a beautiful gift. Within the pages of *Clearly Love* we hear the passionate heart of a loving parent and a courageous pastor. After providing a moving account of her own personal experiences as a parent, Harris presents a clear, concise, and highly readable articulation of the biblical and theological evidence for both affirming and non-affirming perspectives. The church can no longer avoid discussions about its relationship to the LGBTQ+ community. *Clearly Love* will help dispel much of the harmful silence that leaves many congregations naively confused and many of our LGBTQ+ brothers and sisters shamed, excluded, and marginalized from the life and worship of the local church. Any church or small group looking for a springboard to facilitate an informed and sensitive conversation could do no better than to begin that dialogue with *Clearly Love*. Highly recommended.

Brian D. Cunnington, Ed.D, former professor emeritus of counselling at Tyndale University and author of *Open Wide the Gates: An Argument for Welcome, Affirmation, and Inclusion of Gay and Lesbian People in the Local Church*

One of the most conflict-ridden questions in the church today is the question of how the teachings of Scripture should be interpreted and applied when it comes to issues related to same-sex relationships and gender identity. For many Christians, even considering this question can come with a large dose of fear or put them in hot water with their faith community. In *Clearly Love*, Harris shows us that it doesn't have to be this way. Her book is a well-organized roadmap that helps readers to explore various interpretations of biblical texts, equipping Christians to navigate these tough conversations with respectful curiosity, generosity, and integrity.

Katherine Johnson, Th.M, project manager, The Reformation Project

It is uncommon for a book to be at the same time generous, precise, and accessible—but *Clearly Love* is all of that and more. With this lucid and engaging book, Harris frames the sexuality question personally, explains the biblical arguments fairly, illuminates the theology insightfully, and models the debate pastorally. The result is something that many people crave at both the core and the margins of the church: a safe place to consider both sides of the issue with grace and clarity. Because the book is compelling without being alienating, both non-affirming and affirming Christians should feel seen within its pages, even as they disagree. For this reason, it is a gift to church unity as well as to understanding.

Despite having read many popular and academic books on this topic, as I read *Clearly Love* it rose slowly to the top of both sides of my recommendation list. Seminary profs could assign it to prospective pastors, small groups could read it aloud for discussion, and individuals could look to it like a light in the fog. I am immensely grateful that God led Harris to write this book. Not only is it vibrantly illuminating, it is of vital importance for Christians and churches today.

Jon Coutts, Ph.D, associate professor of Christian theology at Ambrose University and author of *A Shared Mercy: Karl Barth on Forgiveness and the Church*

Transparent and caring, thoughtful and thorough, Harris is as careful with her studies as she is with our hearts. The subtitle offers to tell readers what the Bible does and doesn't say about same-sex marriage and LGBTQ+ identities, but it's more than just an objective survey of Bible passages. Harris is crystal clear about her motivations for writing this book—this is the book she as a parent wished that she had. A volume to equip her to support her child's search for an authentic, faithful sexual identity. Harris is also clear about her conclusions and what she wants to accomplish in the hearts and minds of her readers. She hopes to establish that affirming or not affirming same sex-sex is a disputable matter such that Christians who do not affirm same-sex marriage will be able to fully accept Christians who do as fellow believers. In the end, I don't personally believe that argumentation will change many peoples' minds, and so that is why I was both surprised and gratified to see that Harris' conclusion doesn't just sum up the argument and present her findings. Rather, she describes the process of her "heart change" and how it occurred alongside her studies. *Clearly Love* is an invitation to open-hearted, thorough study. If you are ready for that, I highly recommend this book to you!

Jay Mowchenko, D.Min, church planting mentor, leadership coach, and founder of Shalom Leadership

Brace yourself! D. Leanne Harris's *Cleary Love* is a bold invitation to think again about the Bible's teaching on human sexuality. While all readers will not come to the same conclusions, Harris's recounting of her personal story and her deep immersion in the witness of Scripture provides a detailed road map for navigating the complexities of a journey that is too often avoided in the church today. This book is both a primer on a difficult topic and an olive branch for a divided and polarized culture. As a primer, it carefully introduces the reader to the broad range of personal, cultural, and biblical matters that must be considered. As an olive branch, Harris's volume is a loving invitation to sustained dialogue. Amid a polarized culture that prefers debate over dialogue and angry shouting over caring conversation, Harris welcomes the reader to a genuine interchange of ideas in which everyone's voice is heard, everyone's questions are engaged, and the cry of everyone's heart is honored. Most importantly, whether or not one concurs with her conclusions, *Clearly Love* will help every reader become a more understanding, more caring servant of Jesus in today's world.

Douglas Collum, Ph.D, professor of historical and pastoral theology, vice president and dean emeritus at Northeastern Seminary

This book is the result of deeply personal spiritual work and careful biblical study. It is even-handed and generous, something the church desperately needs to find a way to do more often. Harris has created a book that will help churches and families have better conversations and perhaps see each other in a new light. We need *Clearly Love*.

Jared Siebert, church planting consultant, founder of the New Leaf Network, and author of *Gutsy: (Mis)adventures in Canadian Church Planting*

CLEARLY LOVE

What the Bible Says (and Doesn't Say) About Same-Sex Marriage and LGBTQ+ Identities

D. Leanne Harris

Clearly Love: What the Bible Says (and Doesn't Say) About Same-Sex Marriage and LGBTQ+ Identities

DMH Books
PO Box 78003, Taunton Rd
Oshawa, Ontario, Canada
L1K 0H7

ISBN 978-1-7777228-2-1

Dedicated to L:

I am so glad you inspired me to embark on this life-changing journey. Thank you for persevering through my parenting mistakes and for your grace and patience as I did my studying. It fills me with joy to see you living authentically, creating music and art, teaching others, and sharing your gifts with the world. Shine brightly, my beloved.

ACKNOWLEDGMENTS

K: You were the first to passionately introduce me to Jesus, and I am forever grateful to you for your bold, persistent, loving, and patient witness of his presence in my life. Later you would ask me whether the traditional interpretation that same-sex marriage is sinful could be wrong. Thank you for planting that seed too.

R: You welcomed me into your church and your life, and through your witness and example you taught me how to love and serve Jesus. Your continued love and support, even when we interpret the Bible in different ways, means the world to me.

Pastor G: Thank you for teaching me about God's word and God's love in a clear, inviting, and loving way, and for living out God's message of love to me and my growing family in practical ways. I appreciated how you addressed difficult biblical teachings with compassion and sensitivity. Your teaching continues to have a positive influence on me.

My Seminary: Thank you for demonstrating how intelligent, educated, Spirit-led, fully devoted followers of Jesus can interpret the Bible in different ways from each other on many topics. You taught me that although the Bible is not always clear, it is indeed God's word, and it is our responsibility to work hard and pray hard in order to understand it as best as we can. You gave me tools to do this work.

My Church: Thank you for supporting me as I pushed beyond my comfort level and stepped out in various ministry roles. I am grateful for the significant years of my life we were together. To the youth group: Thank you for asking tough questions that kept me thinking about what the Bible says about same-sex marriage.

T: You are the first transgender person I knew both before and after transitioning. I knew you were the same wonderful person after as you were before. I observed that after coming out you seemed more confident and comfortable, and I liked seeing you that way. Thank you for your courage to show your authentic self.

M: Your work has changed many lives, including mine. I can't thank you enough for using your talents and energies to further LGBTQ+ inclusion in the church.

K: Your wisdom and knowledge and your ability to teach gently and effectively is a true gift. Thank you for sharing it with me and so many others.

Y, K, H, and K: Thank you for supporting the vision to share this material in a course format and for helping to make it happen. I couldn't have done it without each one of you and am proud of our Clearly Love team!

Thank you to the participants of the Clearly Love course and discussion groups. Your feedback was instrumental in developing this material.

R, J, and H: Thank you for editing and for the grammar lessons!

My publisher: Thank you for turning this manuscript into an actual book. You continue to amaze and inspire.

My family through birth: The unwavering love and support you have all given me throughout my life has been a strong foundation for me and has shaped me in significant ways. You taught me (and continue to teach me) what unconditional love looks like as you live it out in practical ways. Thank you all from the bottom of my heart.

My family through marriage: Your love and support for me, my family, and our ministry is appreciated more than I have words to say. I have learned much about hard work, perseverance, and generosity in ministry through your examples. Thank you for always being there for us when we needed you, however we needed you.

My kids: You have shaped me and taught me so much. I am so proud of each of you for standing up for what you believed in, even when it was different from what I believed. From your vantage point you could see what I couldn't yet see, but your witness to me has reminded me that God's love is indeed deep and wide, and nothing can come between it and his children. I am so grateful for each one of you and your uncompromising love and support of one another. You make an incredible team.

My husband: I don't think there is a "me" without "you," and I hope I never need to find out. How blessed I am to have spent so many years loving you. You have been there for me and with me during the most difficult and most joyous times in my life. I am infinitely thankful that you are the one with whom I have the privilege of navigating the complexity of life.

CONTENTS

INTRODUCTION

Even before my child came out to me, I had questioned whether I could be a committed, Bible-believing Christian while also being an ally of LGBTQ+ people. I wanted to be loving and inclusive and affirm same-sex marriage, but also uphold the Bible, which I thought taught that same-sex marriages were problematic from God's perspective. I wondered whether expressing support for people's same-sex relationships would ultimately be spiritually harmful to them. I wondered whether supporting same-sex marriage could damage my own relationship with God. I had not yet found any helpful answers to my questions, when my 15-year-old child started dropping hints about being gay, and my need for those answers suddenly became urgent.

When a child comes out, parents have one opportunity to express their initial reaction. They can never take back the first words they say, erase the expression on their face, or interrupt the silence that reveals their struggle to process their thoughts and carefully choose their words. I wish I could have a do-over of the day my child came out to me. Mine wasn't the worst reaction a parent has had to a child's coming out, but although I believed I was being supportive at the time, I now realize that my response was unintentionally hurtful. I would leap at the chance to respond differently, knowing what I know now. At the time though, I knew little about this topic. I knew even less about where to find the information I needed. So, I have written the book that I wish had been available to me.

Although the primary focus of this book is theological, it is my personal experience that motivated my theological journey, so I will introduce you to my personal story before taking a deep dive into conversations about the Bible.

PART I: MY STORY

The Question Becomes Personal

The need to answer the question about whether the Bible prohibits same-sex marriage became personal for me late one November evening. I had picked up my daughter, my son and my son's girlfriend from their high school dance. I parked in the girlfriend's driveway to drop her off, and my son escorted her to her door to say goodnight. As soon as they left the car, my daughter, sitting in the passenger seat beside me, took a deep breath and said, "Mom, I want to tell you about my crush." This was the very first time my daughter had ever mentioned being interested in a boy. She had seemed far too focused on her art and music to be preoccupied with crushes and dating. She had often expressed annoyance when her friends talked about boys. So, I was very curious to hear about the young man who had finally caught her attention.

"Okay, tell me about your crush," I said.

"Well, I just feel so good when I'm near her." The words were barely out of her mouth when my son opened the rear door and jumped back into the car. For the rest of the drive home, that last word rang in my ear. Had she really said "her?" Had she *meant* to say "her?" I wondered whether the word "crush" still meant what I thought it meant. I had heard a straight man talking about his "man crush" recently, so I wondered whether having a crush now meant simply admiring someone.

My daughter was out of the car before I even stopped the engine and was downstairs in her room before I came into the house. I gave her some time to get changed and gave myself some time to collect my thoughts and say a prayer, and then I ventured downstairs and knocked on her door. Trying not to sound awkward, I mentioned the fact that our conversation had been cut short and asked if there was anything else she wanted to tell me about her crush. We talked, with me standing outside the threshold of her door and her keeping hold of its handle, as though ready to shut me out at a moment's notice. She told me a few details, such as how she had met her crush and what she liked about her. She said she didn't know if her crush was interested in girls, and she didn't know how to ask. I asked her if she was worried about having a crush on a girl, and she said she wasn't worried. I told her that she was still young, and she didn't have to have these things figured out yet. I told her that it was normal to have confusing feelings at her age. She nodded, but then told me that she had never had a crush on a boy. The thought suddenly occurred to me that she might think that she could be gay, and, if so, she may be wondering how I would react if she were, so I said, "You know that I love you no matter what, right?"

She answered, "Yes, I know."

I found out later that she believed she had told me that she was gay that night. But in my mind, she had simply confided to me that she had a crush on a girl. I did not equate that with being gay, and I did not, at that point, understand that she identified as gay. She had told me that she wasn't worried about it, so I resolved not to worry about it either. Her comment that she had never had a crush on a boy lingered in my mind though. I had told her that it was normal not to have crushes on boys, but I was surprised by how much I could remember about liking boys, and how early my crushes had started. Remembering my childhood through the lens of my crushes forced me to entertain the possibility that my daughter might *actually be* gay.

A few weeks later, our daughter dropped another hint to my husband when they were alone in the car together. He had asked her about whether there were any boys she liked, trying to dig for more information, and she told him, "No, and I think I like girls." She said "think," so we still didn't know for sure, but the two conversations taken together seemed to be pointing towards a trajectory we hadn't prepared to be on as a family. My husband was an ordained minister in a church denomination that did not affirm same-sex marriage. I was slowly working on my own Master of Divinity degree and was tracking for ordination in the same denomination. The possibility that our daughter might be gay weighed heavily on us. Our response had the potential to have a significant impact on our ministry, which had been the major focus of our life's work. When I emailed a friend asking for prayer for our family, I wrote that we were all healthy and safe, but we needed prayer, and I couldn't bring myself to write my prayer request in words because I didn't want my writing it down to somehow make it true.

My Response

Looking back, I'm ashamed by how devastated I was by the idea that my daughter might be gay. I wish I had felt differently. I hope that my honesty about how I felt will help other parents work through and move on from any such feelings more quickly than I did. I tried to hide my feelings from my daughter, but, while I never told her that I wished she wasn't gay, I unintentionally implied as much when I asked her if she was worried about having a crush on a girl. Simply by asking that question, I was admitting that I thought being gay was something to be worried about. Later, she told me that she knew I had wished she wasn't gay, even though I had never said the words. I could have done better. If I could relive that moment over again, I would simply say, "thank you for telling me about your crush. I am glad you trusted me enough to tell me. You can tell me anything, anytime. I love you." A statement like that would have affirmed her and my love for her, without requiring me to express a position on same-sex marriage if I had not been ready to do so.

Five years later, my child came out as non-binary and then transgender. He uses he/him pronouns and has legally changed his name. With his permission, I used "daughter" and she/her pronouns while telling his coming out story, for the sake of telling the story from my perspective at the time. I am switching to "son" and he/him pronouns while I tell the rest of the story.

The possibility that my son was gay initially filled me with fear and anxiety for three reasons. I was afraid of how it would impact his relationship with God, afraid that he might be rejected by others, and afraid of how it would impact our family's ministry and livelihood. My primary fear was related to my faith. To help readers understand my fear, I will share some of what I believed. I believed that God loves all people and wants everyone to live in a relationship with him, both here and now in this life, as well as forever in heaven. But, because of our decisions to turn our backs on God, we are marred by sin, which needs to be dealt with for us to experience a restored relationship with God.

To understand how I believed sin is dealt with, it is helpful to understand the idea that the nature of God is Triune: Father, Son, and Holy Spirit (some say Creator, Word, and Spirit, to reflect that God is Spirit and not contained within a male gender). God is three persons who share the nature of God and are bound together in a loving relationship. Jesus, the Son (and Word), became human (while remaining God), and came to earth as a baby, miraculously born of a virgin about two thousand years ago. He grew up, taught about God's love, and then demonstrated that love by dealing with the sin of humanity through his death on the cross. God proved his power to provide the eternal life that Jesus promised his followers by raising Jesus back to life after he had been dead for over 30 hours, as well as through Jesus' subsequent ascension into heaven fifty days later. Anyone who trusts in Jesus will be reconciled to God here and now, will have a relationship with God through the Holy Spirit, and will live again in heaven after dying here on earth. Once Christians put their trust in Jesus, they show their love for him by living in a way that honors him. Jesus offers grace and forgiveness for mistakes (which everyone makes), but at some point, if people consistently live in outright disobedience to God without repentance or making an effort to align themselves with his will, it may be that they are no longer trusting him. If people live in persistent, unrepentant sin, God could consider them to have rejected Jesus and his offer of relationship and eternal life.

I was struggling with six verses in the Bible that seemed to clearly condemn same-sex sex. I didn't think it was a sin to *be* LGBTQ+ because I understood that a person's sexual orientation was not within their control, but I *did* believe that gay Christians who wanted to please Jesus should play it safe by remaining celibate. It was the same expectation that I believed to be in place for straight Christians who were unmarried, and until it became personal, the expectation had seemed reasonable. However, suggesting that a hypothetical person should live a celibate life is much easier than telling a beloved child that they should not seek love.

I thought back to when I was a teenager. If someone had told my sixteen-year-old self that I shouldn't even entertain the hope of finding romantic love, it would have felt like a death sentence. I imagined what it would have been like for me, when I was young and in love, if someone had told me that I should remain "just friends" with the man I wanted to marry. Staying "just friends" would have been too difficult, and I am sure I would have eventually had to break off the friendship. Then I imagined what it would be like to have to cut off friendship after friendship when romantic feelings got in the way. At this point, I began to understand how lonely a celibate life could really be, and the suggestion that LGBTQ+ Christians should live celibately suddenly felt uncomfortably harsh.

It was not the life I envisioned for my son. I have loved being married and having children. I wanted him to have the opportunity to have a family of his own, but I thought that in order to get married, he would have to reject Jesus. In my mind, rejecting his faith would be worse than giving up the dream of a spouse and family. The stakes were high. I wanted my son to be happy in this life *and* the next.

The second reason for my anxiety was also motivated by love. I was afraid that he would be ostracized and bullied in school and marginalized in society. I feared that it would be hard for him to find a job. I worried that he would be in physical danger and pictured him being beat up in a bathroom or a back alley. I was concerned that he would not be able to travel freely. I was apprehensive about him joining an LGBTQ+ community which I feared would expose him to sexual promiscuity, substance use, and anti-Christian sentiment, and which would exclude me and the rest of our family. I did not want to lose him to an alternate community.

I can't go any further here without saying that my fears about what an LGBTQ+ community would be like were based on unfair stereotypes and have proven unfounded. I have found accepting, compassionate, and loving LGBTQ+ communities. My kids' LGBTQ+ friends are wonderful people. I regret that I did not make it my priority to help my son get involved in a supportive, life-giving community for people who are LGBTQ+ as soon as he came out to me. I feel like I failed him by trying to dismiss the fact that he needed LGBTQ+ friends and mentors, and I was too afraid to help him find them. I now realize that my perspective about community was backwards. I expected my son to fit into my community, where he could not be himself and therefore felt uncomfortable and anxious. The healthy and inclusive way for us to share a community would have been to find and join a community that embraces LGBTQ+ people like him unreservedly, and which would also accept me. Thankfully, my son has thus far been accepted and supported within school, work, and church communities.

The third reason for my fear and anxiety was practical in nature. As I mentioned, I was worried about how having an out LGBTQ+ child would affect our ministry, which also provided my husband's income. It should not have fallen on our son to have to worry about such things, but the practical reality in any family is that when a parent loses a job, the whole family experiences losses. I worried that the loss of our ministry would require us to pull our children out of school and move to a different city, jobs being scarce at that time. I believed that at my son's stage of life, refraining from dating would be less detrimental to him than moving. He had worked hard to get into a fine arts high school, and I wanted him to be able to stay there. I explained this to him and asked him to wait until he was eighteen to date. I suggested that this would avoid putting his father and I in a situation where we would have either to allow the dating, at the potential cost of our ministry, or disallow it, at the potential cost of our relationship with him. In hindsight, I would have handled the situation differently, because even though it seemed to me like a practical request rather than a moral one, I expect it reinforced the idea that his desires to date a girl were unacceptable. Out of respect for our situation, my son kept his dating discreet.

With the stakes continuing to feel high, we entered a holding pattern of sorts, with tension and strained communication characterizing our relationship. My son struggled with depression and suicidal thoughts. When we learned that he was suicidal, our situation quickly fell into perspective. We knew that his life meant more to us (and, we believed, also to God), than his sexuality did. We learned that tragically, many people who are LGBTQ+ struggle with suicidal thoughts and suicide attempts, and many of them actual do commit suicide.[1] This broke my heart. It weighed heavily on me that the church's traditional response to same-sex marriage is a trigger for these mental health breakdowns, and that as a church leader, I was complicit in that harmful response.

Our Church

As pastors, we did our best to quiet any anti-LGBTQ+ sentiment in our church, in an attempt to avoid causing harm to our son and any

---

1. In Ontario, LGBTQ youth are at 14 times higher risk of suicide and substance abuse than their heterosexual peers. 77% of trans youth have considered suicide and 45% have attempted suicide. CMHA Ontario, *Lesbian, Gay, Bisexual, Trans & Queer identified People and Mental Health,* accessed January 16, 2021, https://ontario.cmha.ca/documents/lesbian-gay-bisexual-trans-queer-identified-people-and-mental-health.

others like him. Since our son was not out at church, we could not tell people that it was personal for us when discussing the topic. During a small group meeting one evening, after someone had made the claim that our church was welcoming to everyone, I tested the waters by asking whether they thought our church would welcome a gay couple into its fellowship. The ensuing discussion taught me that it was best to avoid bringing up the topic, because even if I intended to be supportive of LGBTQ+ people, my comments could stir up a response from others that could cause much harm to those within earshot. After that experience, my husband and I suggested to others in our church that they should always assume that an LGBTQ+ person is in the room whenever we are discussing issues related to same-sex marriage. This would, we hoped, ensure that anything that was said would at least be said respectfully. It did seem to help. For the most part, our church became pretty quiet about the same-sex marriage question.

I have since realized that saying nothing about same-sex marriage was not helpful enough, because whether they have done anything to deserve it or not, churches have inherited a reputation for hatred against LGBTQ+ people. I later found out that since our church didn't explicitly express acceptance for LGBTQ+ people, our son believed that if he were to come out, our church would respond similarly to the worst-case scenarios he read about online, and that he would be rejected and even hated. I knew that most people in our church would have responded lovingly if he had come out, but I also believed that a few would strongly disapprove of same-sex dating, and, as mentioned, I didn't know if we would be able to continue ministering there. Nor was there any way to ask. My son stopped volunteering in the children's ministry, even though he was gifted for the role. He didn't think it was worth upsetting anyone if they found out he was gay. During this time, he continued to struggle with depression and anxiety and withdrew from church and his faith.

Hope

I was continuing to work on my Master of Divinity degree during this time, which involved periodically traveling to my seminary. As I studied, the question of whether God prohibited same-sex marriage was foremost on my mind. I prayed for clarity every day. Without disclosing my situation, I asked my Old Testament professor for his perspective, and he said that he held to a non-affirming view of same-sex marriage, although, I was surprised to hear, not because of the Old Testament verses that prohibit same-sex sex. He said something about how Jesus' sacrifice on the cross has changed our relationship to the Old Testament law, so the Old Testament verses could not be used as the basis for one's view on same-sex marriage. He told me that he based his non-affirming view on Paul's teaching in the book of Romans, in the New Testament.

A few weeks later I conveniently happened to be taking a course on the book of Romans, so I asked my New Testament professor what he believed about same-sex marriage, again without disclosing my situation. He said that he held to a non-affirming view of marriage, but not because of Paul's teaching in Romans. He explained that Paul mentioned same-sex sex in the book of Romans as part of a vice list— a list of actions that society assumed were wrong, which Paul listed to make the case that *all* are guilty of sin so Christians should not judge each other. Because the intention of the passage wasn't specifically to address the issue of same-sex sexual practices, it shouldn't be used as the basis for forming an opinion about same-sex marriage. He said he based his non-affirming view on the book of Leviticus, in the Old Testament. I pondered this discovery, that each of the professors discounted the arguments against same-sex marriage that were based on their own areas of expertise and which they had studied the most thoroughly.

I confided my situation to a fellow student one day during our lunch break and asked him for his thoughts. He told me that he had friends who affirmed same-sex marriage, even while maintaining that the Bible was authoritative as God's word. His friends believed that the verses addressing same-sex sexual practices in the Bible are related to the historical context and that they don't speak to same-sex marriage today. I took advantage of being near a seminary library to start researching that idea. My reading made it clear that same-sex sexual practices during Bible times were quite different from monogamous, covenantal same-sex marriages.

That Sunday, I visited a church that I had briefly attended years ago when I lived in the town. After the service, a woman that I had not seen for five years greeted me. She asked me how my family was doing. Surprising myself, I blurted out, "My daughter is gay." There was no reason for me to have confided with her about something I had been keeping so private, especially not as the first thing I said when chatting in the middle of a busy church!

Her eyes grew wide, but she smiled and leaned in close to me and said, "Did you know mine is too?" I had not known. She told me that her grown daughter was living with a woman, that they had successful careers and were happy, but that as Christian parents, she and her husband had many questions. She told me they had read a book that had given them much to think about, and she recommended I read it. It was called *God and the Gay Christian*, by Matthew Vines.[2] Looking back, I believe that my encounter with that woman was God-ordained. I believe God inspired me to blurt out my situation, because he wanted me to hear about Matthew Vines' book as an answer to my prayers for wisdom and understanding.

My search for his book at the local library back home introduced me to other authors as well. In addition to *God and the Gay Christian*, I read *Generous Spaciousness* by Wendy Vanderwal Gritter and *Torn* by Justin Lee.[3] Each of these books revealed new possibilities to me, slowly opening my heart and mind as they introduced me to the personal stories of gay Christians. They opened my mind to an alternate way of understanding the verses that had been impeding my acceptance of my son's orientation. I remember finishing *Torn* with tears in my eyes and a lightness in my heart, knowing that LGBTQ+ people could love Jesus, love the Bible, *and* engage in a same-sex, sexually intimate marriage. The question of whether same-sex marriage could be blessed by God had become, for me, a disputable matter.

A disputable matter is a question that does not have a clear answer in the Bible. It is an issue that Christians can disagree about yet still consider each other to be Christians. Other examples of disputable matters include whether Christians can drink alcohol, shop on Sundays, or whether churches can ordain female clergy. People (and churches) who land on both sides of the debate can find verses in the Bible to back up their positions. At some point, Christians must make a decision based on their best interpretation of Scripture and their clearest guidance from the Holy Spirit. It is not that the decision about a disputable matter is unimportant, or that people aren't extremely passionate about the side they choose. It is just that the Bible doesn't provide clarity.

I experienced a wonderful sense of peace when I accepted that the question of whether God prohibited same-sex marriage was a

---

2. Matthew Vines, *God and the Gay Christian: The Biblical Case in Support of Same-Sex Relationships* (New York: Convergent, 2014).

3. Justin Lee, *Torn: Rescuing the Gospel from the Gays-vs-Christians Debate* (New York: Jericho Books, 2012).

disputable matter. It meant that my son would not have to give up his faith in order to get married. As long as he didn't feel convicted for willfully disobeying God, I believed there would be grace for him even if his interpretation of Scripture turned out to be wrong. In other words, I believed that, since the Bible isn't clear in what *exactly* it prohibits, Jesus would forgive him if it turned out that he had made a mistake. Feeling peace rather than anxiety allowed me to approach my ongoing studies with a more open mind, having moved from a state of desperation to a state of curiosity. I now understand that the possibility for error exists on both sides, and it may just as likely be the non-affirming church that will need to be the recipient of Jesus' forgiveness if it turns out that it was displeasing him by excluding LGBTQ+ people from full participation and acceptance in the church.

Seeking Deeper Understanding

The question about same-sex marriage deeply impacts lives and is therefore charged with emotion. I am hoping that this book will help Christians who do not affirm same-sex marriage to fully accept Christians that do as fellow believers, once it becomes clear that many of them also uphold the Scriptures and desire to live God-honoring lives. I am hoping that Christians who affirm same-sex marriage will be able to understand that many Christians who don't affirm same-sex marriage genuinely love LGBTQ+ people and want to do right by them. They are trying to follow the Bible and feel that being honest about God's laws is the most loving approach. They believe that if someone is on a path to self-destruction, the most loving response is to warn them and try to convince them to change direction.

The stakes are high on both sides. Upholding a definition of marriage as between one man and one woman severely limits the type of love that LGBTQ+ people can seek and experience. LGBTQ+ people's mental health is negatively affected by the teaching that there is something inherently wrong with their desire for same-sex love, and they are at high risk for depression, anxiety, self-harm, and suicide.[4] There is a potential for this view to result in the breakup of families

---

4. LGBTQ+ youth are 3.5 times more likely to attempt suicide than their heterosexual peers. Ester di Giacomo et al., "Estimating the Risk of Attempted Suicide Among Sexual Minority Youths: A Systematic Review and Meta-analysis," *JAMA pediatrics* 172, no. 12 (2018): 1147.

and friendships if LGBTQ+ people *do* seek out love and are judged for it. An extreme non-affirming view leads some to persecute LGBTQ+ people and commit violence against them.

There are also risks associated with redefining marriage to include same-sex couples. If God *does* prohibit same-sex marriage, people who openly disobey God in this matter could risk damaging their relationship with God here and now as well as and losing the opportunity for eternal life with Jesus after death. Those holding a non-affirming view may also believe that they would be personally subject to spiritual consequences if they teach wrongly about this matter. James 3:1 says, "Not many of you should become teachers, my fellow believers, because you know that we who teach will be judged more strictly."[5] Matthew 18:6 says, "If anyone causes one of these little ones—those who believe in me—to stumble, it would be better for them to have a large millstone hung around their neck and to be drowned in the depths of the sea." Some Christians feel that they would essentially have to give up their own faith (and possibly salvation) in order to affirm same-sex marriage. Many Christians who do not affirm same-sex marriage don't want to judge LGBTQ+ people, because doing so feels unloving, but they don't feel free to affirm them either, so they stay silent.

The stakes are high for everyone. High enough, even, for families and churches to split up over the issue. This is the reason I believe it is of ultimate importance that Christians seek an informed understanding of what the Bible says about same-sex sex. I hope that a broader perspective will enable Christians to love and accept those with differing views.

My primary goal in writing this book is to provide a thorough summary of contrasting perspectives to help Christians make informed decisions about their beliefs regarding whether the Bible prohibits same-sex marriage and the affirmation of LGBTQ+ identities. I am hopeful that the information provided will help to reduce the anxiety that typically accompanies this discussion in Christian circles—anxiety which can become overwhelming when the question is personal. I believe that wise Christians will consider their beliefs around this topic carefully, *before* it becomes personal, because one never knows when a loved one will come out to them, providing them with their one and only opportunity for a first response. I wish

---

5. Unless otherwise stated, all quotations of the Bible are taken from the New International Version (NIV).

I had learned more and processed my beliefs more thoroughly before my child came out to me.

Christian parents who care deeply about what the Bible says and also dearly love their LGBTQ+ children are especially on my mind and in my prayers as I write. This book is also intended for pastors, church leaders, and everyone who considers the Bible to be authoritative and wants to examine it closely in relation to the question of whether it prohibits same-sex marriage. Although I welcome LGBTQ+ readers as well, I am providing a content warning that some of the non-affirming viewpoints that are included could cause emotional distress. There are many other books that present material from a fully affirming viewpoint that may be more suitable reading for anyone who is at risk of being traumatized by reading non-affirming viewpoints stated objectively, or for anyone who prefers to read material presented from a purely affirming perspective.

This book will provide a summary of thoughts from perspectives that affirm same-sex marriage as well as from perspectives that do not, to give readers an awareness of the vast and dynamic conversation currently happening in theological circles and around kitchen tables about whether the Bible prohibits same-sex marriage and LGBTQ+ identities. I hope that readers will be challenged to broaden their perspectives, hold their views with more openness toward the possibility of being wrong, and display more grace towards those who respectfully hold differing views. When I realized that both views stood on solid biblical ground, I was able to fully accept my child's LGBTQ+ identity and orientation even before I became fully affirming myself. The pressure in my heart lifted and I believe the pressure in our home lifted as well. My hope is that readers will also experience freedom and relief from pressure and anxiety related to this topic.

I have nearly given up on this project several times, believing that it could be better written by someone more qualified than I am. However, I continue to have conversations with people and read stories in the news that remind me of the necessity for a book such as this. It is needed to help heal relationships that have been divided by this question and to quell our society's rising animosity towards LGBTQ+ people, especially transgender people. There is a need to consider current information about sexual orientation and new insights into biblical interpretation and ancient culture when determining how to interpret the Bible. More people are coming out as LGBTQ+, making the question personal for many more people.

Churches that hold the traditional view that marriage can only be between one man and one woman may face pressure to make significant changes to their practice and theology, but such changes feel risky. Aside from the risk of making a theological error that is offensive to God, individual churches that choose to support same-sex marriage may face an initial drop in membership and financial sustainability. They may face expulsion from their denomination, which could threaten their survival as a church. Whole denominations that choose to support same-sex marriage risk losing members and financial security. Some Christians worry that interpreting the passages that prohibit same-sex sex to be inapplicable for the church today would mean reconsidering the authority of the Bible itself, which could lead to more and more passages being dismissed or reinterpreted until eventually Jesus might no longer be proclaimed as Lord and Savior.

Tensions run high when the topic of same-sex marriage is discussed. It can be difficult to ask questions and speak openly about it because lives, families, livelihoods, careers, churches, and ministries are, or are perceived to be, at stake. Fears that genuine questions about the Bible might be misinterpreted as being hateful or discriminatory dissuade people from asking them. Many people aren't sure where to turn for reliable information, and when they look, they find information that is one-sided or has strong emotions and personal biases attached to it, which can make it difficult to think objectively about the issues. I am not without my own personal biases and strong emotions related to this subject, but I have tried to keep them in check and leave them out of my writing as much as possible, aside from when I share my own story.

I offer this work not as a last word or an original word, but with the hope that summarizing and organizing the conversation in this way will inspire people to participate in healthy conversations of their own and engage in further research. This is a book that invites critical thinking, and I hope readers will read sections and then pause to consider whether they agree or disagree with the statements made and reflect on their reasons. Readers might find it helpful to keep a journal open while reading, to record questions and reflections. The book also works well to be read in study groups. Consider designating a consistent reader to read each of the three sections aloud for the group (affirming, non-affirming, and background), and then pause for discussion after each section. A fourth leader could serve as a discussion facilitator. Group norms or agreed-upon discussion etiquette should be set up ahead of time to set expectations for respectful conversation.

Preparing for the Study Ahead

Groundwork

There are some definitions and points about style and format that require explanation before we begin. I have chosen to use LGBTQ+ as the primary term throughout this book to represent lesbian, gay, bisexual, transgender, and queer and questioning people, with the plus sign representing anyone else who identifies with the conversation, including asexual, intersex/DSD (Difference in Sexual Development), pansexual, and two-spirit people. I have tried to refer to the groups separately when appropriate, recognizing that each group has their own unique experiences and needs.

Some terms may be unfamiliar to some readers, so they are worth defining. The following definitions are based on the LGBTQ2 terminology glossary on the Government of Canada website.[6] The term "lesbian" describes a female who is sexually and/or romantically attracted to other females. The term "gay" can describe males or females who are attracted to others of the same sex or gender identity as themselves. "Bisexual" people are attracted to two or more genders. It does not mean that they have male and female partners at the same time. Bisexual people who partner with someone from the opposite sex often pass as straight. The term "transgender" describes people who do not identify as the gender they were assigned at birth, or the gender that matches the genitalia they were born with. Some transgender people transition to their identified gender through hormone therapy and/or gender-affirming surgeries, and others may express their gender without transitioning medically, through clothing, hairstyles, and name and/or pronoun changes. Some keep their identity hidden. Some transgender people identify as "non-binary," which means their gender identity is something other than strictly male or female. A non-binary gender identification may include male and female, androgynous, fluid, multiple genders, no gender, or an alternate gender.

---

6. Government of Canada, *LGBTQ2 Terminology: Glossary and common acronyms*, accessed July 26, 2021, https://www.canada.ca/en/canadian-heritage/campaigns/free-to-be-me/lgbtq2-glossary.html.

It can be helpful to think of "gender" as describing someone's self-perception, and the term "sex" as describing someone's physical characteristics, such as genitalia. Transgender people who have not medically transitioned may describe themselves as men or women, using the terms to describe their gender, not their physical bodies. Some people who consider the words "man" and "woman" to describe physical bodies exclusively may feel dishonest if they refer to a transgender person as a man or a woman, when the body they had at birth did not match those designations. Other people believe that words like "man" and "woman" can be used to refer to either gender or sex, and that these terms can be used with integrity to describe people's gender identity even when they don't describe their physical bodies. An affirming view might say that calling a transgender man a man is not lying or being dishonest, if the term is being used to describe his gender identity, or inner self, rather than the physical characteristics of his body (prior to receiving gender-affirming medical care).[7] There are many words in the English language that can have more than one meaning, and "man" and "woman" are among them.

The term "queer" includes a diversity of identities. It was historically used as a derogatory term but is now being reclaimed. It is best to use it only with people's permission, due to its history as a slur. The term "questioning" describes people who are uncertain about their sexual orientation and/or gender identity. Other identities represented by the plus sign include asexual people, who are not sexually attracted to any gender, pansexual people, whose sexual or romantic attractions are not limited to any particular sex or gender identity, and people with DSD, whose sex chromosomes, reproductive organs, genitalia, and/or secondary sex characteristics are different from those typically categorized as male or female. "Two-Spirit" is a term that some Indigenous LGBTQ+ people use to describe their gender identity and/or sexual orientation as comprising both male and female spirits. Sometimes Two-Spirit people are represented with a 2S. Sometimes they are included under the umbrella of the plus sign. Another term worth defining is "cisgender," which refers to a person who does identify as the gender they were assigned at birth. In other words, a cisgender person is someone who is not transgender. The prefix "trans" is Latin and means "on the

---

7. Gender-affirming medical care is used here to include hormone therapy and surgery to change breast size, remove Adam's apple, or alter genitalia.

other side of," and the prefix "cis" is its antonym, meaning "on this side of."

I have chosen to speak of "views" to voice the two primary perspectives shared in this book. The phrase "a non-affirming view" is intended to mean being non-affirming of same-sex marriage and disapproving of medical transitioning and/or identifying as a gender that does not match one's genitalia at birth. The phrase "an affirming view" is intended to mean being supportive of gender-affirming care that is non-medical (including changing clothing, hair, names, and pronouns), and gender-affirming medical care (including hormone therapy and/or surgery) as well as spiritually endorsing marriages for same-sex couples. Because same-sex marriage is legal in Canada, where this book was written, I have used the phrase "spiritually endorses" because some Christians with non-affirming views may support a same-sex couple's legal right to a civil marriage without considering it to be a Christian marriage that is endorsed and blessed by the church. Since same-sex marriage is not legal everywhere, I am considering monogamous, covenantal relationships to be included when I use the term "marriage," assuming that people in such relationships would be legally married if it was permitted. Conversion therapy is discussed from both views in this book, but I want to clearly state that I do not endorse conversion therapy.

Please note that people hold their views for many varied reasons and arrive at them through different circumstances. People who hold an affirming view will inevitably disagree with some of the points I attribute to that view and will likely agree with some points I attribute to the non-affirming view. Likewise, people who hold a non-affirming view will disagree with some of the points I attribute to that view and will likely agree with some points I attribute to the affirming view. At times it may seem like the ideas attributed to the views contradict themselves, but this does not mean that individual people's views are not cohesive. I am painting each view with a wide brush that can't adequately reflect the nuances of each person's individual position.

I am including a wide variety of perspectives that I have read or encountered, even when the points seem weak or unsubstantiated. This is because even weak arguments influence people's perspectives and should be brought into the light so that their influence can be carefully considered. To recognize and honor individual people's unique perspectives and to avoid putting words in anyone's mouth, I have chosen to speak tentatively for each view, using the phrase "might say."

Many people believe that sexual orientations are not chosen, so they do not consider same-sex attraction in and of itself to be sinful, even if they do not affirm same-sex marriage. Others believe same-sex desire itself is sinful and must be resisted. They believe that if an act is sinful, the desire to commit the act is also sinful. For the sake of clarity, the default position in this book will be to discuss behaviors separately from the orientation itself. I use terms like "same-sex sex," "male-male sex / female-female sex," and "same-sex marriage" in order to describe sexual behaviors, separating people's orientation from their sexual activity. As much as possible, I am avoiding use of the word "homosexual" because of its historically negative connotation. To be consistent, I am also avoiding its counterpart word, "heterosexual," and using "opposite-sex sex" instead, once again separating the behavior from the orientation.

In addition to an "affirming view" and a "non-affirming view," there is a third view called an "accommodating view," which supports same-sex marriage as a best moral alternative when celibacy is not possible. An accommodating view might say the Bible does not provide enough evidence to either prohibit or endorse same-sex marriage. It has been described as accepting, rather than celebrating same-sex marriage.[8] Some churches take a similar approach regarding remarriage after divorce, recognizing and possibly even officiating remarriages, even though they don't believe them to be supported from a biblical perspective.[9]

An affirming view might say that an accommodating view is better than an outright prohibition of same-sex marriage, but the idea that they need to be accommodated still teaches LGBTQ+ Christians that there is something inherently wrong with them, causing them to feel like "second class" Christians.

A non-affirming view might say that there isn't much difference between accepting and celebrating a same-sex marriage. If same-sex sex is wrong in God's eyes, accepting it is no less wrong than celebrating it.

For the sake of simplicity, the conversation in this book will primarily be defined in terms of affirming views and non-affirming views. Those who hold an accommodating view might sometimes agree with thoughts attributed to a non-affirming view and other times with thoughts attributed to an affirming view.

---

8. Howard A. Snyder, *Homosexuality and the Church: Guidance for Community Conversation* (Franklin, TN: Seedbed, 2014), 521.

9. Luke 16:18 says, "Anyone who divorces his wife and marries another woman commits adultery, and the man who marries a divorced woman commits adultery."

The objective of this book is to explore the biblical evidence for and against the affirmation of same-sex marriage and LGBTQ+ identities. To keep the conversation focused, this book assumes that sex with unmarried (i.e., non-covenanted) partners is outside of God's plan for sexual intimacy between his people, whether they are LGBTQ+ or straight. It also assumes the definition of marriage to be limited to two people. This commitment to monogamy is based on New Testament teaching. Jesus and Paul inserted the word "two" when quoting Genesis 2:24, saying "the two will become one flesh" (1 Corinthians 6:16; Mark 10:8). In 1 Timothy 3:2 Paul says an overseer is to be the husband of one wife, showing that polygyny, or having multiple wives, was not the ideal lifestyle for Christians. Further conversations around the topics of monogamy vs. polyamory and covenant-based sex vs. consent-based sex are beyond the scope and purpose of this work.

I patterned this book after my own research journey, which started with the study of three Old Testament verses and three New Testament verses that directly address same-sex sex. After that study, I understood that the verses weren't as clear as they had first seemed, and that I was going to need more guidance. I began by reading the entire Bible, taking note of everything I thought was pertinent to the discussion. Then I began reading other books and resources, watching videos, and taking courses, keeping notes of the points made by both sides. That work has resulted in an online course, an online organization for connection and education, and this book.

Like my journey, this book begins by addressing those six passages that directly refer to same-sex sex, as well as a few other passages that shed additional light on them. After examining these passages from a variety of perspectives, it turns to the wider teaching of Scripture to try to discern the overall sense of God's will for his people, touching on multiple topics including: creation and the image of God, procreation, gender complementarianism, marriage, sexual immorality, celibacy, judgment, holiness and obedience, biblical authority, history and tradition, fruitfulness, love, patriarchy and women in ministry, inclusion of sexual minorities, and the gospel. The question of choice and the possibility of change is addressed within the topic of creation and the image of God. Transgender topics are also discussed in that section. I try to provide a thorough overview of the conversation, taking a wide-angled view of biblical teaching that can provide increased understanding and guidance. My hope is that after being introduced to the discussion points, readers will be able to search for deeper explanations of the ideas that are most interesting or pertinent to them.

Reflections on Biblical Interpretation

Background:

Christians hold different understandings about how the Bible communicates God's message to his people. Some say that although the Bible was written down by men, it was inspired by God almost as though God was dictating and man was the scribe, thus the Bible is essentially written by God and is without error. They say that the original manuscript is literally true and authoritative. They believe that God knew that his people would be reading the Bible thousands of years after it was written down and considered contemporary readers to be his audience along with the original hearers. They believe that the Scriptures address contemporary people and situations even as they addressed ancient people and situations. They may point to examples of how the Bible contains layers of meaning, like the prophesy found in Isaiah 7:14, which prophesied that the Lord would give Isaiah the sign of a young woman bearing a son named Immanuel. This prophecy was pertinent to Isaiah himself and his own son while also pointing ahead to Jesus' birth.

Others agree that the Bible was inspired by God and was written down by men but believe that God used humans to contribute to the process of writing the Scriptures, saying that in the same way Jesus is both simultaneously God and man, the Bible is authored by both God and man. They say man's involvement has resulted in some discrepancies, inconsistencies, and cultural biases, but even so, the gospel message of salvation, the standard for Christian living, and an understanding of the nature of God and God's relationship to humanity and the world can be understood through the Scriptures. They believe that the Holy Spirit communes with Christians as they read the Scriptures, illuminating their truth for each new audience. They describe the Bible as infallible rather than without error. They say that the Scriptures themselves never claim to be inerrant and point out that Paul attests that the Old Testament is inspired by God, useful for teaching, reproof, correction and training in righteousness, but does not attest its inerrancy (2 Tim 3:16-17). They say that the Scriptures are trustworthy and authoritative even though there are some minor inconsistencies and inaccuracies. They believe that the Scriptures were inspired and written down for their original, specific, historical context, and readers today best understand their intended meaning by trying to understand what they meant to the original ancient audience. While God knew that people would be reading the Scriptures thousands of years after they were written, God inspired them to be written through people who had no comprehension of future readers' situations. He chose to include people in writing the Bible at specific points in history because it is his character to work with people to accomplish his will in the world, even when it results in imperfections. Although there are Old Testament prophecies that had multiple fulfilments (i.e., one closer to the date when they were written and one pointing to Jesus), this does not mean that all verses and teachings from the Bible can be applied anachronistically to contemporary situations as though they were written to address them. Scripture continues to be useful, instructive, and edifying, and it serves as a conduit for communion with the Holy Spirit. The Bible is the primary way we learn about God, but it was written to an ancient audience, and the context within which it was written needs to be considered to best understand its meaning. They say that translation biases exist in modern versions of the Bible due to human translators making assumptions and reading their own cultural preconceptions into Scripture, making it important to refer to the original manuscripts as much as possible to reduce the incidence of interpretive errors.

For an example of how an understanding of context influences interpretation, they may suggest considering an email written by a pastor to his or her church in Canada, in the year 2020, which says, "be sure to wear masks in church, sit at least two metres away from each other and do not sing out loud." The original congregation reading the email would have interpreted the instructions to be temporary and related to the COVID-19 pandemic restrictions put in place to reduce transmission of disease, but if the email was discovered and still considered authoritative after the context was forgotten, it could lead to a strange and isolating style of worship. People might even wear eye masks to disguise themselves rather than masks that cover their nose and mouth, making church look like a masquerade ball.

A non-affirming view might say:

The Scriptures clearly prohibit same-sex sex, which means same-sex marriage is prohibited. If God had wanted to make an allowance for same-sex marriage he would have said so or provided a positive example of one or more same-sex relationships in the Scriptures.

An affirming view might say:

God inspired the Scriptures to be written in a particular time and place in history. The Scriptures are best understood by considering what they meant to the original audience, which involves looking at the historical and literary contexts and the original language. The Scriptures clearly prohibit the ways same-sex sex was happening during the time and in the location they were written, but these were not within the context of an equal-status, monogamous, covenantal relationship. The Holy Spirit is now inspiring many Christians to understand the Scriptures to allow space for same-sex marriage.

PART II: DOES THE OLD TESTAMENT PROHIBIT SAME-SEX MARRIAGE?

Preparing to Address the Old Testament Passages

The Old Testament is comprised of the books written to and about the Israelite people before Jesus came. Writings about Jesus and the early Christian church are found in the New Testament, which is the second section of the Bible. Jesus' life, death, and resurrection transformed the way Christians encounter grace and forgiveness and changed the nature of Christians' relationship to the Old Testament. Nevertheless, I start this book by addressing some difficult passages in the Old Testament because they have significantly impacted the discussion and sentiment around same-sex sex throughout history. These passages can be disturbing when the context is not understood. I hope any readers who might be new to the Bible will understand that there is much more to God's story than the difficult passages which will be addressed in this conversation.

To prevent these disturbing passages from becoming anyone's first introduction to the Bible, please allow me to frame the conversation by sharing a few more uplifting passages first: "Neither death nor life, neither angels nor demons, neither the present nor the future, nor any powers, neither height nor depth, nor anything else in all creation, will be able to separate us from the love of God that is in Christ Jesus our Lord" (Romans 8:38), and "The LORD is gracious and compassionate, slow to anger and rich in love. The LORD is good to all; he has compassion on all he has made" (Psalm 145:8-9).

God is loving and merciful. He loves all people and wants all people to come to him, and when they do, he promises to show grace and mercy. The apostle Paul teaches that all are guilty of sin. Therefore, we must not judge each other but rather bring our own shortcomings and failures to God for forgiveness and redemption. God's primary message in the Bible is one of hope, grace, and love. With that foundation set, we look now at what the Old Testament says about same-sex sex.

Genesis 19:1-29

Background:

Genesis 19:1-29 tells the second part of a story that began in the previous chapter. In Genesis 18, God tells Abraham that he is sending angels to the towns of Sodom and Gomorrah to see if the people there are as bad as their reputations have suggested. Abraham's nephew Lot lives in Sodom, so Abraham pleads with God to save the city. As per Abraham's request, God agrees to spare Sodom if he can find ten righteous people there.

When the angels, appearing in the form of men, arrive in Sodom, they intend to spend the night in the city square. Lot meets them there and insists that they stay in his home instead. After dinner, all the men from every part of the city, both young and old, surround Lot's house and demand that he should bring the visitors out so they can have sex with them. Lot goes outside to plead with the men of Sodom to leave the visitors alone and offers to send his virgin daughters out to them instead. The men ignore Lot's offer and instead threaten Lot and prepare to break down his door to get to the visitors. Having confirmed Sodom's wickedness and being unable to find ten righteous people, the angels pull Lot to safety, strike the men of Sodom with blindness, and urge Lot to flee with his family before the city is destroyed.

A non-affirming view might say:

God punished Sodom because its men engaged in same-sex sex, which was sinful. This is a warning that those who desire same-sex sex and engage in it, as well as those around them, could be punished for it.

An affirming view might say:

To properly interpret the story, it is necessary to understand something about the culture in which it was first told and recorded. In the highly patriarchal Ancient Near Eastern setting of this story, sex partners were not considered to be of equal status. Women's inferior social status affected the understanding of sexual intercourse. Men played an active, dominant role in sex as the penetrating partner and women played a passive role as the receiving partner.[10] Typical passive partners in male-male sex were slaves, servants, pre-pubescent boys, defeated enemies, or prostitutes. When a man penetrated another man through anal sex, it was understood that he was dominating that man, asserting his power and superiority over him, and shaming him by treating him like a woman. This dynamic of dominance and subservience was present even in the case of consensual intercourse, although it is questionable whether servants, slaves, or boys would have been truly free to refuse.[11] An example of the dominant/subservient understanding of sex is evident in a document from ancient Middle Assyria which outlawed male-male sex from occurring between two equals but allowed it if the penetrated man was of lower social status.[12]

In the Ancient Near East, male-male rape was the "ultimate means of subjugation and domination."[13] Sodom's terrible sin was this intention to inflict violence and humiliation upon the strangers. The men of Sodom's rejection of Lot's virgin daughters demonstrates that they were more interested in humiliating and dominating the strangers than they were in satisfying their sexual lust.[14] That Lot offered his daughters to the men showed that Lot knew the men to be at least just as oriented towards sex with women as they were with men. They were not gay men the way the term is understood today. This is evidenced by the acknowledgement that the men who were engaged to be married to Lot's daughters (and thus presumed to be attracted to women) were among the men at Lot's door. God punished the men of Sodom for their violence and hostility and for being so evil that they would gang rape strangers in their midst. That God condemned the Sodomites' desire to sexually assault the angels does not automatically mean that he also condemns same-sex marriage.

---

10. Martti Nissinen, *Homoeroticism in the Biblical World: A Historical Perspective*, (Minneapolis, MN: Augsburg Fortress, 1998), 26.
11. Robert A. Gagnon, *The Bible and Homosexual Practice: Texts and Hermeneutics* (Nashville: Abingdon, 2002), Kindle ed., Part 1, chap. 1.
12. Nissinen, *Homoeroticism in the Biblical World*, 26.
13. Ibid., 47.
14. Ibid., 48.

A non-affirming view might say:

Even though the sin that sealed Sodom's fate was the intention to commit violent gang rape, it was the fact that it was male-male rape that caused the whole city to be condemned.[15] Male-female rape was not considered to be as serious of an offence (the consequence for raping a woman was paying her father and then having to marry her).[16] The story of Sodom implies that male-male sex commonly occurred among the men in Sodom, and it was the practice of male-male sex that ultimately triggered God's wrath against the city.[17] It didn't matter why the men wanted to have sex with the strangers, or whether they also had sex with women. The intended rape of the strangers was considered so sinful because of its same-sex nature.

Background:

The city of Sodom is mentioned in the New Testament, in Jude 7, where the author writes, "In a similar way, Sodom and Gomorrah and the surrounding towns gave themselves up to sexual immorality and perversion. They serve as an example of those who suffer the punishment of eternal fire" (NIV). The King James Version (KJV) translates it differently. Instead of "sexual immorality and perversion," it says they gave themselves up to "fornication and going after strange flesh." The KJV's use of "fornication and going after strange flesh" is a more literal translation of the Greek text.

A non-affirming view might say:

Jude's reference to "strange flesh" refers to the unnaturalness of same-sex attraction. The flesh was strange because it was of the same sex as the person "going after it" and was thus not the typical type of "flesh" to "go after." Jude considered Sodom's sexual activity to be especially immoral because it involved same-sex sex.

An affirming view might say:

By using the term "going after," Jude is implying a one-sided experience, rather than a mutual encounter. Jude's reference to "strange flesh" may refer to it being the flesh of a stranger (the angels). For Jude, the Sodomites' sexual activity was immoral because it was violent, non-consensual, shaming, abusive, and extremely

---

15. Gagnon, *Bible and Homosexual Practice*, Kindle ed., Part IV, chap. 1.
16. Deuteronomy 22:28-29.
17. Gagnon, *Bible and Homosexual Practice*, Kindle ed., Part IV, chap. 1.

inhospitable to strangers. This story does not reflect the circumstance of same-sex marriage.

The primary sin of Sodom in Genesis 19:1-29 was the absence of hospitality.[18] Ancient Near Eastern culture held to a very strong hospitality code, which meant that people were obligated to welcome strangers, provide for them, and take care of them, even at the expense of their own family's needs.[19] Abraham showed this type of hospitality by washing the angels' feet and feeding them when they visited him. Lot showed this type of hospitality when he invited the angels to share a meal and sleep in his home and when he attempted to protect them at the expense of his and his daughters' safety. The author of the book of Hebrews is likely referring to Abraham and Lot in Hebrews 13:2 when he says, "do not neglect to show hospitality to strangers, for some have entertained angels without knowing it."

The Old Testament often teaches the importance of showing love and concern for strangers. More examples of such teaching can be found in Exodus 22:21, 23:9; Deuteronomy 10:19; Leviticus 19:33-34; Job 31:32; and Isaiah 58:7. When discussing Sodom's guilt, Ezekiel does not even mention sexual sin. In Ezekiel 16:49, God says: "Behold, this was the guilt of your sister Sodom: she and her daughters had pride, excess of food, and prosperous ease, but did not aid the poor and needy." The characteristics of pride, greed, and self-centeredness would all prevent gracious hospitality, the lack of which was Sodom's primary downfall.

In the New Testament, in Luke 9:54, James and John ask Jesus if he wants them to "call fire down from heaven" to destroy a village that did not welcome them, likely referencing the destruction of Sodom. This implies that Jesus' disciples understood Sodom to have been destroyed because of inhospitality. Jesus rebukes them for their intention to inflict violence but does not correct their understanding of the reason for Sodom's destruction. Shortly afterwards, in Luke 10:12, Jesus is talking about a town that did not welcome his disciples, and he says that when the kingdom of God comes it will be more bearable for Sodom than for that town. The context of this conversation had nothing to do with sexuality and was directly addressing a lack of hospitality. This suggests that Jesus, like Ezekiel, recognized Sodom's primary sin as inhospitality toward strangers. For other examples of Jesus' and Paul's emphasis on the importance of

---

18. Ibid.
19. Vines, *God and the Gay Christian*, Kindle ed., 66.

hospitality, see Luke 10:25-37, 14:12-14, Matthew 25:34-46, Romans 12:13, Titus 1:8, and 1 Timothy 3:2, 5:10.

Other verses mention Sodom with no reference to same-sex sex, which further suggests that same-sex sex was not Sodom's primary sin. Isaiah 1:10-17 addresses the rulers of Sodom and the people of Gomorrah, condemning idolatry and ending with "stop doing wrong, learn to do right! Seek justice, encourage the oppressed. Defend the cause of the fatherless, plead the case of the widow." Jeremiah 23:14 condemns God's prophets for committing adultery, living a lie, and strengthening the hand of evil doers, and compares them to Sodom and Gomorrah. Lamentations 4:6 compares the punishment of God's people to the punishment of Sodom but does not mention same-sex sex as part of the sin resulting in their punishment. The fact that same-sex sex is not mentioned when Sodom's sins are mentioned in other parts of the Bible suggests that Sodom's story was not primarily about condemning same-sex sex.

The first to interpret the sin of Sodom as something other than inhospitality was Philo, a philosopher who lived until 50 AD and wrote around the same time as Paul. Philo interpreted Sodom's sin as being about excessiveness, including gluttony, lewdness, and lustful sex with both women and men. Other early Christian thinkers in the first three centuries of the church did not adopt Philo's interpretation and continued to follow the biblical writers in emphasizing the lack of hospitality as Sodom's primary sin. In the late 4th and 5th centuries, the interpretation that Sodom was destroyed for violent same-sex sex rather than inhospitality was promoted by Chrysostom, Augustine, and other influential Christians. The growing belief at that time that any non-procreative sex was sinful may have influenced this shift in thinking. During the Middle Ages, the interpretation of Sodom's sin shifted from violent rape to all same-sex sex.[20] The actual traditional Christian view on this story, however, is that it is condemning inhospitality.

A non-affirming view might say:
The fact that Ezekiel refers to Sodom's sin as pride does not exclude same-sex sex from being the reason for God's judgment

---

20. Brian D. Cunnington, *Open Wide the Gates: An Argument for Welcome, Affirmation and Inclusion of Gay and Lesbian People in the Local Church* (Eugene, OR: Wipf and Stock, 2023), Kindle ed., 3111.

against Sodom.[21] Pride is the root of all sin, including same-sex sex. Pride entices people to turn their backs on God's laws and disobey him, believing they can improve upon God's plan for their lives. For some, this disobedience results in having sex with a same-sex partner. Same-sex sex involves loving someone similar to oneself, and therefore it is a form of self-love, or pride.

Jesus' reference to Sodom in the context of condemning a town for its inhospitality in Luke 10:12 does not mean that Sodom was also condemned for inhospitality. Jesus is comparing punishments for the two towns, which does not require the towns to have committed the same sinful acts. It is not a contradiction for Sodom to have been destroyed because of sins related to same-sex sex, and for the town Jesus is speaking of to be threatened because of inhospitality towards his disciples. However, even if the story of Sodom is primarily about the condemnation of violence and inhospitality, it still depicts God's negative view of same-sex sex.

Judges 19:1-30

Background:

A disturbing story found in Judges 19:1-30 is strikingly similar to the story of Sodom and may shed light on its meaning. Approximately five hundred years after the destruction of Sodom, an Israelite man is traveling through the Israelite city of Gibeah with his servant and his concubine (i.e., a lower-status wife in a polygamous marriage). The travelers enter the city square, where an old man invites them to stay with him for the night. While they are in his house, some of the wicked men of the city surround the house and pound on the door, demanding that the old man bring out the traveler so that the men of Gibeah can have sex with him. The old man goes outside to plead with them and offers to send out his virgin daughter and the traveler's concubine instead. The men of Gibeah reject his offer of the women, but the traveler sends his concubine outside anyway. She is gang raped and abused throughout the night, until she falls at the door where her dead body is found the next morning when the traveler leaves the house. When he informs the rest of the tribes of Israel about the murder of his concubine, with God's help, they destroy not only the

21. Rosaria Champagne Butterfield, *The Secret Thoughts of an Unlikely Convert: An English Professor's Journey into Christian Faith* (Pittsburgh, PA: Crown & Covenant, 2012), 30.

city of Gibeah but also the entire tribe of Benjamin (which fought to defend its city).

An affirming view might say:

Like the story of Sodom, the men's intent in this horrific story was male-male gang rape of the stranger for the purpose of domination and intimidation. In this situation, the traveling man was protected by the hospitable old man and the sacrifice of his concubine. According to the story, the Israelite leaders who decided to destroy Gibeah following the concubine's murder were informed of the rape and murder of the woman, but not of the men of Gibeah's original intent to rape the male traveler. The story condemned their violence against the woman and their robbing the traveler of his honor and his concubine (who would have been considered his possession).

The author and audience of this second story would have been aware of the story about Sodom, which this story deliberately parallels. Since the story of Gibeah is understood to be about condemning the mistreatment of the stranger, it is likely that the story about Sodom was also understood by its earliest hearers to be about condemning the mistreatment of the stranger. The author specifically states that the traveler went to an Israelite city rather than stay in Jebus, a city of foreigners, because the author is trying to show that the Israelites were just as capable of sin as the non-Israelites were. He mirrors the story of Sodom to show that the Israelites had just as much capacity to be sinfully inhospitable as the city of Sodom had been. The comparison of the two stories implies that the author of the book of Judges understood the story of Sodom to be about condemning inhospitality and violence toward the stranger. The lesson to be learned from both stories is that terrible treatment of a stranger is condemned.

A non-affirming view might say:

The death of a woman would be unlikely to have inspired so much anger in the patriarchal cultural setting of this story where women were minimally valued. The audience of this story knew that the men's original intent was to have male-male sex with the stranger, and it can be assumed that the rest of the Israelites who angrily destroyed the city also knew about their intent for male-male sex. The cities of Sodom and Gibeah were both destroyed as punishment for their practice of engaging in male-male sex.

Leviticus 18:22 and 20:13

Background:

The book of Leviticus records the laws and rituals that God gave the Israelites to teach them how to worship and honor him after they had left Egypt and become his chosen people. Most Christians are familiar with the Ten Commandments, which together with the teachings of the book of Leviticus, are often referred to as the law. Christians have a complicated relationship with the law and interpret its authority in different ways. Jesus' death and resurrection means that Christians are not bound by the law the same way the Israelites were. Most Christians believe that Jesus came to fulfill the requirements of the law on their behalf, so that now, instead of receiving atonement and forgiveness by following the law and its system of sacrifices, they receive forgiveness and salvation through faith in Jesus.

Some New Testament passages seem to teach that the law is no longer authoritative for Christians. For example, Romans 10:4 says, "Christ is the culmination of the law so that there may be righteousness for everyone who believes." Hebrews 8:13 says, "By calling this covenant 'new,' he has made the first one obsolete; and what is obsolete and outdated will soon disappear." Galatians 5:1 says, "It is for freedom that Christ has set us free. Stand firm, then, and do not let yourselves be burdened again by a yoke of slavery." Verses 4-6 say, "You who are trying to be justified by the law have been alienated from Christ; you have fallen away from grace. For through the Spirit we eagerly await by faith the righteousness for which we hope. For in Christ Jesus neither circumcision nor uncircumcision has any value. The only thing that counts is faith expressing itself through love." Romans 13:8 says, "Let no debt remain outstanding, except the continuing debt to love one another, for whoever loves others has fulfilled the law."

Some New Testament passages, however, imply that the law is still authoritative for Christians. In Matthew 5:17-18, Jesus says, "Do not think that I have come to abolish the Law or the Prophets; I have not come to abolish them but to fulfill them. I tell you the truth, until heaven and earth disappear, not the smallest letter, not the least stroke of a pen, will by any means disappear from the Law until everything is accomplished." In Luke 16:17, Jesus says, "It is easier for heaven and earth to disappear than for the least stroke of a pen to drop out of the Law." In Romans 3:31, Paul says, "Do we, then, nullify the law by this faith? Not at all! Rather, we uphold the law." In Romans 6:15 he says, "What then? Shall we sin because we are not under the law but under grace? By no means!"

Christians approach the Old Testament law in a variety of ways. Some say that Christ has fulfilled the law, so now Christians observe the law by following Christ. Within this group, an affirming view might say that the prohibitions in Leviticus, including the one against male-male anal sex, are no longer binding on Christians. A non-affirming view within this group might say that God's character, values, and plans for humanity can be understood from the law, and that the law continues to teach Christians how to behave in ways that please God. Although they are not obligated to follow the law, they choose to follow it out of devotion to God.

Some Christians say that the Old Testament law is still authoritative for Christians and that a Christian's new relationship with the law does not give them the freedom to engage in outlawed behavior. Within this group, an affirming view might say that Leviticus prohibits abusive and idolatrous male-male anal sex and does not prohibit covenantal relationships such as same-sex marriage. A non-affirming view within this group might say that the Levitical prohibition refers to all forms of same-sex sex and continues to be authoritative.

Christians who believe that the law is still authoritative face the challenge of explaining why some Levitical laws are followed by Christians and others are not. A common explanation is that the Old Testament laws can be categorized as either ceremonial or moral, and while Christians are not obligated to follow ceremonial laws, moral laws remain binding.[22] They say that ceremonial laws include rules about hand washing, sacrifices, and food, and that moral laws include the Ten Commandments and the sexual purity laws, including the prohibition against male-male sex. They say these are timeless because they are based on God's character and creation design.[23]

Those who believe that Christians are not required to follow the law might say that the moral law vs. ceremonial law distinction is not so simple to make. In the New Testament, James 2:10 says, "for whoever keeps the whole law and yet stumbles at just one point is guilty of breaking all of it." They say that this suggests that the law cannot be separated into ceremonial laws that no longer need to be kept and moral laws that do, and that since the Bible itself does not

---

22. Snyder, *Homosexuality and the Church*, 358.
23. Ibid., 346.

distinguish between ceremonial laws and moral laws, the practice of separating the laws into these categories is arbitrary. They point out that some laws that seem to be more moral than ceremonial are clearly not followed today, such as the rule that if a man rapes an unmarried woman, he must marry her (Deut 22:28), and if a man's brother dies, he must marry his brother's widow (Deut 25:7-8). They also point out that the Sabbath law is an example of a law that does not clearly fit into either a moral or a ceremonial category. The Sabbath law is in the middle of the Ten Commandments, which should solidify its status as a moral law (and thus supposedly still authoritative for Christians), yet most Christians do not follow God's command to rest on Saturdays.

Christians who dismiss the ceremonial vs. moral law explanation of why only certain laws remain binding might suggest that it is the moral logic that undergirds the Old Testament laws, rather than the laws themselves, that should inform Christian practice.[24] They say the Law provides principles and ideals that Christians still seek to embody even if they don't obey the direct commands. They follow the "spirit" of the law rather than the "letter" of the law. They say that the prohibitions in Leviticus are helpful to guide Christian behavior when the moral logic behind them is understood and applied to contemporary contexts.

An affirming view might say:

The moral logic behind the prohibition against male-male sex in Leviticus 18:22 and 20:13 takes into account the way male-male sex was happening in the cultural context when the law was received, as well as when it was written down. Sex that abuses and exploits other people and/or is related to cultic worship is always offensive to God and harmful to humanity, and that is the kind of sex prohibited by Leviticus. An affirming view might say that the over-arching moral logic that encompasses all the prohibitions in Leviticus is to avoid harm. Compared to the laws and purity codes of the other Ancient Near Eastern cultures, Israel's laws were adapted and reformed in the direction of not causing harm.[25] Since in contemporary times we are aware of the harm caused to LGBTQ+ people by their condemnation and exclusion by the church, the church has the responsibility to re-examine its interpretation of the Bible through a life-giving and "do-

24. James V. Brownson, *Bible, Gender, Sexuality: Reframing the Church's Debate on Same-Sex Relationships* (Grand Rapids: Eerdmans, 2013), 278.

25. Ken Wilson, "First, Do No Harm: Foundation for an LGBTQ-Affirming Theology," webinar handout, February 27, 2022.

no-harm" ethical approach. This is the approach that the ancient sages of Israel took when they taught that laws would be set aside when observing them endangered human life.[26]

A non-affirming view might say:

The laws prohibiting male-male sex are clear and can be followed as written. Therefore, they do not need to be interpreted through a "moral logic" lens, as do some of the more obscure laws.

Background:

An affirming view and a non-affirming view might agree that, whether or not Christians interpret the Old Testament laws as binding, Leviticus 18:22 and 20:13 influenced Paul's writing of the New Testament passages that address same-sex sex, and thus need to be considered when discussing the biblical basis for views related to same-sex marriage.

Content Warning: The following Scripture verses can be triggering.

Leviticus 18:22 says, "Do not have sexual relations with a man as one does with a woman; that is detestable." Leviticus 20:13 says, "If a man lies with a man as one lies with a woman, both of them have done what is detestable. They must be put to death" (NIV).

A non-affirming view might say:

These verses clearly prohibit male-male sexual activity. Paul would have understood the prohibition to include all forms of male-male sex and to include female-female sex by implication.

An affirming view might say:

In the original Hebrew, different words are used to describe the two males in Leviticus 20:13. The verse literally says, "If an *ish* (man) also lies with a *zakar* (male)" as he lieth with an *ishshah* (woman)." The use of "man" and "male" implies a power differential and may refer to a man exploiting a boy, who would be called "male," but not "man." If equal-status sex were being considered it could have said if *ish* lies with *ish*, (man with man). The use of *ish* and *zakar* is evidence that equal-status sex is not being referred to here.

---

26. Ibid.

A non-affirming view might say:

The reason the author uses *ish* and *zakar* may have been because *ish* sounds similar to *ishshah*, the word for woman, so it may have confused the listener to use *ish* to describe the second man. *Zakar* can describe a man as well as a boy, so while its use extends the prohibition to sex with boys, it doesn't limit it to pederastic forms of sex. The use of the Hebrew words *zakar* (male) and *ishshah* (woman) in Leviticus 18:22 is significant because *zakar* (male) is paired with *neqevah* (female) in the creation story in Genesis 1:26-27, but *ish* (man) and *ishshah* (woman) are used together in the creation story in Genesis 2:24. Leviticus 18:22 intentionally pulls one word from each of the two creation accounts, which reinforces the idea that the prohibition against same-sex sex is rooted in God's creation design and is therefore to be widely applied.[27]

An affirming view might say:

When considerations related to literary and historical context are examined, additional light is shed on these verses, and they don't seem as clear as they first appear. The historical and literary backgrounds need to be considered to help Christians develop their understanding of Leviticus as well as Paul's related writings.

Historical and Literary Contexts of Leviticus 18 & 20

Background:

Literature discovered from the Ancient Near East shows that the forms of same-sex sex that were happening in the historical context of the Old Testament were not covenantal and monogamous, the way a marriage is. Typically, men who engaged in male-male sex also had wives, or would have gone on to have wives. Evidence suggests that the primary contexts for male-male sex in the Ancient Near East were: the rape of enemies during wartime, sex which elevated the status of the dominant man while shaming the penetrated male, and possibly cultic prostitution.[28]

Archeological evidence of the practice of humiliating male enemies through rape has been discovered. An Egyptian myth called

---

27. Wesley Hill, "Christ, Scripture, and Spiritual Friendship," in *Two Views on Homosexuality, the Bible, and the Church*, ed. by Preston Sprinkle (Grand Rapids, MI: Zondervan, 2016), 133.

28. Nissinen, *Homoeroticism in the Biblical World*, 25-27.

"The Contendings of Horus and Seth" from the late second century BCE describes male-male rape between gods. The story is about sexual aggression and shaming in order to show superiority.[29] A coffin text discovered from ancient Egypt says, "Atum has no power over me, for I copulate between his buttocks."[30] This provides evidence of the perceived superiority of the penetrating man over the penetrated man.

Archeological evidence of sex which elevated the status of the penetrator and shamed the penetrated has also been found. A dream interpretation from Babylon, from the second millennium BCE, says, "if a man copulates with his equal from the rear, he becomes a leader among his peers and brothers."[31] In Mesopotamia, during the middle of the second millennium BCE, a law prohibited a man from having sex with his comrade. As punishment, the man who had committed this crime would be sexually violated by his accuser.[32] This shows that the sex itself was not the crime, or else those administering the punishment would also be guilty of it themselves. The crime was having sex with a social equal, or comrade. Being penetrated was something that caused shame, hence its use as a punishment. This social hierarchy between the penetrator and the penetrated was understood across the Ancient Near East.

In the highly patriarchal Ancient Near Eastern culture, women were devalued compared to men. Being a woman was considered shameful. Acting like a woman by being penetrated was shameful for a man. Note that Leviticus 18:22 and 20:13 specifically mention lying with a man "as with a woman," showing that treating a man like one treated a woman was an important factor influencing why the action is prohibited.

There are different opinions as to how widespread male-male cultic prostitution was at the time Leviticus was written. Some authors say it was prevalent and may have at least partly inspired the prohibition against male-male sex, but others say there is insufficient evidence that it was common enough at that point in time to have been a primary concern of the author of Leviticus.

To understand the Levitical prohibition against same-sex sex, it is helpful to understand what the prohibition meant to its original audience. It is important to examine what is written directly before

---

29. Ibid., 19.
30. Coffin Texts VI, 258 f-g (Westendorf, "Homosexualitat," 1272), quoted in Robert A. Gagnon, *Bible and Homosexual Practice*, Kindle ed., Part I, chap. 1.
31. Ibid., 27.
32. Nissinen, *Homoeroticism in the Biblical World*, 25.

and after the verse as well as what is written in the rest of the book and in the Bible in general. A brief study of the literary context of Leviticus will show that the purpose of the law is to separate the Israelites from the surrounding nations by prohibiting them from participating in the idolatrous and harm-inflicting activities engaged in by the surrounding nations. It will show that of the many laws listed in Leviticus, some are still followed by Christians, and some are not. It will show that the punishments prescribed for breaking the law are not usually followed today and do not consistently match the severity of the offense according to today's perspectives.

Leviticus 18

At the point in history described in Leviticus, God had just rescued his newly formed people, the Israelites, from slavery in Egypt, and was leading them towards Canaan, the land he had promised to give to them. Leviticus 18 begins with God warning the Israelites against doing as the people do in Egypt, where they had just come from, as well as in Canaan, where they were going. This warning communicates an expectation that the Israelites were to be set apart by behaving differently from the nations surrounding them. Leviticus 18:24 says, "do not defile yourselves in any of these ways, because this is how the nations that I am going to drive out before you became defiled." Leviticus 18:27 says, "for all these things were done by the people who lived in the land before you, and the land became defiled." Verses 29 and 30 say, "Everyone who does any of these detestable things—such persons must be cut off from their people. Keep my requirements and do not follow any of the detestable customs that were practiced before you came and do not defile yourselves with them. I am the Lord your God."

An affirming view might say:

The warning against following the customs of the Canaanites suggests that Leviticus is prohibiting male-male sex specifically in the way that it was practiced by the surrounding nations. This primarily involved the violent, sexual domination of men defeated in battle, the sexual exploitation of slaves or servants, including prepubescent boys, and possibly cultic prostitution. In these situations, the penetrated male was shamed for being placed in a woman's role. Covenantal same-sex relationships akin to a marriage were rare to non-existent.

Background:

Leviticus 18 prohibits men from having sex with other specific types of people, including their close relatives, their mothers or their fathers' other wives, their sisters, their granddaughters, their aunts by blood or by marriage, their daughters-in-law, and their sisters-in-law. A man was prohibited from having sexual relations with both a woman and her daughter, granddaughter, or sister, his neighbor's wives, and women who were unclean from menstruation. The menstrual period was typically measured as seven days after regular menstruation begins, or seven days after irregular bleeding ends.

A non-affirming view might say:

This list of prohibited sex acts is common sense and largely still endorsed by Christians today. The list also prohibits men having sexual relations with a man as one does with a woman, and this should also still be endorsed today.

An affirming view might say:

The prohibitions are intended to avoid causing harm, which is why most of them still resonate as common sense today. However, most Christians would not prohibit sex for seven days after menstruation begins or after irregular bleeding ends. This prohibition may have been related to the idea that it was sinful to waste semen and/or seed on non-procreative sex during a woman's infertile time of the month. Since there is at least one prohibition in this passage which Christians no longer consider to be authoritative based on new cultural practices and understandings, it is possible that other prohibitions, such as the one against male-male sex, may likewise no longer be authoritative.

A non-affirming view might say:

Leviticus 18:26 says, "The native-born and the foreigners residing among you must not do any of these detestable things." The fact that foreigners are expected to comply with the Israelite prohibition against male-male sex further supports its universal applicability.[33]

An affirming view might say:

For the good of the community, Leviticus expects foreigners to comply with avoiding violent, abusive, exploitative, and/or cultic,

---

33. Hill, "Christ, Scripture, and Spiritual Friendship," in *Two Views on Homosexuality, the Bible, and the Church*, 133.

male-male sex. This is a timeless prohibition in keeping with God's loving character.

Leviticus 18:21 addresses the worship of other gods, saying, "Do not give any of your children to be sacrificed to Molech, for you must not profane the name of your God." One of the ways the Canaanites worshiped their god Molech was to sacrifice their own children, likely killing them by passing them "through the fire," or possibly dedicating them to Molech to be temple priests or prostitutes.[34] This practice of child sacrifice is referenced in Deuteronomy 12:31 and 2 Kings 16:3, where it is described as *to`ebhah* (an abomination, detestable, or religiously offensive). Psalm 106:35-38 suggests that the Israelites, at least for a time, also participated in this idolatrous practice. Here in Leviticus 18:21, God is prohibiting the Israelites from worshiping Molech through child sacrifice. Immediately after this prohibition, Leviticus 18:22 says, "Do not have sexual relations with a man as one does with a woman; that is detestable." Verse 22 is likely connected to verse 21, in that one of the ways the Canaanites worshiped their gods was through child sacrifice (v. 21), and another way was through cultic male-male sexual activity (v. 22).[35] The connection between cult prostitution and child sacrifice can be seen in 2 Kings 23:7-10 and Isaiah 57:5-7, where the two practices are mentioned together.

Worship of the god Ishtar involved prostitution with the belief that men who penetrated a male prostitute were accessing Ishtar's power.[36] Ishtar was considered to be Molech's spouse. Because the prohibition against engaging in male-male sex follows directly after the prohibition against child sacrifice, it seems that the two are connected, relating to the prohibition of the idolatrous worship of the divine spouses, Molech and Ishtar. Jeremiah 44:15-18 mentions the "Queen of Heaven," which could be a reference to Ishtar. If so, it would provide evidence to support the possibility that worship of Ishtar through cultic male-male sex was a cultural practice and could have at least partially inspired the Levitical prohibition.

---

34. N. H. Snaith, "The Cult of Molech," *Vetus Testamentum* 16, no. 1 (1966): 123.

35. Gagnon, *Bible and Homosexual Practice*, Kindle ed., Part VII, chap. 1.

36. Ibid., Part I, chap. 1. See also Nissinen, *Homoeroticism in the Biblical World: A Historical Perspective*, 27.

Leviticus 19

Background:

Although Leviticus 19 does not directly address same-sex sex, it provides further context for chapters 18 and 20. Chapter 19 contains another list of rules. It starts with the command, "Be holy because I, the LORD your God, am holy." Then it goes on to instruct the Israelites to respect their parents, observe the Sabbaths, and eat the fellowship sacrifice within two days (adding that anyone who eats it on the third day or later must be cut off from their people). It instructs them to leave the edges of their fields unharvested and to leave unharvested grapes for the poor. It warns the Israelites against idol worship, stealing, lying, deceiving one another, swearing falsely by God's name, robbing their neighbor, holding back wages, cursing the deaf, and putting a stumbling block in front of the blind. It says to not pervert justice but rather to judge fairly, without partiality. It goes on: do not spread slander; do not endanger your neighbor's life; do not hate your brother; rebuke your neighbour frankly so you don't share in his guilt; do not seek revenge or bear a grudge; love your neighbor as yourself. The instructions continue: do not mate different kinds of animals; do not plant two different kinds of seeds in one field; do not wear clothes that are woven of two kinds of materials; if a man sleeps with a slave girl, he must bring a guilt offering to the LORD; refrain from eating the fruit of a tree for the first three years, then offer the fruit to the LORD in the fourth year, and eat it in the fifth year; do not practice divination or sorcery; do not cut the hair at the sides of your head or clip off the edges of your beard; do not cut your bodies for the dead or put tattoo marks on yourselves; do not make your daughter a prostitute; have reverence for the LORD's sanctuary; do not turn to mediums or seek out spiritists; do not mistreat the stranger living in your land, but treat him as one of your native-born; and finally, use honest scales and weights.

An affirming view might say:

Christians continue to follow many of the laws listed in Leviticus 19 but consider others to no longer be authoritative. It would be inconsistent to use Leviticus to prohibit all forms of same-sex sex while allowing Christians to break other laws by doing things like wearing cotton-polyester blend clothing, cutting the sides of their hair and shaving their beards, getting tattoos, and neglecting to keep the Sabbath on Saturdays. There are several commands in Leviticus 19 that prohibit telling lies. Many LGBTQ+ people who are not allowed to come out and live authentically feel like they are living a lie. Leviticus 19:16 says, "do not do anything that endangers your neighbor's life. I am the LORD," but non-affirming theology endangers LGBTQ+ people's lives because it inspires violence and discrimination against them and leads many LGBTQ+ people to feel unworthy of God's love and to attempt or commit suicide.

Many of the prohibitions listed in Leviticus 19 function to protect people from harm. When following a law causes harm to people, Christians should examine the law closely to see if they have misunderstood it.

A non-affirming view might say:

The laws prohibiting same-sex sex are among the Levitical laws that remain authoritative because they are reinforced by Paul in the New Testament. Non-affirming theology is not responsible for people hiding their sexuality or taking their own lives. People have other options, including putting their identity fully in Jesus and living celibate lives.

Leviticus 20

Background:

Like chapter 18, chapter 20 starts by reminding the Israelites to live differently than their Canaanite neighbors. The instructions in chapter 20 vary only slightly from the ones in chapter 18. The primary difference is that chapter 20 outlines the punishments for breaking some of the commands given in chapter 18. Chapter 20 lists the death penalty as the punishment for: sacrificing children to Molech, being a medium or spiritist, cursing one's parents, committing adultery with another man's wife, lying with a male as one lies with a woman (with both men being punished), marrying both a woman and her mother, and having sexual relations with an animal. Being cut off from the people is the punishment listed for a number of actions, including: turning a blind eye to the practice of sacrificing children to Molech, prostituting oneself to Molech, turning to mediums and spiritists, marrying one's sister, lying with a woman during her menstruation period, and having sexual relations with one's aunt. After listing the punishments, chapter 20 gives reminders that God has set Israel apart from the nations to be his own people, that Israel is to be holy because he, the LORD, is holy, and that therefore God's people are to behave differently than the surrounding nations.

A non-affirming view might say:

That both males involved in male-male sex were punished shows that one was not oppressing the other, because God would not have punished an innocent man.[37] The level of severity of the punishments can serve as an indicator of the severity of the sin. That the death penalty was the punishment for male-male sex shows that its prohibition was important to God. Since the stakes are high, it is best to err on the side of caution by prohibiting all same-sex sex.

An affirming view might say:

In the ancient culture around Israel, a man who penetrated a slave or prostitute was not considered guilty of a crime.[38] The Levitical law including punishment for the penetrator shows a greater degree of fairness for the penetrated man by not singling him out for condemnation (i.e., punishing him for crossing gender boundaries by shamefully acting like a woman). This law meant that in Israel, a perpetrator of male-male rape or abusive sex would be punished even if the victim was a slave or subservient man. The law may have deterred abuse. This is a departure from the consistent practice of the surrounding nations, which cast shame only on the penetrated man.

The other sexual sins listed in Leviticus 20 (adultery, incest, bestiality, and sex during menstruation) also involved punishing both parties with death or excommunication. The animals involved in bestiality were to be killed, even though they could not have been complicit in the act. Women in that ancient patriarchal culture may not have had freedom to refuse sex, yet they were also to be punished in incestuous relationships along with the men. The mutual punishment for both males involved in male-male sex does not prove a mutual relationship existed between them, just like the punishment of an animal victim of bestiality, or a powerless, female participant in opposite-sex incest in a highly patriarchal culture does not prove them to have been mutual partners. The level of severity of a punishment should not be used to determine whether a command is permanently authoritative, as there are examples of offenses with severe punishments in Leviticus that are not followed today. For example, the punishment for having sex with a woman during her period was being cut off from one's people.

---

37. Preston Sprinkle, *A People to be Loved: Why Homosexuality Is Not Just an Issue* (Grand Rapids, MI: Zondervan, 2015), 48.

38. Nissinen, *Homoeroticism in the Biblical World*, 72.

Leviticus 20:3-5's references to "giving children to Molech" and "prostituting [oneself] to Molech" suggest a context where the discussion of male-male sex in verse 13 could also be related to cultic worship practices. If cultic prostitution was in view in 20:13, the reason the passive man was condemned along with the dominant man was because he was worshiping idols by serving as a temple prostitute. The knowledge that Molech's spouse, Ishtar, was worshiped through cultic prostitution supports a connection between the worship of Molech and same-sex cultic prostitution.

A non-affirming view might say:
The reason the reference to Molech is included in a list of other prohibited sexual practices is because children are the result of sex, so giving children to Molech (child sacrifice) is categorized as a prohibited sexual practice along with all forms of same-sex sex. The fact that Molech is included in this list does not imply that the prohibition against same-sex sex is related to idol worship but rather suggests that both child sacrifice and same-sex sex were classified as sexual sins because of their negative impact on procreation.

Additionally, if we decide that same-sex sex is acceptable, even though it appears on Leviticus's list of prohibited activities, this may lead us also to accept activities like bestiality and incest, since the prohibitions will no longer carry any authority.

An affirming view might say:
When marriage is defined as being between two consenting human adults, boundaries can still be placed on sexual activity, such as requiring that it occur within a marriage relationship. This would rule out incest and bestiality. Other appropriate boundaries are that sexual activity must not be abusive or exploitative.

The Word To`ebhah (Detestable)

A non-affirming view might say:
The fact that Leviticus 18:22 and 20:13 use the word to`ebhah—translated as "detestable" or "abomination"—to describe male-male sex underscores the severity of these prohibitions.

An affirming view might say:
Leviticus 18:26-27 and 29-30 use the word to`ebhah (detestable/abomination) to describe sexual relations with the whole list of prohibited partners (including menstruating women) as well as

sacrificing children to Molech. The male-male sex is not the only act described as detestable.

The book of Deuteronomy repeats the message of Leviticus, which is that God wants his people to avoid behaving like the nations whose land they are about to enter. Of Deuteronomy's sixteen usages of the word to`ebhah, twelve describe the worship of foreign gods or improper worship of Israel's God. In the rest of the Old Testament, to`ebhah frequently has the sense of being religiously offensive, referring to idolatrous practices or practices committed by the surrounding nations that can be assumed to be idolatrous. Idolatry is treated very seriously throughout the Bible. The first two of the Ten Commandments pertain to avoiding idol worship.[39] 2 Chronicles 7:19-22 warns the Israelites that if they worship and serve other gods, God will bring disaster upon them. See 2 Chronicles 17:3-4, 21:11-15, and Psalm 44:20 for further evidence that God was adamant that his people must avoid idolatry. The strict prohibition against male-male sex seen in Leviticus 18:22 would be expected if same-sex sex was most often happening in the context of idolatrous prostitution.

In light of the usage of the word to`ebhah in Deuteronomy and elsewhere in the Old Testament, the male-male sex described as "detestable" in Leviticus can be understood as something offensive to God, related to cultic prostitution and/or sex that oppresses the poor or powerless. Equal-status, monogamous, covenantal same-sex sex would not be religiously offensive and thus would not be to`ebhah.

A non-affirming view might say:

The ancient Israelites did not distinguish between religious and non-religious aspects of life and therefore all of life could be considered religious. An act such as same-sex sex could have been offensive to God even if it was not associated with idolatry or abuse. Deuteronomy also uses the word to`ebhah to describe forbidden foods (14:3-10), wearing the opposite sex's clothing (22:5), dishonest trade (25:16), and remarrying a previous wife after she has been divorced or widowed (24:4). Since these four practices do not refer to cultic worship, it cannot be assumed that the prohibition against male-male sex is related to idolatry, simply because it is described as to`ebhah. To`ebhah is always used to describe prohibited acts. The fact that male-male sex in Leviticus is described as "abominable" or "detestable" shows that it is offensive to God and must be avoided, but it does not prove that the sex in view is necessarily related to idolatry. If the

---

39. Exodus 20:1-6.

author of Leviticus had intended specifically to prohibit sex related to cultic prostitution, he could have used more specific language. The author deliberately chose to use words that encompass every form of male-male sex; therefore, it is evident that he was not prohibiting only cultic male-male sex.

An affirming view might say:

Some of the non-idolatrous activities that are prohibited in Deuteronomy seem to relate to the idea of crossing creation categories or mixing types. For example, the Israelites are allowed to eat animals that chew their cud and have a divided hoof but are not allowed to eat ones that chew their cud but do not have a divided hoof. They are also not allowed to eat creatures that live in the water but do not have fins and scales.[40] In Deuteronomy 22:9-11, the Israelites are prohibited from planting two kinds of seeds in a vineyard, plowing with an ox and a donkey yoked together, and wearing clothes of wool and linen woven together. The avoidance of mixing types may have reminded the Israelites to keep themselves separate from the surrounding nations. Crossing creation categories in these ways may have been religiously offensive to God at the time, but Christians don't typically consider these actions to be problematic today. The prohibition against wearing the opposite sex's garments (22:5) could also be seen as avoiding the crossing of creation categories. If male-male sex was prohibited in Leviticus specifically because it crossed creation categories (inasmuch as a male was acting like a woman), then the prohibition against it should be no more authoritative for Christians today than the law against eating pork or shellfish or wearing mixed-fiber clothing.

Re-marrying a previous wife after she has been divorced or widowed is described as to`ebhah (Deut 24:4) but would not be considered problematic by many Christians today, who might even see it as a positive restoration. Dishonest trade, also described as to`ebhah (Deut 25:16) is a form of exploitation. The offenses that are described as to`ebhah (detestable) in Deuteronomy are either idolatrous or exploitative, or else they cross creation categories, and/or they are no longer considered detestable today. Idolatrous and exploitative behavior is still considered problematic, but same-sex marriage is not either of those, so it does not fit in with the other activities described as to`ebhah (detestable).

---

40. See Deuteronomy 14:3-10.

A non-affirming view might say:

The concept of crossing creation categories is not taught in the Bible. It has been suggested as a way of making sense of some prohibitions but should not be assumed to be a biblical concept. Whether or not the word *to`ebhah* describes actions that are prohibited contextually or timelessly, male-male sex is viewed negatively in Leviticus and is prohibited without qualification regarding the specific nature of the same-sex sex. While the other offenses, such as eating unclean food, were dismissed in the New Testament as no longer authoritative for Christians, the prohibition against same-sex sex was reinforced by Paul and should continue to apply today.

An affirming view might say:

Deuteronomy 27 contains a list of prohibited behaviors that the Levites (the priests) were instructed to recite to all the Israelites. People who were guilty of these prohibited behaviors faced the consequence of being cursed. The list of prohibited behaviors includes making an idol, dishonoring one's father or mother, moving one's neighbor's boundary stone, leading the blind astray on the road, withholding justice from the stranger, fatherless or widow, having sex with one's father's wife, sister, half-sister, or mother-in-law, having sexual relations with an animal, killing one's neighbor secretly, and accepting a bribe to kill an innocent person. The absence of the prohibition against male-male sex within this list is notable and suggests that the prohibition against male-male sex was understood to be included within the prohibition against making an idol (i.e., worshiping other gods). This supports the hypothesis that the prohibition against male-male sex was against specific forms of sex related to idol worship.

Besides the possibility that male-male sex was associated with idolatry, other spiritual reasons why male-male sex was religiously offensive was that it was aggressive and violent and that it shamed and oppressed the penetrated man, who was often poor and powerless. A cultural reason for its prohibition may have been that it was understood to waste semen, which was thought to contain tiny babies that could grow if inserted into a woman's womb. Equal-status sex within a same-sex marriage is not aggressive, shaming, or oppressive to the poor and powerless, nor is it an element of idol worship. It is now known that semen does not contain babies that are wasted on non-procreative sex. Therefore same-sex marriage should not be considered to be religiously offensive today and should not be prohibited based on Levitical laws designating it as *to`ebhah*.

The literal interpretation of Leviticus 18:23 implies a prohibition of anal sex. Other forms of same-sex erotic activity between men and women are not prohibited. Even if the law was still authoritative today, a male-male couple that avoids anal sex or a female-female couple would not technically be breaking this law. Female-female sex was not specifically prohibited in Leviticus. Reasons for this omission could be that it was not happening in the context of idolatry, or it did not shame or exploit a man. The reference to female bestiality in Leviticus 18:23 demonstrates that the author was aware of female sexual practices, which makes the absence of a prohibition against female-female sex notable. The fact that female-female sex was not included in the prohibitions suggests that the prohibition against male-male sex is contextual rather than universal. The absence of a prohibition against female-female sex provides further weight to the hypothesis that it was sex in the context of idol worship and/or the shaming and exploitation of the penetrated man that inspired the prohibition.

A non-affirming view might say:
Although female-female sex is not specifically addressed in the Old Testament, it can be assumed that female-female sex is prohibited along with male-male sex.[41] It may not have been necessary to specifically prohibit female-female sex at the time because it was unlikely to occur or to be known to have occurred in a patriarchal society that held a high value on female chastity.[42] Or, if it was known to be happening, it may not have been considered to be real sex because it did not involve semen. Paul seemed to interpret female-female sex as being prohibited when he condemned unnatural female intercourse in Romans. The logic of the law implies that if anal sex is sinful, any form of same-sex erotic activity is sinful.

An affirming view might say:
It is not clear that Paul condemned female-female sex in Romans 1:26. He may have been condemning another form of unnatural sex that females were participating in, possibly non-procreative sex with their husbands.

---

41. Jay Sklar, *Leviticus*, Tyndale Old Testament Commentaries Vol 3, ed. by David G. Firth and Tremper Longman III (Downers Grove, IL: IVP Academic, 2014), 237.
42. Gagnon, *Bible and Homosexual Practice*, Kindle ed., Part VII, chap. 1.

Conclusion to Part II

Some Christians believe that in the story of Sodom, God condemned the Sodomites' desire to sexually assault and dominate the angels instead of showing them hospitality. They believe that this story does not address equal-status, same-sex sex within a covenantal relationship or marriage. Others believe that the Sodomites' desire to sexually assault the angels implies that it was the practice of male-male sex that triggered God's wrath against Sodom.

The Old Testament Levitical laws prohibit male-male sex and punish it with severe consequences. Some Christians believe that since Jesus has fulfilled the law for us, Levitical teaching should not be used to prohibit same-sex marriage. Some Christians believe that Leviticus prohibits only specific forms of male-male sex, and that the prohibition does not apply to same-sex marriage today.

Some Christians believe that the prohibition in Leviticus refers to all forms of male-male sex (and female-female sex by implication), and that the prohibition is still to be upheld. They observe that the passages in Leviticus clearly depict God as viewing same-sex sex negatively, and that there are no qualifications identifying specific forms of same-sex sex, so they believe that these prohibitions can be assumed to apply broadly. They say that since Paul reinforces the prohibition in the New Testament, it is still relevant today.

Personal Reflection

Following my research on the Old Testament, I believed that, while Christians were no longer obligated to follow the law, it did still instruct us on the types of behaviors and attitudes that please God. I came to believe that the story of Sodom and the teaching in Leviticus were addressing specific forms of abusive or idolatrous same-sex sex, and they did not give guidance regarding same-sex marriage. I shifted my focus of study to the New Testament verses, hoping they would help guide my response to the question of whether to affirm same-sex marriage and LGBTQ+ identities.

PART III: DOES THE NEW TESTAMENT CONDEMN SAME-SEX MARRIAGE?

Romans 1:26-27

Background:

The three passages that directly address same-sex sex in the New Testament are found in letters attributed to the Apostle Paul, written to newly formed Christian churches after Jesus' death and resurrection. Of the three passages, Romans 1:26-27 is the most complex and is the only one to address women's sexual practices. There are a lot of ideas to unpack in this passage, so the following discussion on Romans is organized around themes, including: creation, idolatry, covenantal relationships, pederasty, patriarchy, hierarchy, shameful lusts, unnatural behavior, extreme vices and their punishments, and Paul's primary purpose.

The Apostle Paul sent this letter to the church in Rome from the city of Corinth, likely around the year 57 CE. Paul had not yet met the Roman church, so his letter introduces himself and includes a review and application of the message of Jesus (i.e., the gospel). He also introduces plans to ask for their support to enable him to travel to Spain after he visits them. The church receiving his letter was divided. The Jewish Christians had recently returned to Rome from five years of forced exile by Emperor Claudius. They had re-joined the church, which had consisted of the Gentile Christians who had not been exiled. Paul encourages reconciliation between the two factions and makes the point that they should not judge each other.[43] As usual, it

---

43. Colby Martin, *Unclobber: Rethinking Our Misuse of the Bible on Homosexuality* (Louisville, KY: Westminster John Knox Press, 2016), 118.

is helpful to read the broader passage to provide context for the verses of particular interest. Romans 1:18-2:1 says:

> The wrath of God is being revealed from heaven against all the godlessness and wickedness of people, who suppress the truth by their wickedness, since what may be known about God is plain to them, because God has made it plain to them. For since the creation of the world God's invisible qualities—his eternal power and divine nature—have been clearly seen, being understood from what has been made, so that people are without excuse.
>
> For although they knew God, they neither glorified him as God nor gave thanks to him, but their thinking became futile and their foolish hearts were darkened. Although they claimed to be wise, they became fools and exchanged the glory of the immortal God for images made to look like a mortal human being and birds and animals and reptiles.
>
> Therefore God gave them over in the sinful desires of their hearts to sexual impurity for the degrading of their bodies with one another. They exchanged the truth about God for a lie, and worshiped and served created things rather than the Creator—who is forever praised. Amen.
>
> Because of this, God gave them over to shameful lusts. Even their women exchanged natural sexual relations for unnatural ones. In the same way the men also abandoned natural relations with women and were inflamed with lust for one another. Men committed shameful acts with other men, and received in themselves the due penalty for their error.
>
> Furthermore, just as they did not think it worthwhile to retain the knowledge of God, so God gave them over to a depraved mind, so that they do what ought not to be done. They have become filled with every kind of wickedness, evil, greed and depravity. They are full of envy, murder, strife, deceit and malice. They are gossips, slanderers, God-haters, insolent, arrogant and boastful; they invent ways of doing evil; they disobey their parents; they have no understanding, no fidelity, no love, no mercy. Although they know God's righteous decree that those who do such things deserve death, they not only continue to do these very things but also approve of those who practice them.
>
> You, therefore, have no excuse, you who pass judgment on someone else, for at whatever point you judge another, you are condemning yourself, because you who pass judgment do the same things.

Creation

A non-affirming view might say:

In verse 20, when Paul teaches that God's attributes can be known through his creation, he wants his use of the word "creation" to cause his readers to think of the creation stories in Genesis 1 and 2. Paul specifically directs his readers' thoughts to the creation story in Genesis 1 by repeating the words used in the Greek translation of Genesis 1:26: *eikōn* (likeness), *homoioma* (image), *anthropos* (human being), *peteinon* (birds), *tetrapous* (four-footed beasts) and *herpeton* (reptiles).[44] Paul uses the words *arsen* (male) and *thēlus* (female), words previously used in the Greek translation of the original Hebrew Scriptures. By using the same words as appear in Genesis, Paul intends to demonstrate that God's plan for human sexuality is known through human beings' anatomical and physiological design, which was established during creation. An essential element of honoring God involves honoring God's plan for exclusively male-female sexual intercourse, which is evident by the way male and female genitalia are designed to fit together for procreation and mutual pleasure.

In verses 25-32, when addressing same-sex sex, Paul uses words from Genesis 3's story of the fall from grace, including the words *pseudos* (lie), *aschēmosunē* (shame), and *thanatos* (death). Paul's references to creation and the fall through his use of the same words used in Genesis suggest that he believes same-sex sex to be contrary to God's creation design and therefore prohibited by God.

An affirming view might say:

Verses 19 and 20 say that creation plainly reveals information about God, specifically his eternal power and divine nature. They do not say that creation reveals anything about human nature or God's plans for human sexuality.[45] Paul's reference to creation is not intended to teach his readers about human sexuality, but rather to remind them that by contemplating creation, people can understand enough about God to know that he is superior to idols.

Rather than alluding to Genesis 1 and 2 to cause people to think about creation and how God created people as male and female, Romans 1:20 actually alludes to the apocryphal book the Wisdom of Solomon,[46] which was written about one hundred years before Paul's time and would have been familiar to Paul and his audience. When the passages from Romans and the Wisdom of Solomon are compared side by side, it becomes clear that Paul intentionally mirrors the Wisdom of Solomon, and his reason for alluding to creation also becomes clear: to show that all have sinned and need God's grace. This is, essentially, the message of the gospel.

---

44. Sprinkle, *People to be Loved*, 91-92.
45. Brownson, *Bible, Gender, Sexuality*, 241.
46. Karen R. Keen, *Scripture, Ethics, and the Possibility of Same-Sex Relationships* (Grand Rapids, MI: Eerdmans, 2018), 43.

In the Wisdom of Solomon 13:1, 5, and 8-9, it says:

> For all people who were ignorant of God were foolish by nature; and they were unable from the good things that are seen to know the one who exists. ... For from the greatness and beauty of created things comes a corresponding perception of their Creator. ... Yet again, not even they are to be excused, for if they had the power to know so much that they could investigate the world, how did they fail to find sooner the Lord of these things?[47]

Romans 1:19-20, 22 says:

> For what can be known about God is plain to them, because God has shown it to them. Ever since the creation of the world his invisible nature, namely, his power and deity, has been clearly perceived in the things that have been made. So they are without excuse. ... Claiming to be wise, they became fools...

The parallel point made in both passages is that, in their foolishness, the Gentiles failed to perceive God from the things God had created, and for this they have no excuse.

The Wisdom of Solomon 13:10 says: "But miserable ... are those who give the name 'god' to the works of human hands, gold and silver fashioned with skill, and likenesses of animals." Romans 1:34 says: "[they] exchanged the glory of the immortal God for images made to look like a mortal human being and birds and animals and reptiles." The parallel point made in these passages is that instead of worshiping God, people fashioned and worshiped idols made to look like animals.

The Wisdom of Solomon 14:12, 24-27 says:

> For the idea of making idols was the beginning of fornication, and the invention of them was the corruption of life. ...they no longer keep either their lives or their marriages pure, but they either treacherously kill one another, or grieve one another by adultery, and all is a raging riot of blood and murder, theft and deceit, corruption, faithlessness, tumult, perjury, confusion over what is good, forgetfulness of favors, defiling of souls, interchange of sex roles, disorder in marriage, adultery and debauchery. For the worship of idols not to be named is the beginning and cause and end of every evil.

Romans 1:24-31 says:

> Therefore God gave them over in the sinful desires of their hearts to sexual impurity for the degrading of their bodies with one another. They exchanged the truth about God for a lie, and worshiped and served created things rather than the Creator. ... Because of this, God gave them over to shameful lusts. Even their women exchanged natural sexual relations for unnatural ones. In the same way the men also abandoned natural relations with women and were

---

47. New Revised Standard Version: Catholic Edition.

inflamed with lust for one another. Men committed shameful acts with other men, and received in themselves the due penalty for their error. Furthermore, just as they did not think it worthwhile to retain the knowledge of God, so God gave them over to a depraved mind, so that they do what ought not to be done. They have been filled with every kind of wickedness, evil, greed and depravity. They are full of envy, murder, strife, deceit and malice. They are gossips, slanderers, God-haters, insolent, arrogant and boastful; they invent ways of doing evil: they disobey their parents; they have no understanding, no fidelity, no love, no mercy.

The parallel point made in both passages is that idolatry is the cause of human immorality, which includes sexual immorality.

The similarities between these verses in Romans 1:18-32 and the Wisdom of Solomon are striking. Both books imply that creation itself should provide people with enough evidence to know and worship God. Both say that people who don't recognize God from his creation are foolish. Both describe people worshiping idols instead of God and both provide a list of vices that result from the idol worship. Both vice lists include sexual impurity. Both documents seem to be criticizing the Gentiles who disregard God. These similarities provide evidence that Paul deliberately alludes to the Wisdom of Solomon in this passage. After following it so closely, he then makes an abrupt change and makes a statement that contrasts the Wisdom of Solomon. This is where it gets interesting.

The Wisdom of Solomon 15:1-4 says:

But you, our God, are kind and true, patient, and ruling all things in mercy. For even if we [the Jews] are yours, knowing your power, but we will not sin, because we know that you acknowledge us as yours. For to know you is complete righteousness, and to know your power is the root of immortality. For neither has the evil intent of human art misled us.

Verses 16:1-3 say:

Therefore those people [the Gentiles] were deservedly perished through such creatures, and were tormented by a multitude of animals. Instead of this punishment you showed kindness to your people, and you prepared quails to eat, a delicacy to satisfy the desire of appetite; in order that those people, when they desired food, might lose the least remnant of appetite because of the odious creatures sent to them, while your people after suffering want a short time, might partake of delicacies…

In contrast to this, Romans 2:1-11 says:

Therefore, you have no excuse, O man, whoever you are, when you judge another, for in passing judgment upon him you condemn yourself, because you, the judge, are doing the very same things. We know that the judgment of God rightly falls upon those who do such things. Do you suppose, O man, that when you judge those who do such things and yet do them yourself, you will escape the judgment of God? Or do you presume upon the riches of his kindness and forbearance and patience? Do you not know that God's kindness is meant to lead you to repentance? But by your hard and impenitent heart you are storing up wrath for yourself on the day of wrath when God's righteous judgment will be revealed. For he will render to every man according to his works: to those who by patience in well-doing seek for glory and honor and immortality, he will give eternal life, but for those who are factious and do not obey the truth, but obey wickedness, there will be wrath and fury. There will be tribulation and distress for every human being who does evil, the Jew first and also the Greek, but glory and honor and peace for everyone who does good, the Jew first and also the Greek. For God shows no partiality.

The Wisdom of Solomon implies that the Gentiles deserve to be judged for the behaviors listed in the vice list and elevates Jewish people as morally superior to the Gentiles. In contrast, Romans says that it is hypocritical for the Jews to judge the Gentiles, because all are guilty, including the Jews. God will treat Jews and Gentiles equitably and without partiality. This difference between the Wisdom of Solomon and Romans in these passages suggests that the vice list and allusion to the Wisdom of Solomon in Romans 1 function as a set-up. Paul wants his readers to agree that the Gentiles who do these sinful things are deserving of judgment so that he can turn around and show those within the church that they are also guilty and in need of grace themselves, and that the same grace they receive should be extended to the Gentiles. His primary intention is not to condemn the Gentiles, but rather to inspire the church to have more grace and to seek grace through Jesus because all need it, including the church itself.

By closely following the pattern in the Wisdom of Solomon, Paul sets his Jewish readers up to anticipate the further condemnation of the Gentiles, as occurs in the Wisdom of Solomon. When Paul says the opposite of what they are expecting to hear, which is that they also need God's grace, he intends to catch them off guard and cause them to take notice of what he is saying. This "bait and switch" technique can be observed in a simple reading of Romans 1 and 2 alone but is even clearer when we consider Paul's references to the Wisdom of Solomon.

Idolatry

Background:
Romans 1:22-24 says that because people rejected God and worshiped idols, God gave them over to their sinful sexual desires.

Same-sex sex is listed alongside idol worship as a primary behavior resulting from people's rejection of God. Other vices included on the list are envy, murder, strife, deceit, and malice. The vice list also identifies people who are gossips, slanderers, God-haters, insolent, arrogant, boastful, disobedient to parents, and without understanding, fidelity, love, or mercy.

An affirming view might say:

Paul may have been addressing same-sex sex in the context of idolatry, possibly including cultic prostitution. In this case, his condemnation would not apply to covenantal same-sex relationships today. Paul's mention of sexual impurity in verse 24 is inserted between two verses that describe idol worship. The references to idolatry in verses 23 and 25 provide evidence that same-sex sex in the context of idol worship may have been on Paul's mind as he wrote verse 24. In verse 26, Paul says that God gave the people up to shameful lusts because of their worship of idols. This would make the most sense if the shameful lusts were referring to cultic or idolatrous sexual practices.

The Wisdom of Solomon 14:23-26 (which Paul mirrored, as previously discussed) contains a vice list that is suggestive of vices related to idolatry, such as killing children during initiations and holding "frenzied revels with strange customs." It is further connected to idolatry through its closing statement in verse 27: "for the worship of idols not to be named is the beginning and cause and end of every evil." Paul may have condemned the sexual practices he mentions because they were performed as part of idolatrous, cultic worship. The similarity between the passages in the Wisdom of Solomon and Romans 1, and the clear connection between idolatry and the vice list in the Wisdom of Solomon 14, supports the possibility that Paul is also referring to sexual sin in the context of idolatry in Romans 1.

A non-affirming view might say:

Paul includes offenses in his vice list that are not necessarily associated with cultic worship. Therefore, his reference to same-sex sex should not be assumed to be related to idolatry or cultic worship simply because idolatry is also listed as a vice.

Male-male sex in the context of cultic prostitution was not common in Israel and the surrounding nations immediately prior to and during Paul's time, so it would not have been on Paul's mind as he wrote Romans.[48] Paul mentions same-sex sex in the context of idolatry because he is saying that people's choice to worship idols has led them to engage in sinful behavior, including same-sex sex. Paul is not saying that same-sex sex is only wrong when it is part of idolatrous worship, but rather that people engage in it, and other sinful behaviors, because they have forsaken God. Harshly, Paul says that God's decree is that those who do the things on the vice list are deserving of death. This shows that these sins are serious.

An affirming view might say:

Even if it is the case that Paul is not referring to same-sex sex in the context of idolatry, it does not mean that all same-sex sex is sinful. The way same-sex sex was practiced during Paul's time was not within a model of equal status, monogamous, committed relationships. During Paul's time it was occurring within a context of abuse, exploitation and/or idolatry. When Paul says that God's decree is that those who commit these behaviors are deserving of death, it suggests that Paul is talking about something abusive, exploitative, and/or idolatrous, not an equal-status, monogamous, covenantal relationship. Paul includes greed, envy, gossip, deceit, malice, slander, arrogance, boastfulness, disobedience to parents, and lack of understanding, fidelity, love and mercy along with some type of same-sex sex in his statement about God's decree. It is inappropriate to single out same-sex sex to say it was deserving of death in isolation from the entire vice list. Paul uses vice lists to show that all are guilty. In Romans 6:23 Paul teaches that the wages of all sin is death, so that he can also teach that the gift of God is eternal life in Christ Jesus, who offers forgiveness for sin.

Covenantal Relationships

A non-affirming view might say:

Equal-status same-sex relationships *did* exist during Paul's time,[49] and Paul likely knew about relationships that were similar to same-sex marriages today. Four hundred years prior to Paul's time, Plato wrote *The Symposium*, which contains a mythical creation story about exclusive same-sex desire, which gives evidence that it was understood to exist even at that time. The emperor Nero was a well-known man,

---

48. The widespread presence of male-male cultic prostitution in the Ancient Near East and Israel is disputed amongst scholars. Keen, *Scripture, Ethics, and the Possibility of Same-Sex Relationships*, 29.

49. Sprinkle, *People to be Loved*, 62.

contemporary to Paul, who was consecutively married to two other men. There are examples of loving, same-sex relationships in ancient literature, such as Pausanias and Agathon, and Achilles and Patroclus.[50] Paul *would* have been considering people who were in loving relationships when he wrote this passage, therefore his condemnation applies broadly to all forms of same-sex sex.

An affirming view might say:

Paul was not condemning people who were in equal-status, monogamous, covenantal same-sex relationships because these types of relationships would have occurred very rarely, if at all, during his time, and would not have been on his mind. Paul's society didn't understand the concept of sexual orientations, which have only started to be understood in the past century. He was not condemning people for having exclusive same-sex attractions or covenantal relationships, because he did not understand such relationships to be a possibility.

Same-sex sex in Paul's world would have been extra-marital, and in addition to, not instead of opposite-sex sex. The penetrated males were often pre-pubescent or feminized men. Since women's virginity had to be protected until marriage, some unmarried men turned to feminized men or boys to fulfill their sexual desires. Some who were already married were looking for lustful extramarital sex beyond what they could have with their wives.

None of the examples of ancient male-male sexual relationships, real-life or fictional, were equivalent to same-sex marriage because they were not monogamous and the relationships were not equal-status, but rather involved a social hierarchy between men. The emperor Nero's marriages included an unhealthy power imbalance, as evidenced by Nero having had one of his male spouses forcibly castrated, which indicates that he treated his spouse like a slave.[51] The origin story recounted by Plato described people searching for their "other half" from whom they had been physically detached and separated. The myth describes deviant people, not typical people. The opposite-sex people seeking each other were adulterers and adulteresses. The men seeking a male partner were seeking a pederastic relationship with a prepubescent male. This created a logistical problem whereby two males were supposedly split from a

---

50. Ibid.
51. Ibid., 60.

single being but were different ages when they reunited with each other. This logistical problem was easier for ancient people to accept than the unthinkable idea of two men of the same age and status having sex. Philo, a philosopher who wrote in Alexandria during and just after Jesus' time, opposed the theory of innate same-sex attraction, showing that it was not widely accepted during Paul's time.[52] In the examples from literature, Agathon and Pausanias started their same-sex relationship as pederasty, but then they stayed together beyond the accepted age. They were mocked for their relationship and had to maintain strict roles aligning with gender roles, so even theirs was not an example of an equal-status, covenantal relationship that was recognized by society, like a marriage relationship. Achilles and Patroclus, male characters from Homer's Iliad, had a life-long loving relationship, however it was not a sexual relationship and both men had sex with women. Some later readers interpreted their relationship as sexual, however these readers assumed it would have been a hierarchical, pederastic relationship, showing that they did not understand same-sex relationships to be equal-status. If this was a sexual relationship, it was not monogamous or covenantal.

Paul was intelligent and well-read, but even so, it cannot be assumed that he would have known all the literature available during his day, so he may not have been aware of these literary characters. Even if he was aware, his readers may not have been, so he would not have been referring to literary characters in his letters. Paul and his original readers would have understood male-male sex to be excessively lustful, to be engaged in by men who also had opposite-sex sex, to be shaming of or abusive to the penetrated male, and to be extra-marital. Paul would not have been considering an equal-status, monogamous, covenantal same-sex relationship when he wrote Romans. Even the passage itself shows that faithful, loving relationships were not on Paul's mind, because in Romans 1:31 he says that the people he is referring to have no fidelity and no love.

A non-affirming view might say:

Romans 1:27 uses the phrase, "inflamed with lust for one another." "One another" implies a mutual relationship. Paul was not addressing rape or sex that is forced through an imbalance of power. Paul *is* prohibiting equal-status, consensual same-sex sex.[53]

---

52. Keen, *Scripture, Ethics, and the Possibility of Same-Sex Relationships*, 41.

53. Loader, "Homosexuality and the Bible," in *Two Views on Homosexuality, the Bible, and the Church*, 39.

An affirming view might say:

The phrase "one another" means it is male-male sex. It doesn't imply mutual desire between the males. Paul's statement in verse 32, that some of the Romans approve of the same-sex relationships he is describing, shows that the relationships are not mutual or exclusive. The types of same-sex relationships that were culturally accepted in Paul's time were hierarchical encounters or relationships with slaves, prostitutes, prepubescent males, or foreigners. It would have been highly unlikely that the Romans would have approved of an equal-status, monogamous, covenantal relationship, partly because of the way they understood the receptive partner to be shamed through the act of same-sex sex.

Pederasty

An affirming view might say:

As already alluded to, male-male sex in ancient Greco-Roman culture frequently involved pederasty, which was a practice where an older man penetrated a prepubescent male. There were differences in the ways ancient Greeks and Romans practiced pederasty. For the ancient Greeks, the men in these pederastic relationships fulfilled a paternal role of sorts, providing for the boy and teaching him to become a man.[54] The men were called the *erastes* (lovers), and the boys were called the *eromenos* (beloved). Since the practice was intended to be educational and prepare the boy for civil life, the *eromenos* had to become a free citizen, (thus he could not be a slave or a foreigner). There were strict expectations that the *eromenos* would not experience sexual pleasure but would submit dutifully. If he did not experience sexual pleasure, there would be no shame associated with being in the relationship, and the practice was supported by society, including the boy's parents. There may have been a belief that the man's character traits could be passed on to the boy through the passing of the semen into his body, so mothers would even help pick out a choice lover for their sons. It was considered shameful if the boy enjoyed the sex. In such a case, he would become a *pornoi*, or a *kinaidos* (sexual deviant). The *kinaidos* had minimal honor and were unable to hold public office.

The *erastes* were not yet married when they were involved sexually with their *eromenos* but would later go on to marry women. They typically stopped their pederastic relationship once married, frequently becoming friends instead of lovers. The age difference

---

54. Nissinen, *Homoeroticism in the Biblical World*, 58.

between the men and the boys could be as small as a couple of years, making it appear to be equal status, however there was always a clear set of role expectations that the men were dominant and the boys did not experience pleasure. Society did not approve of them staying together after the boy became a man. It was not an equal-status, marriage-type relationship. Because women were inferior to men, some Greeks thought that a deep, loving relationship was not possible between a man and a woman, and that the pederastic relationship was the purest form of love.[55]

Pederasty was common among the ancient Romans as well, but Roman relationships could be more violent and aggressive. The boys were slaves or foreigners and were shamed by the relationship. Both Greek and Roman cultures influenced Paul's writing. Translations such as the NIV, which read, "Men committed shameful acts with other men," slightly but significantly alter the original meaning of Romans 1:27. The original Greek uses the word *arsenes,* which means "males" more broadly, rather than "men" specifically. It is possible, therefore, that the original text had pederastic relationships in view, but most modern English translations restrict the meaning of the word, making it seem like the two males were always both adults.[56] Among other specific forms of same-sex sex, Paul has men having sex with prepubescent males in mind when he condemns male-male sex in Romans 1:27.

A non-affirming view might say:

An age difference between the men and the boys in a pederastic relationship would not have been Paul's reason for condemning male-male sex, because a significant age difference was also common in opposite-sex marriages at that time, with girls being married around age twelve or thirteen. In the Greek relationships, the youth had some amount of control over the men who were attracted to them, and there is evidence of them bragging about being courted by men, suggesting that these were not abusive relationships.[57] Paul did not indicate that he was thinking of pederastic relationships when he condemned same-sex sex, and pederasty was not the only form of male-male sex that was happening, so his condemnation was not restricted to specific forms of same-sex sex. This is further evidenced by his condemnation of female-female sex, which would not have

---

55. Ibid., 59, 64.

56. Cunnington, *Open Wide the Gates*, Kindle ed., 6753.

57. Greg Johnson, *Still Time to Care: What We Can Learn from the Church's Failed Attempt to Cure Homosexuality* (Grand Rapids, MI: Zondervan, 2021), 170.

been pederastic, showing that his condemnation was not restricted to pederasty.

Patriarchy / Hierarchy

An affirming view might say:

The highly patriarchal, shame/honor culture of Paul's world significantly shaped its understanding of sex. Sex was always associated with a power dynamic and was never between equal-status partners, even when it was male-female in nature. Society during Paul's time considered women to be inferior to men, so through the act of male-male intercourse, the male who took the "woman's position" as the penetrated male was shamed, while the dominant man rose in social stature. It was important for a man's honor that he be the active partner during sex, but it mattered less whether the receptive partner was male or female.[58] Acting like a woman was considered shameful. Paul may have condemned male-male sex because of the unloving way it inflicted shame on the penetrated male.[59]

The Romans tolerated male-male sex with a prepubescent boy, foreigner, slave, or a prostitute, but same-sex sex between men of equal status was not accepted and may have been illegal.[60] Male prostitutes were primarily slaves and foreigners, rather than free Roman citizens.[61] Same-sex sex amongst equal-status peers was rare and would not have been accepted by society.[62]

A reason why female-female sex may have been considered an offense was because it was a form of sex that occurred between two individuals with similar social standing, which contradicted the cultural hierarchical dynamic of sexual conduct, and because it transgressed gender role boundaries.[63] Because of strict gender role codes during Paul's time, female-female sex would have been deemed "unnatural" because of the way a woman subverted her gender role by playing the role of a man, essentially "undermining the male privilege of penetration" through artificial means.[64] The strict

---

58. Sprinkle, *People to be Loved*, 58.
59. Nissinen, *Homoeroticism in the Biblical World*, 43.
60. Ibid., 65, 69.
61. Ibid., 67.
62. Sprinkle, *People to be Loved*, 56.
63. Nissinen, *Homoeroticism in the Biblical World*, 87.
64. Ibid.

patriarchal gender role delineations within ancient Roman culture meant that female-female sexual activity was not acceptable.

A non-affirming view might say:

Paul did not share his culture's low level of respect for women, as evidenced by his affirmation of female leaders in his own ministry (see Romans 16:1-15). Since gender roles were not Paul's primary concern, his reason for condemning male-male sex was not because it shamed the penetrated male for acting like a woman, nor did he condemn female-female sex because women were inappropriately acting like men. Since his condemnation of same-sex sex was not based on gender role nonconformity, it should not be dismissed on this basis.

Or a non-affirming view might say:

Gender roles were established by God in creation and are evident through his design of male and female bodies. Paul gives different instructions to husbands than he gives to wives in Ephesians 5, showing that gender roles are a timeless reality rather than a cultural practice to be dismissed as being from an ancient society. Patriarchy was established by God when he told Eve her desire would be for her husband and he would rule over her in Genesis 3:16, and this was confirmed by Paul in Ephesians 5:23 when he says, "the husband is the head of the wife." Paul's condemnation of same-sex sex may have rightly been based on the way it conflates gender roles, and this remains a valid reason to condemn it today. It continues to be shameful for a male to take a woman's role in male-male sex and for a woman to take a man's role in female-female sex. That reason for condemning same-sex sex has not changed.

An affirming view might say:

Although Paul did elevate women to a higher status within his ministry, he also accommodated his cultural circumstances and did not push change beyond what at least some people were prepared to accept. Like Jesus, Paul prioritized spreading the gospel message over bringing about sudden widespread changes to the social hierarchy. Since he supported patriarchal household codes subjecting slaves and women to the male household leaders, Paul would likely have upheld the traditional sexual gender role norms even if he personally felt they were too strict and even though he was willing to make leadership exceptions within his own ministry.

It should be noted that Paul doesn't specify that he is talking about female-female sex. It may be that the condemnation of female "unnatural sex" was not describing female-female sex at all, but rather non-procreative sex between women and men. When Paul says, "In the same way, men … were inflamed with lust for one another," a common interpretation is that the words "in the same way" indicate that the female unnatural sex was with the same sex, in the same way that the men were engaging in same-sex sex. However, the phrase "in the same way" could describe the women engaging in non-procreative sex with men, with the similarities being the wastage of semen. The reason the women may have been condemned for the non-procreative sex instead of their husbands is that they were requesting it to avoid becoming pregnant.

A non-affirming view might say:

There is evidence of an awareness of female-female sex found in second century literature, including fictional work about women in equal-status sexual relationships on the island of Lesbos and a story about an Egyptian king's daughter and her female love. Female-female sex would have been equal-status, consensual, non-exploitative, and between adults. A lack of a power imbalance in the women's relationships rules out the possibility of Paul's reason for condemning male-male sex being due to power imbalance between the men. The plainest reading of Romans 1:26 is that Paul is condemning female-female sex, but even if he is merely condemning non-procreative sex, it still stands that same-sex sex is not open to procreation and that is a valid reason for it to be considered sinful.

An affirming view might say:

Second century literature that describes female-female sexual love is written over one hundred years after Paul's time, so the existence of this literature does not mean that Paul was aware of female-female covenantal relationships happening during his time. Even if he does intend to condemn female-female sex, the phrase "in the same way" could imply the excessive lust or idolatry that characterized typical male-male sex at the time, with these characteristics being the problem rather than the same-sex aspect of the sex. During the drunken idolatrous parties held by the Roman elite in Paul's time, men would have sex with multiple women, and at the same time the women would likely engage sexually with each other as part of the whole sex event. Paul may have been condemning excessively lustful, idolatrous orgies.

Shameful Lusts

An affirming view might say:

Romans 1:26 says, "Because of this, God gave them over to shameful lusts." The "this" in question is idol worship, which was described in verse 25. Idol worship is not commonly considered to be a reason why people are same-sex attracted, so it would make the most sense for Paul to be saying that a particular behavior, rather than a sexual orientation, is shamefully lustful. The behavior that was considered to be sinful and to result from idol worship was excessive, out-of-control, lustful same-sex sex. Paul's culture believed that male-male sexual passion was an excess or overflow of the same desire that inspired male-female passion.[65] The issue was understood to be lack of self-control. It was believed that any man who did not control his desires could find himself attracted to other males.

Both the women and the men are described as "exchanging" or "giving up" natural relations, which implies a giving up of opposite-sex sex with their spouses. It was thought that some people were unable to satisfy their sexual desires within their marriages because of excessive lust, which led men to seek sex with other men instead of with their wives, and women to seek some form of unnatural sex, possibly with other women. The belief that same-sex attraction was an overflow of lust rather than an intrinsic, exclusive, fixed attraction was prevalent during Paul's time, as seen in Philo's writing:

> Incapable of bearing such satiety, plunging like cattle, they threw off from their necks the law of nature and applied themselves to deep drinking of strong liquor and dainty feeding and forbidden forms of intercourse. Not only in their mad lust for women did they violate the marriages of their neighbours, but also men mounted males without respect for the sex nature which the active partner shares with the passive; and so when they tried to beget children they were discovered to be incapable of any but a sterile seed.[66]

This understanding continued after Paul's time, as seen in writings by first century Roman orator Dio Chrysostom, who says:

> The man whose appetite is insatiate in such things [sex with women], when he finds there is no scarcity, no resistance, in this field, will have contempt for the easy conquest and scorn for a woman's love, as a thing too readily given—in fact, too utterly feminine—and will turn his assault against the male quarters,

65. Hill, "Christ, Scripture, and Spiritual Friendship," in *Two Views on Homosexuality, the Bible, and the Church*, 65. See also Vines, *God and the Gay Christian*, 38, 104-105.

66. Philo, quoted in Brownson, *Bible, Gender, Sexuality*, 155.

eager to befoul the youth who will very soon be magistrates and judges and generals, believing that in them he will find a kind of pleasure difficult and hard to procure.[67]

There is evidence that in ancient culture, female-female sex, like male-male sex, was considered to be caused by an excess of lust. About four hundred years prior to Paul's time, Plato wrote, "I think that the pleasure is to be deemed natural which arises out of the intercourse between men and women; but that the intercourse of men with men, or of women with women, is contrary to nature, and that the bold attempt was originally due to unbridled lust."[68]

The type of female sexual behavior that Paul is referencing in Romans 1 is not clearly stated, but whether it is female-female sex, female-male sex, or even masturbation, it is a behavior that Paul considers to be fueled by an excessive lust. It would be unjustified to ban female-female sex today based on an assumed meaning of one unclear verse.

Paul was condemning the most common forms of male-male sex in his culture, which were extra-marital, shameful, excessively lustful, abusive, or idolatrous. When churches use Paul's teaching to prohibit same-sex marriages today they are not taking Paul's teaching literally but rather are extrapolating to make it refer to a practice that Paul was not considering when he wrote Romans 1:26-27.

A non-affirming view might say:

Paul's use of the term "shameful lusts" to describe same-sex sex indicates that he considers all forms of same-sex sex to be lustful and shameful. He doesn't specify a form of same-sex sex (i.e., abusive or idolatrous), so his condemnation can be assumed to apply to all forms of same-sex sex. Even though Romans 1:26 does not clearly say that the women are being condemned for female-female sex, female-female lustful and sexually indecent acts are implied by Paul's use of the phrase "in the same way," to compare the women's "unnatural sexual relations" to the men being "inflamed with lust for one another and committing indecent acts with other men." Female-female sex is thus condemned along with male-male sex. Since women are less

---

67. Dio Chrysostom, quoted in: The Reformation Project, *Brief Biblical Case for LGBTQ Inclusion*, accessed May 6, 2021, https://reformationproject.org/case/tradition.

68. Plato, *Laws*, Book 1, trans. Benjamin Jowett, Sue Asscher and David Widger (The Project Gutenberg ebook, 2013), accessed May 28, 2021, https://www.gutenberg.org/files/1750/1750-h/1750-h.htm#link2H_4_0008.

susceptible to sexual passion and therefore would not have been motivated by excessive lust, it follows that male same-sex sex was not condemned purely because it was excessively lustful.[69]

An affirming view might say:

The wording of the text in the original Greek implies that the phrase "in the same way" in Romans 1:27 can refer not only to the women's exchange of natural for unnatural sexual relations in 1:26, but also to the other "exchanges" of things that are good for things that are bad. In 1:23 they exchanged the glory of the immortal God for images resembling a mortal human being or animals. In 1:25 they exchanged the truth of God for a lie and worshiped and served created things rather than the creator. In 1:26 their women exchanged natural sexual relations for unnatural ones. And in 1:27 the phrase "in the same way" could imply a fourth exchange—men abandoning natural relations with women and being inflamed with lust for one another. It is common to apply the phrase "in the same way" to the preceding verse, emphasizing the similarity between the women's and men's sexual behaviors, however the similarity could be between all four descriptions of sinful behavior (worshiping idols, worshiping and serving created things, women's unnatural sexual relations, and lustful relations between men). Consequently, just because the men's unnatural behavior is same-sex sex, it does not necessarily follow that this is the behavior Paul has in mind when discussing the women, in the same way that his reference to idol worship is not necessarily a reference to same-sex sex. Conversely, it may mean that the women's and the men's sexual behavior are both associated with idol worship, as are the first two exchanges to which they are compared.[70]

A non-affirming view might say:

Literary authors from the first, second, fourth, and fifth centuries AD depict an understanding of innate same-sex attraction, including: Phaedrus (a first century fable writer), Soranus (a second century Greek physician), Polemon (a second century philosopher), and Firmicus Maternus (a fourth century astrologer). In the fourth century BCE, both Aristotle and Plato comment on loving, male-male relationships, and such relationships are depicted by the characters Hippothoos and Hyperanthes in the *Ephesian's Tale* (ca. the second

---

69. Sprinkle, *People to be Loved*, 99.

70. Jamie A. Banister, "'Ομοίως and the Use of Parallelism in Romans 1:26-27," Journal of Biblical Literature 128, no. 3 (2009): 588. See also Brownson, *Bible, Gender, Sexuality*, 224.

century AD).[71] Paul would have understood that male-male relationships could be equal-status and loving, but he did not make any qualifications to say that he did not condemn the same-sex sex in these types of relationships.

An affirming view might say:

The second, fourth, and fifth centuries were after Paul's time. In *The Symposium,* Plato wrote about a story accounting for same sex attractions well before Paul's time. Equal-status, monogamous, covenantal relationships would have been rare during Paul's time, so they were not what he was condemning. Paul did not know his letters would be shared and read hundreds and thousands of years after he wrote them. He wrote his letters to particular people and churches in particular situations. He referenced the behavior that was causing problems in his society at that time and that would have been pertinent to the people who were the direct recipients of his letters. He was not writing to warn future readers in the twenty-first century not to marry a same-sex spouse; he was writing to warn the people in his churches not to do what their non-Christian neighbors were doing.

The Meaning of the Word "Unnatural"

A non-affirming view might say:

Paul describes same-sex sex using the word *para physin* (unnatural) to emphasize its contradiction of God's creation design for opposite-sex sex. Same-sex sex is unnatural, and therefore it is outside of God's plan even when it happens within an equal-status, monogamous, covenantal relationship.

An affirming view might say:

The use of the word "unnatural" could also describe people going against their innate, natural desires, such as would be the case for a straight person engaging in same-sex sex or for a gay or lesbian person engaging in opposite-sex sex.[72]

A non-affirming view might say:

Paul would not have considered opposite-sex sex to be "unnatural" for anyone because he would not have understood the concept of a fixed same-sex attraction. While opposite-sex sex would

---

71. Johnson, *Still Time to Care*, 174.
72. Sprinkle, *A People to be Loved*, 97.

feel unnatural to an exclusively gay or lesbian person, this was not what Paul would have meant by the word.

An affirming view might say:

For the first three hundred years of its existence, the church understood the women's "unnatural relations" in 1:26 to refer to women engaging in non-coital/non-procreative sex with men (possibly oral or anal sex).[73] Saint Augustine wrote, "if one has relations even with one's wife in a part of the body which was not made for begetting children, such relations are against nature and indecent."[74] Semen was understood to be the sole source of a baby, and its wastage was a concern in both male-male sex and non-procreative male-female sex.[75] The belief at the time was that semen was limited and could run out, rendering the man infertile, thus it should only be spent on procreative sex.[76] Teaching based on avoiding the wastage of semen is not applicable today, as it is now known that the supply is not limited and semen does not contain tiny, whole babies. The fact that Leviticus does not specifically prohibit female-female sex suggests that what mattered most to ancient Israelite society was what was happening with the semen, and that female-female sex was not considered to be real sex. This supports the possibility that Paul's use of the word "unnatural" is referring to non-procreative male-female sex in Romans 1, as was the understanding of the early church. Since Paul may have been referring to women having non-procreative, opposite-sex sex when he described their behavior as unnatural, the condemnation of the women's behavior should not be used to support the condemnation of equal-status sex between committed same-sex partners today.

A non-affirming view might say:

Paul did not specify that the sex was unnatural on account of it being non-procreative, so that cannot be assumed to have been his concern. Non-procreative sex would not have been off-limits for Paul, because Paul did not believe that procreation was the only acceptable purpose for sex. In 1 Corinthians 7:9 he says that marriage

73. Brownson, *Bible, Gender, Sexuality*, 109.
74. Augustine, quoted in Martin, *Unclobber*, 131.
75. Gagnon, *Bible and Homosexual Practice*, Kindle ed., Part VII, chap. 1.
76. William Loader, "Homosexuality and the Bible," in *Two Views on Homosexuality, the Bible, and the Church*, ed. by Preston Sprinkle (Grand Rapids, MI: Zondervan, 2016), 28.

can also be entered into in order to avoid "burning with passion."[77] If Paul was merely referring to women taking a dominant role or engaging in non-procreative sex with men, he would have condemned the men who were involved, along with the women. This is especially true since the men, who had the authority and power in the relationship, would have been the ones most responsible and therefore most culpable for the couple's actions.[78]

An affirming view might say:

There are many circumstances in patriarchal cultures where blame for the sexual behavior of an opposite-sex couple is placed on the woman rather than shared by both partners. Consider the story of the woman about to be stoned for being caught in the act of adultery in John 8:1-11. Although she was caught "in the act"—presumably with her male partner—the male partner is not also facing a potential barrage of stones.

A non-affirming view might say:

The word *para physin*, translated as "unnatural" in verses 26-27, refers to physical nature. This is its meaning in Galatians 4:8, which says that idols "by nature are not gods," and in Romans 11:24, which discusses being grafted "against nature" from a wild olive tree into a cultivated olive tree. Paul is calling the prohibited sex "unnatural" because it goes against God's biological creation design for sex between a man and a woman.

An affirming view might say:

Contemporary readers are inclined to consider the word "unnatural" to refer to a genetic/biological state, but the Greek word *para physin* would have been understood by its original hearers to be used for a variety of possible meanings, including "unconventional" or "not customary."[79] This is its meaning in 1 Corinthians 11:14, where Paul discusses the hair length of women and men, saying that it is "according to the nature of things" that men have short hair and women have long hair. This is obviously cultural rather than biological. Paul himself possibly had long hair for a time, during a

---

77. Sprinkle, *People to be Loved*, 94.

78. Loader, "Homosexuality and the Bible," in *Two Views on Homosexuality, the Bible, and the Church*, 38.

79. Nissinen, *Homoeroticism in the Biblical World*, 113.

period when he had taken a Nazarite vow.[80] Romans 11:24 says: "After all, if you were cut out of an olive tree that is wild by nature, and contrary to nature were grafted into a cultivated olive tree, how much more readily will these, the natural branches, be grafted into their own olive tree!" Paul is saying that God grafted the Gentiles into the people of God against nature. This shows that the term "against nature" cannot be assumed to describe something that is always to be avoided, because God himself went "against nature" to include the Gentiles.[81] The more probable translation of *para physin* as "unconventional" means that engaging in same-sex sex could have been condemned because it went against cultural expectations by disrespecting gender roles, rather than because it went against God's creation order.

Paul and his society were influenced by a system of philosophical beliefs called Stoicism. The Stoics believed that harmony with nature meant having self-control, complying with social and cultural sexual norms, and engaging in sex only for the purpose of procreation. According to Stoic philosophy, unnatural sex would have been lustful, non-procreative sex that defied patriarchal social norms.[82]

A non-affirming view might say:

Paul was not a Stoic, as evidenced by the fact that the Stoic philosophers rejected him in Acts 17:18, and it is unclear whether Stoic philosophy widely influenced his culture.

An affirming view might say:

Romans 1:28 points back to idol worship or insufficient worship of God as the reason for the sinful behavior it describes, reinforcing the fact that Paul is speaking about people who do not worship God. In verses 29-31, he describes other attitudes and actions that God gave the people up to, including being "filled with every kind of wickedness, evil, greed and depravity ... [being] full of envy, murder, strife, deceit and malice, and [being] gossips, slanderers, God-haters, insolent, arrogant and boastful." He says they "invent ways of doing evil ... disobey their parents ... have no understanding, no fidelity, no love, no mercy." The passage seems to imply that God gave people up to many extreme vices, which include sexual lusts as well as these

80. David B. Capes, Rodney Reeves, and E. Randolph Richards, *Rediscovering Paul: An Introduction to His World, Letters and Theology* (Downers Grove, Ill: IVP Academic, 2007), 154.

81. Martin, *Unclobber*, 132.

82. Vines, *God and the Gay Christian*, Kindle ed., 37.

others. It would be expected that people who were engaging in same-sex sex would display many of these other sinful traits, but LGBTQ+ people do not naturally exhibit these other types of sinful attitudes and behaviors to a greater degree than straight, cisgender people. The sexual sins being condemned by Paul were part of a comprehensively and extremely sinful and idolatrous lifestyle and are not representative of a same-sex marriage relationship.

Paul may have had the households of Emperor Gaius Caligula and Emperor Nero in mind as he wrote Romans 1. Gaius had a reputation for excessive, violent, out-of-control, lustful sexual relations with both men and women, including incestuous sex with his sisters. These activities took place in the public context of banquets, thus were common knowledge.[83] If Paul was referring to Gaius' sisters when he refers to "their women," the term "unnatural" could refer to the incestuous aspect of their sexual relations. Gaius was associated with idolatry, to the point of attempting to put a statue of himself up in the Jewish temple. The theory that Paul was alluding to Gaius Caligula and the immoral behaviors of Gaius' household in Romans 1 seems to fit the fuller description of the evil attitudes and actions listed in Romans 1:29-31. Paul's statement in verse 27 that "they received in themselves the due penalty for their error" also seems to fit this theory because Gaius was murdered by a military officer whom he had sexually humiliated. According to legend, the officer stabbed Gaius in his genitals. This happened about fifteen years before Paul wrote his letter to the Romans. The emperor in power during the time Paul wrote the letter was Nero, who had a reputation for excessively lustful and abusive sexual behavior. The reference to these men would have surely been understood by his readers, and Paul may have alluded to these powerful rulers, who would have been hated by the Jews and Gentiles alike, to further foster unity between factions within the church.[84]

A non-affirming view might say:

Paul's list of extreme vices demonstrates that same-sex sex is a serious sin, and not to be taken lightly. God is deeply passionate about the prohibition against same-sex sex. Paul implies that there is a serious consequence for same-sex sex when he says that men received the "due penalty for their error" in Romans 1:27. People who affirm

---

83. Brownson, *Bible, Gender, Sexuality*, 153-155.
84. Cunnington, *Open Wide the Gates*, Kindle ed., 6961.

same-sex marriage are complicit along with those who marry a same-sex spouse. Among other punishments, the "due penalty" Paul warned about can impact all of society, taking the form of diseases, natural disasters, and tragedies such as mass shootings.[85]

An affirming view might say:

The phrase "due penalty for their error" in verse 27 implies a natural consequence, rather than a spiritual judgment. If Paul was not referring specifically to Emperor Gaius Caligula's death, he was likely implying that the men would suffer the consequence of cultural shame and dishonor as well as the negative impact of living a life lacking self-control. There is no basis for blaming the sexual behavior of LGBTQ+ people for societal problems like natural disasters, illness, and war.

Paul's Primary Purpose in Romans 1

An affirming view might say:

Romans 2:1 reveals that Paul's primary purpose in Romans 1 was not to condemn people for specific sins but rather to set up his introduction to the gospel message by establishing that everyone is guilty of sin and each person needs Jesus' grace. Because his purpose was to establish the universal need for Christ rather than to make a clear statement about same-sex sex, it is not appropriate to use Romans 1:18-32 as a definitive statement to enforce a permanent prohibition on all types of same-sex sexual practices. Paul assumed that his readers would agree with his condemnation of all the items on his vice list, including same-sex sex. This suggests that he is referring to something other than equal-status, monogamous, covenantal relationships, as such relationships would have been unknown to the recipients of his letter. Paul was referring to forms of same-sex sex that would have been commonly known about and agreed upon by Christians as being sinful, such as those that were excessively lustful, abusive, exploitative, idolatrous, and/or extra-marital.

---

85. For example, in response to Disney World's Gay Days, Pat Robertson said, "I would warn Orlando that you're right in the way of some serious hurricanes, and I don't think I'd be waving those flags in God's face if I were you ... It'll bring about terrorist bombs; it'll bring earthquakes, tornadoes, and possibly a meteor." Leslie Bentz, "The Top 10: Facebook 'vomit' button for gays and other Pat Robertson quotes." *CNN*, July 9, 2013, https://www.cnn.com/2013/07/ 09/us/pat-robertson-facebook-remark/ index.html. Accessed June 1, 2024.

In Romans 2:1, Paul says, "at whatever point you judge another, you are condemning yourself, because you who pass judgment do the same things." He equated judgmentalism with the items on the vice list, including idolatry and out-of-control lustful sex. The commonality between judgmentalism and these other actions and attitudes is that they all "attempt to advance one's own honor, status and will at the expense of others."[86] The Gentiles referred to by the vice list abused and oppressed each other in a quest for honor, while the Jews sought self-honor and a superior status through strict observation of the law.[87] Paul's point is that both groups must recognize their need for God's grace through Jesus.

A non-affirming view might say:

Romans 1:26-27 refers to all forms of same-sex sex among women (described as "exchanging natural sexual relations for unnatural ones,") and among men (described as "abandoning natural sexual relations with women and being inflamed with lust for one another"). Paul's use of negative terms, including "shameful lusts," "unnatural," and "sexual impurity," to describe the people's sexual behavior clearly shows that same-sex sex is sinful. Paul would have understood Leviticus 18:22 to prohibit all forms of same-sex sex, and in Romans 1:18-32 he confirms this Levitical law to be timeless and valid for Christians in all contexts. Even if Paul's point was to teach that all people need God's grace, the understanding that same-sex sex is outside of God's will can be understood from his inclusion of it as an example of sinful behavior.

1 Corinthians 6:9

Many of the points about the historical context outlined in the previous discussion of Romans 1:26-27 also apply here and in the upcoming discussion of 1 Timothy 1:10. To reduce repetition, I have tried to keep comments focused on the new ideas brought forward in each passage.

Background:

The second of the three New Testament verses that specifically address same-sex sex is found in Paul's letter to the Corinthian church,

---

86. Brownson, *Bible, Gender, Sexuality*, 151.
87. Ibid.

believed to be written around 55 AD, in the city of Ephesus. Corinth was a busy Greek city that served as a centre of trade and commerce. Idolatry, sexual immorality, and slavery were common in Corinth.[88] One of Corinth's cultic temples was a grand temple dedicated to Aphrodite, the goddess of love, which is said to have housed over a thousand temple prostitutes.

1 Corinthians is a letter written by Paul in response to communication he had received about issues or incidents within the church. We do not have access to the original communication informing him of the concerns, but they seem to have related to the sexual sins of a particular member of the church, church members taking each other to secular court, and church members engaging in prostitution. 1 Corinthians 6:9 is part of an overall message in 1 Corinthians 6:1-11, which points out that Paul wants the more powerful and wealthy Christians to stop taking their poor fellow believers to court to be judged by non-Christian Gentiles.[89] 1 Corinthians 6:1-11 says:

> If any of you has a dispute with another, do you dare to take it before the ungodly for judgment instead of before the Lord's people? Or do you not know that the Lord's people will judge the world? And if you are to judge the world, are you not competent to judge trivial cases? Do you not know that we will judge angels? How much more the things of this life! Therefore, if you have disputes about such matters, do you ask for a ruling from those whose way of life is scorned in the church? I say this to shame you. Is it possible that there is nobody among you wise enough to judge a dispute between believers? But instead, one brother takes another to court—and this in front of unbelievers! The very fact that you have lawsuits among you means you have been completely defeated already. Why not rather be wronged? Why not rather be cheated? Instead, you yourselves cheat and do wrong, and you do this to your brothers and sisters. Or do you not know that wrongdoers will not inherit the kingdom of God? Do not be deceived: Neither the sexually immoral nor idolaters nor adulterers nor men who have sex with men nor thieves nor the greedy nor drunkards nor slanderers nor swindlers will inherit the kingdom of God. And that is what some of you were. But you were washed, you were sanctified, you were justified in the name of the Lord Jesus Christ and by the Spirit of our God.

---

88. G. Lacoste Munn, "The Historical Scriptural Background of First Corinthians," *Southwestern Journal of Theology* Vol 3 (Fall, 1960), accessed March 9, 2021, https://preachingsource.com/journal/the-historical-Scriptural Background-of-first-corinthians.

89. Cunnington, *Open Wide the Gates*, Kindle ed., 4540.

An affirming view might say:

Paul seems to include men who engage in same-sex sex in a list of vices along with idolaters, adulterers, thieves, greedy people, drunkards, slanderers, and swindlers. The vice list is used to illustrate his point, but it is not the point itself. Paul lists these vices to demonstrate that the Corinthian church should not subject its own members to being judged by Gentiles who are guilty of those vices. In 1 Corinthians 6:1 Paul says, "If any of you has a dispute with another, do you dare to take it before the ungodly for judgment instead of before the Lord's people?" The word translated as "ungodly" is the Greek word *adikos*. It means unjust or unrighteous. The same word is translated by the NIV as "wrongdoers" in 1 Corinthians 6:9, where he says, "Or do you not know that wrongdoers will not inherit the kingdom of God?" In 6:1, *adikos* clearly refers to those who are outside the church, or non-Christians. It could also imply non-Christians in 6:9, as in "ungodly or unjust non-Christians will not inherit the kingdom of God."

In 1 Corinthians 6:8 Paul writes, "instead, you yourselves cheat and do wrong, and you do this to your brothers and sisters." Paul has already specified that the wrong they have been doing to their brothers and sisters is taking them to Gentile court. After this, in verse 9, he lists the vices and the consequences for committing them. Then in verse 11 he says, "And that is what some of you were. But you were washed, you were sanctified, you were justified in the name of the Lord Jesus Christ and by the Spirit of our God." This once again signals that he is describing non-Christian Gentiles in his vice list.

As previously stated, the forms of male-male sex that were common during Paul's time were extra-marital, excessively lustful, pederastic, abusive, or idolatrous, and they shamed the penetrated male for taking the woman's role. Paul is thinking specifically of these types of same-sex sexual activities when he writes in 1 Corinthians 6:11, "this is what some of you were." Paul was aware that he would be speaking to slaves who might have been victims of sexual abuse, men who had been in pederastic relationships when they were younger, and slaveholders and men who were or had been the abusers.[90] Since the vices listed were things that some of the people in the Corinthian church had been or had done, and since equal-status, monogamous, covenantal same-sex relationships were rare to non-existent during Paul's time, Paul is not referring to same sex marriage

---

90. Ibid., 4810.

types of relationships. Since covenantal, equal-status same-sex relationships (such as we see in same-sex marriages today) were rare, he would not have claimed that some of the people reading his letter had participated in such relationships.

A non-affirming view might say:

No qualifications or exceptions are stated, so the condemnation applies to all forms of same-sex sex. The same-sex nature of the sex is part of why Paul condemns it, and that element is still present in same-sex marriages today, even if other elements of the relationships are different. Paul would still have condemned same-sex marriage if such marriages were an option during his time.

Paul teaches that, along with people who engage in the other sinful behaviors listed, men who have sex with other men will not inherit the kingdom of God, implying they will not have eternal life in heaven. The severity of this consequence reveals God's passion against same-sex sex.

1 Corinthians 6:12-20 says,

> "I have the right to do anything," you say—but not everything is beneficial. "I have the right to do anything"—but I will not be mastered by anything. You say, "Food for the stomach and the stomach for food, and God will destroy them both." The body, however, is not meant for sexual immorality but for the Lord, and the Lord for the body. By his power God raised the Lord from the dead, and he will raise us also. Do you not know that your bodies are members of Christ himself? Shall I then take the members of Christ and unite them with a prostitute? Never! Do you not know that he who unites himself with a prostitute is one with her in body? For it is said, "The two will become one flesh." But whoever is united with the Lord is one with him in spirit.
>
> Flee from sexual immorality. All other sins a person commits are outside the body, but whoever sins sexually, sins against their own body. Do you not know that your bodies are temples of the Holy Spirit, who is in you, whom you have received from God? You are not your own; you were bought at a price. Therefore honor God with your bodies.

Sexual sins committed by Christians are of a more serious nature than other forms of sin because, as verses 18 and 19 reveal, Christians' sexual sins are against their own bodies, which are temples of the Holy Spirit. The seriousness of sinning against one's own body is emphasized in 1 Corinthians 3:17 which says, "If anyone destroys God's temple, God will destroy that person; for God's temple is sacred, and you together are that temple." Same-sex attracted people should honor God with their bodies (his temples) by remaining celibate or by entering an opposite-sex (mixed orientation) marriage, so as not to destroy their bodies, which are God's temples.

An affirming view might say:

When Paul says, "you together are that temple" in 1 Corinthians 3:17, he is referring to the people of God (i.e., the church) forming the temple. Previously in verse 16, when he asks, "Don't you know that you yourselves are God's temple and that God's spirit dwells in your midst?" Paul reveals that he is referring to a group of people, since God wouldn't dwell "in the midst of" one person. Since Paul refers to the temple as the spiritual bond between a group of Jesus' followers, he isn't referring to an individual person's physical body when he says, "you together are the temple" and warns that God will destroy anyone who destroys God's temple (1 Cor 3:16, 17). An "individual body as temple" interpretation seems to fit for its usage in 1 Corinthians 6:19, which instructs Christians to honor God with their bodies, but it does not automatically follow that 1 Corinthians 3:17 also refers to the individual's body. Therefore, it is inappropriate to use 1 Corinthians 3:17 to threaten individual people with destruction for sexual sin. The admonition to honor God with their bodies in 1 Corinthians 6:19 is not attached to a consequence. The threat of destruction seems to be a consequence for destroying God's temple, defined as the community of believers. The controversy about whether Christians should affirm same-sex marriages is causing serious division within the community of believers and may in this sense be an instance of "destroying God's temple."

1 Corinthians 6:18-19 teaches that sexual sins, as sins against one's own body (which is the temple of the Holy Spirit) are serious, however it is a statement made in the context of discussing prostitution, not talking about sex within a same-sex marriage.

Background:

Different versions of the English Bible translate 1 Corinthians 6:9 in different ways. In the original Greek, Paul uses two different words, *malakoi* and *arsenokoitai*, to describe the men. The words have sometimes been translated into English in ways that hide this fact that the original Greek uses two different words. Examples include: "men who have sex with men" (NIV, TLB), "men who practice homosexuality" (ESV, NLT), "homosexuals" (RSV 1946 version and NASB), "sexual perverts" (RSV), and "practicing homosexuals of whichever sort" (New Testament for Everyone). Some translations maintain the two separate words, such as: "effeminate" and "abusers of themselves with mankind" (KJV), "homosexuals" and "sodomites" (NKJV), "effeminate" and "homosexuals" (NASB 1995), "male prostitutes" and "sodomites" (NRSV), "male prostitutes" and "men who engage in illicit sex." (NRSVue), "male prostitutes" and "those who practice homosexuality" (NLT), and "effeminate [by perversion]" and "those who participate in homosexuality" (Amplified Bible).[91]

The words *malakoi* and *arsenokoitai* were first combined and translated into the word "homosexuals" in the 1946 RSV New Testament. When the translation committee was challenged on that decision, they agreed with the challenger's points and changed their translation to "sexual perverts," which does not restrict the sexual sin that the verse describes to being same-sex in nature. The RSV was not re-printed for ten years however, and during that time the NIV, TLB, and NASB also translated the two words *malakoi* and *arsenokoitai* with the single word "homosexuals," following the example of the RSV without doing independent research.[92] In their more recent updates, the NIV and TLB now translate the words as "men who have sex with men," still not yet acknowledging that two different words appear in the Greek, but now indicating that same-sex behavior is in view, rather than people with same-sex attraction.

An affirming view might say:

The use of the word "homosexuals" was inappropriate for a few reasons. One reason is that the concept of homosexuality as an exclusive orientation was not understood in Paul's time, so Paul would not have considered *malakoi* and *arsenokoitai* to be referring to people with exclusive same-sex attraction the way the word "homosexuals" is used today. Paul would have been referring to people as defined by their behavior, not by their sexual desires. Some translators try to capture this by defining the behavior rather than the people. Much psychological damage has been caused to LGBTQ+ Christians who are told that they are sinful simply for being same-sex attracted, whether they have a sexual or romantic relationship with a same-sex partner or not. Another reason why it is inappropriate to translate the words as "homosexuals" is because of the ambiguity regarding the meaning of the words *malakoi* and *arsenokoitai*. This ambiguity is

---

91. TLB is The Living Bible, ESV is the English Standard Version, NLT is the New Living Translation, RSV is the Revised Standard Version, NASB is the North American Standard Bible, KJV is the King James Version, NKJV is the New King James Version, NRSV is the New Revised Standard Version, NRSVue is the New Revised Standard Version updated edition.

92. *1946: The Mistranslation That Shifted Culture*, directed by Sharon Roggio (Acowsay, 2022).

evidenced by the previous conversation about the variety of ways the words are translated today. These translation difficulties will be discussed further at a later point in this book. A third reason has already been discussed: same-sex sex in Paul's time was known to be lustful, abusive, exploitative, and/or idolatrous, which is not true of all same-sex relationships today. Paul was condemning those characteristics of male-male sex rather than all forms of same-sex sex. A fourth reason is that Paul's language referred directly to males, but the word "homosexuals" includes females who are same-sex attracted. Translations that suggest Paul condemns female-female sex in 1 Corinthians and 1 Timothy go beyond the literal meaning of the text.

A non-affirming view might say:

The original text clearly references male-male sex in a negative way. It is dangerous to go against this direct teaching to say that certain forms of same-sex sex are accepted or even blessed by God. Since Paul included women in his condemnation of same-sex sex in Romans 1, it is reasonable to assume he would also condemn female-female sex in 1 Corinthians, and that he intended to encompass all forms of same-sex sex, making the word "homosexual" an appropriate translation. When translations say, "men who have sex with men," the teaching can be reasonably applied to females who have sex with females as well. The words *malakoi* and *arsenokoitai* label people, not their behaviors, as does the word "homosexuals." Some defend the use of the word "homosexuals," which describes people who have same-sex desires, because if the behavior is sinful, the desire for that behavior is also, by implication, sinful.

Background:

This leads to a sidebar conversation about whether attractions and desires can be sinful (meaning the translation "homosexual" could be appropriate), or whether it is only the acting out of sinful desires that should be condemned (meaning the translation choice should describe the behavior rather than the person). Some people believe that a desire for sinful behaviors are sinful in and of themselves. There are people with affirming views and non-affirming views who hold this belief. They say that Paul's reference to "dishonorable passions" in Romans 1:26 shows that desires can be sinful, or dishonorable. They point out Jesus' teaching that looking with lustful intent is the same as adultery in Matthew 5:27-28 and that anger is the same as murder in Matthew 5:21-22. They also point out that James 1:14-15 says, "but each person is tempted when they are dragged away by their own evil desire and enticed. Then, after desire has conceived, it gives birth to sin; and sin, when it is full-grown, gives birth to death." They say that since James called the person's desire evil, desires are not neutral, and evil desires lead to sin and death.

A non-affirming view that holds the belief that desires can be sinful may say that recognizing same-sex desires as sinful and labeling them as a problem helps people resist and overcome them. Calling the desires wrong does not mean they are unforgivable, because all people need Jesus' grace, regardless of sexual orientation.

An affirming view that holds the belief that desires can be sinful may say that same-sex marriage is not a sin, so a desire for it is not sinful. They may say that when James, Paul and Jesus talk about dishonorable passions, lust, anger, and evil desires, they are describing something different from a desire for a same-sex marriage relationship. Even if some feelings and desires can be sinful, same-sex attractions are no more sinful than opposite-sex attractions. They point out that James 1:14-15 uses the word *epithumia*, which is translated as "desires." However, in Romans 1:24, the same word *epithumia* is translated as "lust." *Epithumia* therefore likely describes excessive desire in this context. James warned that excessive desires, or lust, can drag a person away and lead them to sin. This is also true for heterosexual lusts and other excessive desires. Jesus's teaching that looking lustfully at a person is wrong does not mean that desiring a relationship with a person is wrong. Lust is an excessive, out of control desire. This does not describe all sexual or romantic desires.

Some people say that since a person's attractions and desires are not always within their control, it is only the behaviors that are condemned. There are those with affirming views and non-affirming views who hold this belief. They point out that Jesus' instruction in Matthew 5:22, that "anyone who is angry with a brother or sister will be subject to judgment," needs to be nuanced. The original Greek implies that he is discussing an anger that is without cause. Being angry without cause suggests an actively nurtured feeling, or something that can be controlled. Jesus' subsequent teaching in the second half of the verse, that anyone who says *raca* (you fool) is answerable to court also implies a behavioral component to the anger (i.e., name calling). Paul says in Ephesians 4:26, "in your anger do not sin," making a distinction between the emotion of anger and the behavior of acting out due to the anger. They say that when Jesus taught that looking lustfully at a woman is akin to adultery, it should be recognized that "look" is a verb, a behavior that can be controlled, so is different from simply having a desire. A non-affirming view that holds this belief might say that it is acceptable to be LGBTQ+, but that people should remain celibate or marry someone of the opposite sex. An affirming view that holds this belief might say that neither the desires for same-sex marriage nor the actual marriage are sinful.

Having taken time to discuss the nuances of whether only behavior or both attractions and behavior are culpable for condemnation, and therefore should be depicted in translation, the conversation will now return to other issues related to translation.

When Paul condemned the *malakoi* and *arsenokoitai*, it is not clear exactly who he was referring to, because the definitions of these two words are ambiguous. Paul appears to be the first person to record the word *arsenokoitai*, and the word *malakoi* can have multiple meanings.

Paul uses the term *arsenokoitai* here and again in 1 Timothy 1:10, but neither of these contexts clearly show what the word means. Other than these two places, the word does not appear anywhere else in the New Testament. *Arsenokoitai* is a compound word made up of the words for "male" and "bed," or "laying down." Compound words often do not reflect the literal meaning of the words they join together. This means that the claim that *arsenokoitai* means "men who have sex with men" makes an assumption that this compound word can be understood literally without nuanced meaning. Additionally, while it could refer to a man "bedding" another male, it could also refer to a man "bedding" a female, similar to the way the term "rapist" does not indicate the sex of the victim. The word *arsenokoitai* is found in vice lists within other ancient writings after Paul's time, but surprisingly, it has been found within the sections of the lists relating to economic exploitation, rather than the sections relating to sexual sins. This suggests that *arsenokoitai* could relate to economic exploitation through sexual means, or sexual exploitation for economic gain.[93] Old German translations translated *arsenokoitai* as "boy molesters," reflecting the practice of pederasty. This is the traditional interpretation of the protestant church. The word "homosexual" did not replace "boy molesters" in German translations until 1983.

---

93. Dale B. Martin, "Arsenokoites and Malakos: Meanings and Consequences," in *Biblical Ethics & Homosexuality: Listening to Scripture*, ed. by Robert L. Brawley (Louisville, KY: Westminster John Knox Press, 1996), 122.

A non-affirming view might say:

Paul's coining of the word *arsenokoitai* was inspired by the Greek translation of Leviticus 18:22 and 20:13, which use the words *arsenos* (male) and *koiten* (bed). Since these verses in Leviticus do not qualify specific forms of same-sex sex, Paul's use of *arsenokoitai* likely refers to all instances where men have sex with men, too.

An affirming view might say:

The early German Bibles translated Leviticus 18:22 as "a man shall not lie with young boys as he does with a woman." They also use "young boys" in their translation of Leviticus 20:13.[94] If the early German Bibles interpreted Leviticus the same way Paul himself did, Paul may have been primarily referring to pederasty as the form of male-male sex being condemned. That the German Bibles only added the word "homosexuals" at a late date and under the influence of American Christian culture is significant because the concept of homosexual orientation was first developed in Germany nearly one hundred and twenty years prior to the term entering the German Bible, and for all of that time the Germans did not think Paul was describing homosexuality in 1 Corinthians and 1 Timothy.[95]

There were other words available to Paul to describe same-sex sex which were commonly understood, but he chose to create a new word, seeming specifically to reference Leviticus.[96] Leviticus's primary message was that the Israelites were to separate themselves from the pagan nations around them through their holy behavior. Paul may be using the same words to make his point that the Christians are also to separate themselves from the sinfulness of their surrounding culture by living holy lives. This is a theme he emphasizes in 1 Corinthians

---

94. Ibid.

95. Ed Oxford, "Has 'Homosexual' always been in the Bible?" *Forge* (March 21, 2019), accessed July 19, 2021, https://www.forgeonline.org/blog/2019/3/8/what-about-romans-124-27.

96. "Paul had a number of options for the words he could have used to describe whatever was in his mind. These included, for example, *paiderast?s* [sic], *pallakos*, *kinaidos, arrenomanos,* and *paidophthoros*. There are also technical terms, such as the lover (*erastos*), the beloved (*eromenos, paidika*), to give the body for purposes of intercourse (*charis, charidzesthai*), as well as slang terms that could have been used to indicate various forms of culturally accepted homosexuality, or even homosexuality in general. Paul doesn't use any of these." Graeme Codrington, "The Bible and Same Sex Relationships, Part 8: Male-Bedders – The Meaning Of 'Arsenokoitai'" FutureChurchNow (August 24, 2015). Accessed March 2, 2024, https://www.futurechurchnow.com/2015/08/24.

1:2, 1 Corinthians 10:6-7, 1 Corinthians 10:14, and 1 Corinthians 15:33-34.

The purpose of Leviticus 18:22 and 20:13 may have been to prohibit participation in cultic male prostitution. The prostitutes may have been primarily young slaves, offered as a sacrifice to the gods to be temple prostitutes. Temple prostitution was also occurring in Paul's cultural context, and if he had intended to include cultic sex on a vice list, it would have made sense for him to use the words *arsenos* and *koiten* from the Greek translation of Leviticus, rather than the more commonly used words to describe male-male sex. This prostitution theme aligns with 1 Corinthians 6:15-16, which says that members of Christ should not be united with a prostitute, and that those who have sex with a prostitute become one body with her.[97] Paul might be telling the church to avoid cultic prostitution with both male and females prostitutes.

The word *malakoi* has multiple meanings, most of which do not refer to the penetrated male in male-male sex. Paul could have used the word *kinaedoi*, which was a more specific word to describe the penetrated male, but instead chose *malakoi*, which literally means soft, and can be a general word for moral failure. It can refer to men who are effeminate, lazy, cowardly, who lack self-control, love luxury, pretty themselves up to attract women, have affairs with women, engage in traditionally feminine roles, or are the penetrated male in male-male sex.[98] As previously mentioned, Paul was speaking to some people who had been slaves or adolescent boys used for sex. Since it seems he did not expect them to understand the term *malakoi* as referring to themselves, it likely means more to Paul than simply the penetrated male.[99] There is no reason *malakoi* must be paired with *arsenokoitai*, because the rest of the vice list is not organized in word pairs. It may even be that the "soft" men refer to the rich men who are unjustly exploiting the poor. If the words are intended to be paired, and *malakoi* does refer to the penetrated male, Paul's use of it alongside *arsenokoitai* shows that he considers the two males to have different roles associated with different statuses in the sexual act.[100]

---

97. Ibid.

98. Martin, "Arsenokoites and Malakos," 125. See also Megan K. DeFranza, "Journeying from the Bible to Christian Ethics in Search of Common Ground," *Two Views on Homosexuality, the Bible, and the Church,* ed. by Preston Sprinkle (Grand Rapids, MI: Zondervan, 2016), 79.

99. Cunnington, *Open Wide the Gates,* 4810.

100. Brownson, *Bible, Gender, Sexuality,* 273.

Paul was not thinking about an equal-status relationship like a same-sex marriage.

A non-affirming view might say:

Paul's condemnation of the *malakoi*, or penetrated male, shows that his condemnation of same-sex sex was for reasons other than it being abusive. If the *malakoi* were boys or slaves who were victims of abuse, Paul would not have been condemning them.

1 Timothy 1:10

Background:

The third and final passage in the New Testament to address same-sex sex directly is 1 Timothy 1:10. This is a letter from Paul to Timothy, the pastor of the church in Ephesus. Paul writes to encourage Timothy to stand up to false teachers and maintain a strong theology.

1 Timothy 1:8-11 says:

> We know that the law is good if one uses it properly. We also know that the law is made not for the righteous but for lawbreakers and rebels, the ungodly and sinful, the unholy and irreligious, for those who kill their fathers or mothers, for murderers, for the sexually immoral, for those practicing homosexuality, for slave traders and liars and perjurers—and for whatever else is contrary to the sound doctrine that conforms to the gospel concerning the glory of the blessed God, which he entrusted to me.

The second use of the word *arsenokoitai* in the New Testament is found in verse 10. As with 1 Corinthians 6:9, *arsenokoitai* has been translated in different ways. Early German Bibles translate it as "boy molesters."[101] The RSV says, "men who engage in illicit sex." The KJV and NKJV translate it as "them that defile themselves with mankind." The ESV says, "men who practice homosexuality." The TLB and the NASB translations use "homosexuals," which includes women and encompasses the person's identity along with their sexual behavior. The NIV and the NLT use language that includes women but differentiates between the people and the activity, saying, "those practicing homosexuality," and "people who practice homosexuality," even though the word *arsenokoitai* refers specifically to men. The translation of the word *arsenokoitai* has considerable influence over how this passage is interpreted and how the church responds to people with non-heterosexual orientations. The meaning of

---

101. Oxford, "Has 'Homosexual' always been in the Bible?"

arsenokoitai is unclear, but it is clearly included within a list of extremely sinful people.

A non-affirming view might say:

As he does in 1 Corinthians 6:9, Paul references the Greek words *arsen* (male) and *koiten* (bed) when he uses the word *arsenokoitai,* both of which were used in the Greek translation of Leviticus. It means male-male sex, with no qualifications indicated as per the type of sex, so it can be assumed to include same-sex marriage.

An affirming view might say:

Within the vice list, the word *arsenokoitai* is located after the word *pornos* (prostitute or sexually immoral) and before the word *andrapodistēs* (slave traders or kidnappers), which suggests that its meaning reflects the concept of sexual and financial exploitation, as it likely does where it is found in subsequent ancient, non-biblical writings.[102] Paul may have been listing prostitutes (*pornos*), those who visit prostitutes (*arsenokoitai*), and those who traffic prostitutes (*andrapodistēs*). At least twenty percent of the residents of Rome were slaves, and many of them were used for sex. Boys were kidnapped and castrated, turning them into eunuchs to be trafficked and sexually exploited.[103] Such a terrible practice is appropriately placed in a vice list. This interpretation aligns with the early translations of *arsenokoitai* as "boy molester."

A non-affirming view might say:

Paul modeled his vice list after the Ten Commandments listed in Exodus 20:1-17. The vice of being unholy and irreligious relates to the first four commandments (do not have other gods before me, do not make graven images, do not take the name of the Lord in vain, and honor the Sabbath). Killing their fathers and mothers relates to the fifth commandment (honor your father and mother). Murdering relates to the sixth commandment (do not kill). Sexual immorality relates to the seventh commandment (do not commit adultery). Slave trading (stealing children) relates to the eighth commandment (do not steal). Lying and perjuring relates to the ninth commandment (do not lie). The point made here is that Paul's placement of the word

---

102. Martin, "Arsenokoites and Malakos: Meanings and Consequences," 122.
103. DeFranza, "Journeying From the Bible to Christian Ethics in Search of Common Ground," 274.

arsenokoitai between the words for sexually immoral and slave traders is not intended to signify the use of trafficked and exploited boy prostitutes. The reason it is placed there is because that is where it fits in the order of the Ten Commandments.[104]

An affirming view might say:

If Paul was following the structure of the Ten Commandments, *arsenokoitai* could have fit within the command about stealing, with the slave traders, rather than the command about adultery. The broader context of 1 Timothy 1:10 is that Paul is encouraging Timothy to command certain people not to teach false doctrines. In 1 Timothy 1:5-7 Paul says that some who want to be teachers of the law are ignorant, and seem to have departed from having pure hearts, good consciences, and sincere faith. He corrects their false teaching about the law by asserting that the law is good, if used properly, and reminds them that the law was made for sinners, such as those listed in the vice list, rather than for the righteous. Paul's purpose in this verse is not to provide teaching specifically on same-sex sex or on the definition of marriage. He assumes that Timothy and any other readers agree that these *arsenokoitai* were sinning. Paul broadened the vice list at the end to include *anything* that is contrary to sound doctrine conforming to the gospel. Paul includes men who engaged in some form of male-male sex as an example of sinners in need of grace. He is therefore referring to the forms of same-sex sex that were clearly sinful and commonly occurring during his time, such as extra-marital, lustful, pederastic, exploitative, abusive and/or cultic sex. Although his point is not clearly stated, it seems to be similar to his point in Romans 1, that sinners need grace through faith in Jesus, and that *all* are sinners and share this need.

A non-affirming view might say:

The inclusion of male-male sex within yet another vice list confirms that Paul considered it to be a serious sin, and that the prohibition against it first given in Leviticus continues to be relevant for Christians today.

---

104. Johnson, *Still Time to Care*, 160.

Conclusion to Part III

Paul assumed that Christians would agree that same-sex sex between men was sinful, as evidenced by his inclusion of it in three vice lists found in Romans, 1 Corinthians, and 1 Timothy. He may have assumed that same-sex sex between women was also agreed upon to be sinful, possibly alluding to it in one vice list in Romans. Same-sex sex in Paul's culture rarely (if ever) happened within equal-status, monogamous, covenantal relationships. Some Christians believe that Paul was condemning certain types of same-sex sex which were happening during his time. Other Christians believe Paul condemned all forms of same-sex sex. Among these Christians, some believe that Paul condemned the same-sex desires themselves, and others believe that Paul only condemned having sex with a same-sex partner.

Personal Reflection

Learning that the verses that directly address same-sex sex were talking about different sexual situations than occur in same-sex marriage today helped me understand that the church's prohibition against same-sex marriage does not have the unwavering biblical support I had assumed it had. However, I thought there were still biblical principles that suggested that a celibate life was the safest choice for LGBTQ+ people who wanted to avoid sinning against God. For example, I thought God's will could be known through his creation of our bodies as male and female for procreation. But since celibacy felt like a surprisingly harsh demand to come from a loving God, I continued to read, watch, listen, and pray, turning my focus to the principles taught in the wider canon of Scripture, which are discussed next in Part IV.

PART IV: DO BIBLICAL PRINCIPLES PROHIBIT SAME-SEX MARRIAGE?

Although there aren't any other verses that directly address same-sex sex in the Bible, many other biblical teachings and concepts inform Christians' views about whether or not the Bible prohibits same-sex marriage and LGBTQ+ identities. The second half of this book will examine these guiding biblical principles, with conversations about creation, procreation, gender complementarianism, marriage, sexual immorality, celibacy, judgment, holiness, obedience, biblical authority, history, tradition, fruitfulness, love, patriarchy, women in ministry, inclusion of sexual minorities, and the gospel. I hope these discussions will inspire further conversation, thinking, and research. As was the case with the previous conversations about the verses that directly address same-sex sex, views that affirm and views that do not affirm same-sex marriage are presented. Some verses and points of discussion are relevant to more than one topic, and the format of this book has made some degree of repetition unavoidable. I have tried to keep repeated comments brief and to add new ideas or nuances when the verse or concept re-appears.

Creation

Background:
This significant topic addresses themes including the image of God, undoing the fall versus diversity in creation, transgender identities and gender-affirming medical care, new creation, conversion therapy, and the physical act of anal sex.

The Image of God

The understanding that humankind is created in the image of God is foundational to the Christian faith. Genesis 1:26-27 says:

> Then God said, "Let us make mankind in our image, in our likeness, so that they may rule over the fish in the sea and the birds in the sky, over the livestock and all the wild animals, and over all the creatures that move along the ground." So God created mankind in his own image, in the image of God he created them; male and female he created them.

A non-affirming view might say:

God revealed his plan and pattern for marriage and sex when he created humankind as male and female. Genesis 1:26-27 associates being made in the image of God with being male and female. Jesus quoted Genesis 1:27, saying "the Creator 'made them male and female'" (Matt 19:4), emphasizing the lasting importance of the association. God's image is primarily reflected by people through the marital union of a man and a woman. Single people can also reflect God's image through participation in complementary gender roles in society, but it takes male and female people partnering together to mirror God's image.[105] Same-sex marriages therefore do not reflect the image of God.

An affirming view might say:

Adam and Eve were the first parents, from whom a diverse range of people descended, including LGBTQ+ people. Adam and Eve's relationship as the first couple did not serve as a pattern that everyone after them must follow.[106] Genesis 1:27's statement that males and females reflect the image of God is a celebration of diversity that doesn't rule out further gender diversity. The focus is not that the two sexes are required to partner together to reflect God's image, but rather that females, as well as males, reflect God's image. This idea would have been contrary to some of the patriarchal views at the time

---

105. Linda Rice. "A Heavenly Purpose of Marriage: Image-Bearing." Biblical Counseling for Women. https://bc4women.org/a-heavenly-purpose-of-marriage-image-bearing. Accessed June 1, 2024. See also Pope Francis, "The Married Couple is the Image of God," Inside the Vatican: Pope Francis' General Audience on the Sacrament of Marriage (St. Peter's Square, Vatican City, April 2, 2014). https://insidethevatican.com/popeswords/married-couple-image-god. Accessed June 1, 2024.

106. DeFranza, "Journeying from the Bible to Christian Ethics in Search of Common Ground," 90.

Genesis was recorded, which said that men were the reflection of God's image, and women were the reflection of men. The logical extrapolation of Genesis' teaching is that all humans reflect God's image, regardless their gender. Although marriage is the only lifestyle presented in the creation story, the church allows for people to remain single and celibate. The fact that singleness is affirmed in the New Testament shows that Adam and Eve's pattern of opposite-sex marriage is not prescriptive, or in other words, it does not need to be followed by all people. Since at least one other option is acceptable, it follows that other options may also be acceptable.

Matthew 19:3-6 says:

> Some Pharisees came to him to test him. They asked, "Is it lawful for a man to divorce his wife for any and every reason?"
>
> "Haven't you read," he replied, "that at the beginning the Creator 'made them male and female,' and said, 'For this reason a man will leave his father and mother and be united to his wife, and the two will become one flesh'? So they are no longer two, but one flesh. Therefore what God has joined together, let no one separate."

Jesus' quote of Genesis 1:27 in Matthew 19:4 references the first marriage, between Adam and Eve, in the context of his teaching about divorce and the permanence of marriage. His emphasis was on the spouses being one flesh and permanently bonded to each other, not on the genders of the spouses.

One way to understand what it means to be made in the image of God is that we reflect God as a relational being by loving others the way the members of the Triune God (Father/Creator, Son/Word, and Holy Spirit) love each other. This divine relationship of love does not require male and female gendered persons or sexual relationships, so it can be assumed that human relationships do not require both sexes in order to reflect the image of God. It is the love between people that allows a relationship to reflect God's image.

2 Corinthians 4:4 says that Jesus is the image of God. 1 Corinthians 15:49 says, "Just as we have borne the image of the man of dust, we shall also bear the image of the man of heaven." This verse explains that Christians should aspire to bear the image of Jesus, who is the new Adam.[107] Jesus was single. The New Testament compares his relationship with the church to that of a groom and his bride. It is a sacrificially loving relationship but not a sexual relationship.

---

107. Lianne Simon and Megan DeFranza, *Intersex Christians and the Image of God*, video, accessed May 26, 2021, https://www.youtube.com/watch?v=331 smwhg0gM.

Reflecting the image of Jesus does not require a sexual marriage relationship or even a relationship that fulfills specific gender roles. Rather it involves loving the world as Jesus loved the world. Jesus loved sacrificially, inclusively, compassionately, and with grace and mercy. In Colossians 3:10, Paul says that Christians have "put on the new self, which is being renewed in knowledge in the image of its Creator." In verses 12-14 he describes what this looks like, saying:

> Therefore, as God's chosen people, holy and dearly loved, clothe yourselves with compassion, kindness, humility, gentleness and patience. Bear with each other and forgive one another if any of you has a grievance against someone. Forgive as the Lord forgave you. And over all these virtues put on love, which binds them all together in perfect unity.

None of these qualities that reflect the image of the Creator involve gender roles or opposite-sex marriage. Paul was also unmarried and even taught that being single was the preferred state for the Christian.[108] Paul would not have taught this if being unmarried meant missing out on the opportunity to reflect God's image.

Undoing the Fall vs. Diversity in Creation

A non-affirming view might say:

Genesis 1:27 says that God made Adam male and Eve female. God's creation plan is for humans to be either male or female and to be attracted to the opposite sex. This means that intersex/DSD bodies, transgender (including non-binary) genders, and same-sex attractions are not part of God's plan and are the result of humanity's fall from grace, which happened when Adam and Eve ate the forbidden fruit and were evicted from the Garden of Eden. The fall marred God's image in humanity and resulted in health problems, disability, and death. Transgender identities and same-sex attractions may result from psychological dysfunction, possibly because of trauma, social conditioning, or a disruption in genetic codes. Christians do not typically embrace illness, disability, or dysfunction, but rather seek healing from them. Transgender Christians should therefore reject or suppress their inclination to identify as any gender other than the one that matches the body given to them by God at birth, and they should not try to circumvent God's plan for their bodies by undergoing hormonal treatments or surgeries to change their bodies. Instead, they should seek therapy and spiritual support

---

108. See 1 Corinthians 7.

to help them come to peace with their bodies. Same-sex attracted people should root their identity in Christ, rather than in their sexual orientation, and should avoid acting out on their same-sex attractions. In the case of children with DSD, parents and doctors can discern the appropriate gender and proceed with appropriate surgeries and hormonal treatments to enable them to live as male or female.

An affirming view might say:

God created a broader diversity of life than is specifically stated in Genesis. When Genesis 1:3-5 describes God creating light, separating it from the dark, and making day and night, it is inferred that dawn and dusk are included as part of his intentional creation. While the Bible says God created land and water, it is understood that he also created swamps, bogs, and rivers that exist as something in between land and sea. While the Bible says God created land creatures and sea creatures, it is also known that he created amphibians, which can breathe both in water and on land.[109] There is much more diversity in nature than is expressed in the creation story found in Genesis 1, and this diversity includes broader expressions of gender than male and female, and broader expressions of sexuality than opposite-sex marriage. Just like God planned for diversity within the rest of creation, he also planned for diverse sexual orientations and genders. LGBTQ+ orientations are not something to be accommodated, but rather to be celebrated as God's good intention. When Genesis says, "God created them male and female," it is descriptive of what he did, not prescriptive of what he always will do. It does not say that people are always created male or female, just that the first people were created male and female.

There is natural variation in the genitalia, chromosomal configuration, and hormonal balance of humans, providing a natural biological spectrum spanning between male and female.[110] Some of these variations are observable, while some are invisible. About 1.7% of babies' bodies do not fit into the expected standards for male or female. The term to describe people who are neither fully male nor fully female is "difference in sex development" (DSD), previously called "intersex." About 0.05% of babies have abnormal genitalia at birth that results in recommended surgeries to conform to an assigned

109. DeFranza, "Journeying from the Bible to Christian Ethics in Search of Common Ground," 90.

110. The Gender Dysphoria Bible, "But the Chromosomes!!!" accessed May 26, 2021, https://genderdysphoria.fyi/gdb/chromosomes.

gender.[111] The fact that they have DSD is often hidden by such surgical intervention. Sometimes the gender assigned at birth is mistaken, creating confusion and heartbreak as people with DSD grow up in social roles or with surgically modified bodies that do not match their gender identity.[112] The affirmation of people with DSD recognizes diversity in God's creation and removes pressure for them to fit into prescribed gender roles and/or undergo medically unnecessary surgeries and invasive treatments.

Psalm 139:15-16 says, "My frame was not hidden from you when I was made in the secret place, when I was woven together in the depths of the earth. Your eyes saw my unformed body; all the days ordained for me were written in your book before one of them came to be." Christians ought to accept and affirm each person as God's good creation, regardless their gender or sexual orientation. The acceptance of LGBTQ+ people as they have been created is a way of honoring God's creation. Since transgender people were created to be transgender, their experience should be honored. God didn't make a mistake when he created transgender people, and they are not defying his will by medically or socially transitioning. Rather, they are using their creative agency, given to them by God, as they reflect the image of the creator God. Since the fall, people have used medications, medical procedures, rehabilitative devices and other means to change various biological characteristics that they find distressing or undesirable. Using bodies in ways that go beyond their clear anatomical design is not usually considered to be displeasing to God. God-given creativity can be used to change bodies to match gender identities and to express love through same-sex sex within marriage or covenantal relationships.

It is not fair to single out LGBTQ+ orientations and identities by saying that they result from the fall as though straight, cisgender people's orientations and identities have not been affected by the fall. In Genesis 3:16, God tells Eve her husband will rule over her because of her sin, revealing that patriarchy resulted from the fall. Many male and female identities and roles are wrapped up in the patriarchal lens through which Christians tend to see the world.

---

111. Interact Advocates for Intersex Youth, "FAQ: What is Intersex?" May18, 2020, accessed January 16, 2021, https://interactadvocates.org/faq/#howcommon.

112. Austen Hartke, *Transforming: The Bible and the Lives of Transgender Christians* (Louisville, KY: Westminster John Knox Press, 2018), 141.

A non-affirming view might say:

Diverse gender identities such as non-binary and transgender identities are a recent phenomenon and are the result of a trend or a fad. Transgender people are unhappy with their lives and, under the influence of culture, they use gender change as one way to try to change their lives to achieve happiness when they should be turning to God to experience joy.

An affirming view might say:

Gender-diverse people have been around throughout history. The ancient Jewish people understood gender diversity, partly because they closely examined babies' genitals in relation to the practice of circumcision. Their legal traditions include eight gender variations, including: male (*zachar*), female (*nekevah*), characteristics of both male and female (*androgynos*), lacking sexual characteristics (*tumtum*), identified female at birth but later developing male characteristics naturally (*ay'lonit hamah*), identified female at birth but later developing male characteristics through human intervention (*ay'lonit 'adam*), identified male at birth but later developing female characteristics naturally (*saris hamah*), and identified male at birth and later developing female characteristics through human intervention (*saris 'adam*).[113] Indigenous people in North America recognized and honored their community members who carried both male and female spirits within them. Being able to see through both masculine and feminine lenses gave them unique insights and they were often healers and visionaries. Two Spirit people lost their respect and honor when colonization and residential school indoctrination enforced heteronormative and homophobic attitudes.[114] Transgender people existed in the decades and centuries prior to current cultural awareness and understanding, even if they did not have the terms to describe their experiences and connect with each other, or the tools to fully transition.[115]

---

113. Rachel Scheinerman, "Gender and Sexuality: The Eight Genders in the Talmud," *My Jewish Learning*, accessed April 13, 2024, https://www.myjewishlearning.com/article/the-eight-genders-in-the-talmud.

114. Isabella Thurston, "The History of Two-Spirit Folks," *The Indigenous Foundation*, June 29, 2022, accessed April 13, 2024, https://www.theindigenousfoundation.org/articles/the-history-of-two-spirit-folks.

115. Laine Kaplan-Levenson, "NPR's Embedded All The Only Ones," *NPR*, November 2, 2023, accessed April 13, 2024, https://www.npr.org/series/1212940848/nprs-embedded-all-the-only-ones.

A non-affirming view might say:

God would not have intentionally created people to be transgender, because life is so hard for transgender people and so many of them struggle with mental health. This would not be God's plan.

An affirming view might say:

Many of the difficulties faced by transgender people are due to actual or feared non-acceptance and discrimination. If families and society in general accepted and celebrated transgender people, their lives would not be so difficult. Life is and historically has been extremely hard for other marginalized or oppressed groups of people, but this is not usually used as an argument to say that God would not have created them to have characteristics that marginalize them, such as a specific race or sex.

Transgender Identities and Gender-Affirming Medical Care

A non-affirming view might say:

Deuteronomy 22:5 says, "A woman must not wear men's clothing, nor a man wear women's clothing, for the LORD your God detests anyone who does this." This verse prohibits transitioning from one gender to another.

An affirming view might say:

The original Hebrew language of Deuteronomy 22:5 suggests that it is discussing something other than simply wearing clothing pertaining to the opposite sex. It says that it restricts items that pertain to a man, which implies weapons, tools, ornamentation and clothing, from being upon a woman. The word used for man describes a mighty man, or warrior, which supports the idea that the items in question are armour or weapons. The second part of the verse restricts men from wearing women's garments, using a Hebrew word that describes a cloak or outer garment. The prohibition may have been to prevent men from attacking women with weapons, to prevent women from being conscripted to fight, or to prevent women from disguising themselves as men to fight in battle. It may have also been intended to prevent warriors from disguising themselves as women to avoid being conscripted to fight, or to avoid being attacked by other men.[116] The prohibition against wearing opposite-sex garments and apparel could also have been related to cultic worship of the god Ishtar, where cross-dressing was part of worship. It is taking the verse out of context to use it to restrict clothing options for people today or to say it addresses questions related to transgender identities.

A non-affirming view might say:

God gave people a physical body as well as a spiritual soul, or inner self, connected to that body. When a person rejects the body that God has given them, they are separating their body from their inner self and are prioritizing their inner self over their God-given body in a form of individualistic self-expression.[117] In doing so, they dishonor the gift of body that God has given them. If a choice needs to be made between the body and the inner self, the body should have primacy.[118]

An affirming view might say:

Scripture does not directly prohibit Christians from identifying as transgender or from transitioning through gender-affirming medical care. God made Adam and Eve male and female, but that does not preclude God from creating subsequent people to be transgender or non-binary. When a transgender person undergoes gender-affirming medical treatment such as hormones or surgery, they are valuing their body, not rejecting it. They are not denying the unity of their body and their inner self or spirit, rather they are aligning their body with their inner self. Once their body and inner self are integrated, they can feel whole and can love and honor their body more, which sets them up to be able to love others and serve God more effectively.[119]

Christians frequently undergo surgeries to improve the way their bodies function. Gender-affirming medical care, or medical transitioning, is a medical intervention to treat the painful and distressing experience of gender dysphoria. Gender dysphoria results

---

116. Calum M. Carmichael, *The Laws of Deuteronomy* (Ithica, NY: Cornell University Press, 1974), 147, quoted in Justin Tanis, *Transgendered: Theology, Ministry, and Community of Faith* (Cleveland, OH: The Pilgrim Press, 2003), 64.

117. Carl Trueman, *Strange New World: How Thinkers and Activists Redefined Identity and Sparked the Sexual Revolution* (Wheaton, Ill: Crossway, 2022), 178, 182.

118. Nancy Pearcey, *Love Thy Body: Answering Hard Questions about Life and Sexuality* (Grand Rapids, MI: Baker Books, 2018), 34.

119. Katherine Johnson, "A Biblical Theology of Gender," The Reformation Project Leadership Development curriculum (The Reformation Project, 2023), 21.

from having a body that is incongruent with one's sense of self. Gender dysphoria can cause so much distress that many people would rather die than live in a body or identify as a gender that does not match their self-perception. Studies suggest that 41% of transgender people in the United States have attempted suicide.[120] Many aspects of our bodies in the fallen world are not as they are designed to be and using medical intervention to reduce pain and distress is a common way of coping with this reality. Jesus cared about restoring peoples' bodies to wholeness and relieving physical and emotional distress. Gender-affirming care relieves distress for transgender people and is consistent with how Jesus helped people with their physical needs.

Prioritizing the body over the inner self is not a biblical principle. Rather it is the inner self that communes with the Holy Spirit and worships God. There are places in Scripture where the spirit or inner self is given priority over external realities. Matthew 10:28 says "Do not fear those who kill the body but cannot kill the soul." 2 Corinthians 4:16 says, "So we do not lose heart. Even though our outer nature is wasting away, our inner nature is being renewed day by day." 2 Corinthians 4:18 says, "we look not at what can be seen but at what cannot be seen, for what can be seen is temporary, but what cannot be seen is eternal."[121] Scripturally, when there is a misalignment between the inner self and the outer self, the inner self takes precedence.

A non-affirming view might say:

Young people who transition are making high-stakes decisions impacting their future fertility and health that they are not yet mature enough to make. Those who transition sometimes regret their decision, but the effects are irreversible. Many are succumbing to social pressure to be LGBTQ+ and they are not actually transgender. Supporting minors to medically transition is akin to child abuse because it damages their bodies and confuses their identity.

---

120. Jaime M. Grant, Lisa A. Moffet and Justin Tanis, "Injustice at Every Turn: A Report of the National Transgender Discrimination Survey," (Washington, DC: National Center for Transgender Equality and National Gay and Lesbian Task Force, 2011), 82.

121. Johnson, "A Biblical Theology of Gender, 22-23.

An affirming view might say:

By the time people are in their late teens, they tend to be sure about their gender identity. Living in the world as a transgender person is difficult and people who try it will typically stop if it is not right for them or they are doing so merely due to social pressure. Doctors look for signs that people are persistent, insistent, and consistent about their transgender identity before undergoing any irreversible treatments, and they usually insist that people begin with reversible changes such as names, pronouns, hairstyle, and clothing, in order to be sure prior to making more permanent changes.

In some cases, puberty blockers are used to allow time for a young teen to mature cognitively and emotionally without having to suffer from dysphoria resulting from going through puberty in a body that does not align with their inner self. This allows them to wait until they are older to make a more permanent decision. Once they come off puberty blockers, they either go through puberty with the sex they were assigned at birth, or they take hormones and go through puberty according to their gender identity. Health risks related to the use of puberty blockers and hormones are often more acceptable to patients and their parents than the risk of death by suicide. Use of puberty blockers can affect bone density, but even so, bone density stays within the normal range between cisgender males and females. In other words, transgender people may lose bone density, but only to the point that their risk of osteoporosis is similar to that of cisgender females.

Fertility loss is a weighty concern for many and is the primary reason people regret transitioning. Plans for future sexual function and fertility can be considered when determining a timeline for treatment. Transgender girls can wait to use puberty blockers until their penis has developed so that it will be functional for urinary and sexual purposes and in case the tissue is needed for future surgery, although it should be noted that the vast majority of transgender women do not undergo bottom surgery. Sperm can be harvested prior to starting puberty blockers or hormones. Transgender men may still be able to get pregnant if they stop taking testosterone. They can also harvest eggs prior to gender affirming treatment. Some transgender people say that if they had not received gender affirming care, they would likely not be alive to bear children anyway, so transitioning is worth the cost of infertility.

The health risks associated with gender-affirming medical care are not excessive and can be managed through monitoring and medical means. Many transgender people are prepared to face health risks because gender-affirming treatment improves their mental health, quality of life, and life expectancy.[122]

While regret after transitioning is rare, those rare cases are widely publicized. A 2021 study of eight thousand teens and adults from the US, Canada, and Europe showed that 1% of people who had transitioned expressed regret related to transitioning. Half of those (0.5%) expressed regret specifically due to their decision to change their gender. Some regret was due to poor surgical outcomes and/or dissatisfaction with the aesthetic outcome rather than uncertainty or fluctuations in their gender identity. The other half of the one percent had regrets due to the social stigma and discrimination they faced after transitioning. In other words, if they had not experienced rejection and discrimination, they likely would not have experienced regret. Only a small number of the one percent that expressed regret detransitioned.[123] Aside from regret, other reasons for detransitioning are involuntary, such as lack of access to hormone treatment, often for financial or political reasons. Regret is common after other types of surgery (e.g., knee replacements, plastic surgery), but these do not result in the surgeries being banned.

People who do not have transgender family or friends might contemplate the risks involved with undergoing gender affirming medical care but they may not be privy to the risks of not receiving that care (e.g., depression, suicide, failure to thrive) or to the benefits of receiving care (e.g., relief from distress, desire to live, improved self-esteem, increased confidence, greater productivity, more social engagement). Many people express concern and compassion for the one percent of people who may later regret medically transitioning and may desire to see a ban on gender-affirming care to prevent anyone from experiencing such regret. These people may not be considering the many transgender people whose lives are improved and even made possible because of being able to transition, who would suffer if denied access to gender-affirming care. Supporting young teenagers to use puberty blockers and late teenagers to

---

122. Shauna Lawlis, Understanding Transgender Healthcare and Wellness: Expert Panel, Moderator Lucas Hall, May 21, 2023, accessed July 17, 2023, https://us06web.zoom.us/rec/play/VSF_na0AVitswGfXzJVkyuNxzxLAjoHAAc gO7TWVmOh2qQzJa8DCwzvdHSh3Z9MBAnaUTvHdL55K4Yb.pcsVYqj6UW6 F4hB1?autoplay=true&startTime=1684709995000.

123. Valeria P. Bustos et al., "Regret after Gender-affirmation Surgery: A Systematic Review and Meta-analysis of Prevalence," *Plastic and Reconstructive Surgery Global Open* 10, no. 4 (2021):11.

medically transition through gender-affirming care is not child abuse, rather it is supporting their mental health and increasing their life expectancy. Medical considerations related to risks and benefits of transitioning are medical issues to be considered by doctors, patients, and parents, not moral issues to be judged by the church.

A non-affirming view might say:

Inclusion of transgender people in society creates confusion and complexity which denies cisgender people their rights, risks their safety, and limits their opportunities. Parental rights are being subverted when schools teach children about different gender identities and allow children to use different pronouns or names without parents' awareness and permission. Transgender people using public bathrooms and changerooms make children and women uncomfortable and put them at risk of harm. Transgender women and girls have an unfair advantage in female sports. When transgender women are given opportunities in society that are reserved for women, it takes those opportunities away from cisgender women.

An affirming view might say:

The complex issues related to the inclusion of transgender people (e.g., educational approaches, parents' and children's rights, safe washroom and changeroom spaces, participation in sports, and protecting women's opportunities in society) are challenges for our society to face, but they are not evidence that gender-affirming care itself is immoral. They are practical issues to be solved rather than moral issues to be judged by the church.

Schools do not try to influence cisgender students to become transgender. Rather, they try to support transgender students in accepting themselves and teach other students to accept transgender people. Learning about the existence of transgender people does not cause cisgender people to become transgender. People don't become transgender, rather they discover that they are transgender. Occasionally it takes children some time to experiment in order to make that discovery. Rules that require teachers to disclose students' requests to use different pronouns or names to their parents put teachers in a difficult position because they know that some parents may react in ways that harm their children. For example, some teenagers are kicked out of the home when they come out to their parents. Teachers cannot discern ahead of time which students will be at risk of harm if prematurely outed to their parents. It is the child's right to decide when to come out to their parents. Teachers do not have the right nor the responsibility to "out" a student. If teachers decline to use the name and pronouns a student wants to use, it can lead students to experience further depression and distress. Many teachers are aware of the high rates of suicide associated with being transgender and want to help students avoid that outcome. Many students need some time to try out a name and pronouns at school so they can be sure before coming out to their parents and facing the overwhelming risk of rejection from the ones they love and depend on the most. Many parents of transgender teens who came out initially at school are thankful that their children had a safe place to be themselves when they weren't ready to come out at home. They recognize that schools met a need for their children which supported their mental health.

Use of public bathrooms and change rooms is a complex issue, but restricting people to the bathroom designated for the sex that was assigned to them at birth does not mitigate and actually increases the risk of men entering women's bathrooms or change rooms for the purpose of harming women or girls. This is because many transgender men have facial hair, deep voices, and muscular builds that make them difficult to differentiate from cisgender men. Having these transgender men (who were assigned female at birth) entering women's bathrooms and change rooms would likely make women more uncomfortable than having transgender women in those spaces. It would create an opportunity for cisgender men to enter women's bathrooms and claim to be transgender men if anyone were to question them as they entered or exited. Transgender women are not likely to be abusive towards women in women's spaces and they are at higher risk of being abused and harassed themselves. Transgender women are at risk of being assaulted and abused in men's bathrooms and change rooms. Many transgender people limit their drinking and eating during the day so they won't need to use public washrooms. This practice leads to health complications. A solution to the bathroom issue is to offer gender neutral bathrooms and changerooms, with private individual stalls or showers, which also helps families, parents with young children, and people with disabilities.

Competitive sports where transgender women are competing against cisgender women is a topic that is difficult to navigate. While transgender women may have a height advantage over cisgender women, their strength advantage is minimized by hormone therapy. There is a wide variation in height for cisgender women as well, and competitive sports do not usually accommodate for these differences. Perhaps an alternate way to determine which people should compete against each other in sporting events could be implemented, which could help sports become more inclusive for all people, including cisgender people who may be naturally smaller statured.

If such insufficient opportunities exist for women in society that cisgender women feel they cannot afford to share these opportunities with transgender women, the solution is to create more opportunities for women in general, rather than to try to exclude transgender women from participating as women in society.

New Creation

An affirming view might say:
The trajectory of Christianity is looking ahead to a new creation, not trying to somehow re-create the conditions of the Garden of Eden prior to the fall. This means we shouldn't feel a need to copy the dynamics of the first marriage relationship in current relationships. The prayer Jesus taught his followers to pray in Matthew 6:10 says, "your Kingdom come," implying that something new is coming, rather than something old returning. A return to the conditions of the Garden of Eden would mean losing the diversity of languages and cultures that resulted after God scattered people for trying to build the Tower of Babel (Gen 11:8-9). However, Revelation 7:9 suggests that this diversity will not be lost in the Kingdom of God. John recounts his vision of heaven, saying, "there before me was a great multitude that no one could count, from every nation, tribe, people and language, standing before the throne and before the Lamb."[124] Gender diversity and ethnic diversity may not have been initially created in the Garden of Eden but that does not mean they are displeasing to God or that they weren't created by him.

Paul teaches that in Christ there is neither male nor female (Gal 3:28), and Jesus teaches that people won't marry nor be given in marriage at the resurrection (Matt 22:30). The coming new creation does not emphasize marriage or gender roles, so churches should not prohibit same-sex marriage or exclude people who don't conform to customary gender identities or roles, believing they somehow need to return to the way life was in the Garden of Eden. Christians are not

---

124. Lianne Simon and Megan DeFranza, *Intersex Christians and the Image of God*, video, accessed May 26, 2021, https://www.youtube.com/watch?v=331 smwhg0gM.

on a quest to "undo" the effects of the fall, but rather to help usher in a new Kingdom.

Conversion Therapy

Content Warning: This discussion may be upsetting, especially for those who have been through or promoted conversion therapy. Please do what you need to do to take care of yourself and skip ahead to the next section if this topic is too difficult.

Background:

Until recently, a central belief of Christians who do not affirm same-sex marriage has been that people can change their sexual orientation from gay to straight through a form of therapy and prayer called conversion therapy. Awareness is growing about the significant harm that has been inflicted upon LGBTQ+ people and their families through conversion therapy, also called reparative therapy. These so-called therapies have occurred in different formats and styles and under different names, but all of them are attempts to influence someone to decrease or eliminate same-sex attraction or to refrain from acting upon same-sex attraction. As I address conversion therapy, I acknowledge that some readers and some churches, being ignorant of the harm it caused, may have genuinely thought that it was a loving approach. Without dismissing the harm done or the repentance or relational healing work that needs to happen, for the purposes of this book, the focus will be on doing better now that we know better. Some non-affirming views continue to believe change therapy is an appropriate option, and others do not. The promotion of conversion therapy is illegal in Canada. This book does not promote or endorse conversion therapy, and the author believes it to be harmful to those who receive it. Some Christians still hold views that support change therapy, so it is helpful to identify such views in order to engage in an open and transparent conversation about them.

A non-affirming view might say:

Non-heterosexual sexual orientations and non-cisgender identities are not God's plan for his people. LGBTQ+ orientations and gender identities have various causes, including physical or psychological trauma, genetic changes, hormone imbalances in the womb, societal pressure, or underlying sin and a rejection of God. Therapy or spiritual practices have attempted to change LGBTQ+ people's orientation or identity to conform to God's original intention with some success.[125] There are public examples of LGBTQ+ people who have been able to change, including author and speaker Rosaria Butterfield, author and speaker Beckett Cook, and singer/songwriter Dennis Jernigan.[126] Christians should not put limits on what God can do. People who want to change should be encouraged and supported to undergo therapies to help them meet their goals.

An affirming view might say:
Sexual orientations are unlikely to be able to be changed due to desire, effort, therapy, or prayer. The idea that LGBTQ+ orientations are caused by childhood sexual abuse is misleading. Not all people who have experienced emotional and physical trauma from sexual abuse have become LGBTQ+, and not all LGBTQ+ people have experienced emotional and physical trauma from sexual abuse. The cause of diverse sexual orientations is not understood, but many people attest to having been aware of their orientation since childhood and to being unable to change, even after earnest attempts to do so. Attempts that have been made to help people undergo orientation change through conversion therapy or reparative therapy have been overwhelmingly unsuccessful in changing people's orientation. One research study found conversion therapies to have a success rate of only 15%, and in such cases, "success" may have been defined as a change in actions/lifestyle rather than a change in attraction.[127] Such attempts to change have caused significant emotional, psychological, spiritual, and financial harm to the individuals and has negatively impacted their family relationships. Conversion therapy practices are now illegal in Canada, due to a recognition of the harm they cause.

The harm is multi-faceted. Some conversion therapies directly or indirectly teach LGBTQ+ people to loathe their intrinsic desires, which can lead them to loathe their whole selves. This is deeply

125. Stanton L. Jones and Mark A. Yarhouse, "Ex Gays? An Extended Longitudinal Study of Attempted Religiously Mediated Change in Sexual Orientation," *Sexual Orientation and Faith Tradition Symposium; APA Convention* (2009), 10.

126. Beckett Cook and Brett McCracken, "From Gay to Gospel: The Fascinating Story of Beckett Cook," *The Gospel Coalition*, accessed August 18, 2021, https://www.thegospelcoalition.org/article/gay-gospel-becket-cook; Rosaria Champagne Butterfield, "Rosaria's Story," accessed August 18, 2021, https://rosariabutterfield.com/biography; Dennis Jernigan, *DJ's Testimony*, accessed August 18, 2021, https://www.dennisjernigan.com/djs-story.

127. Jones and Yarhouse, "Ex Gays? An Extended Longitudinal Study of Attempted Religiously Mediated Change in Sexual Orientation," 10.

psychologically damaging.[128] Some conversion therapy practices teach LGBTQ+ people that faulty parenting is an underlying cause of their same-sex attraction, and that identifying and confronting suppressed anger towards their parents can help reduce their same-sex attractions. Even people who initially have good relationships with their parents can be pressured to identify and confront problems in those relationships. This can cause people to alienate themselves from their parents and to resent or even hate them. It can also lay an unnecessary burden of guilt on parents' shoulders. The theory that faulty parenting causes same-sex attraction was accepted and promoted with no evidence of its accuracy and has had, and continues to have, devastating consequences on individuals and families. Conversion therapy is expensive in terms of both time and money. When it offers false hope for a change in orientation that is unlikely to occur, it amounts to consumer fraud. When people are unsuccessful in changing their orientation, some conversion therapists say that the clients lack commitment or motivation, and recommend increasing the frequency of therapy sessions, causing further psychological and financial harm. Some clients experience the pressure to enter a mixed-orientation marriage to be a form of sexual abuse. Survivors of conversion therapy have reported that it caused them to suffer depression and suicidal ideation. It gave them post-traumatic stress disorder, taught them to hate their parents, wasted valuable years of their youth, created financial hardship, and made them afraid to enter a church. Survivors of conversion therapy often require years of regular therapy to help them heal from their experiences. Some require regular therapy but are afraid to trust another therapist or are unable to afford the help they need. Some people may desire conversion therapy to help them change, but this desire is often due to having been taught that God will accept them only when they change or while they are trying to change.

The overwhelming number of failed attempts to change sexual orientation and the very few stories of actual changes in orientation demonstrate that one's sexual orientation is not a choice. The

---

128. In a 2020 National Survey of over 40,000 LGBTQ youth aged 13-24, those who have had someone try to convince them to change their sexual orientation or identity were more than twice as likely to attempt suicide as those who did not. The Trevor Project, "Conversion Therapy & Change Attempts," *National Survey on LGBTQ Youth Mental Health* 2020, accessed February 19, 2021, https://www.thetrevorproject.org/survey-2020/?section=Conversion-Therapy-Change-Attempts.

presentation of a few people who have changed their orientations as evidence that similar change is possible for the majority is misleading, painful, and confusing for those who try but cannot change. Not everyone can participate in an opposite-sex marriage or live celibately for their entire life.

Many people who claim to have undergone successful conversion therapy have not actually changed their orientation or attractions but rather have been able to accept celibacy or enter a mixed-orientation marriage. Some who presented as gay or lesbian but are actually bisexual may have found opposite-sex partners while also remaining same-sex attracted. Some bisexual women who identified as lesbian in order to protest patriarchy may have changed their political views. People who had been abused by someone of the same sex may have had confusing sexual and romantic desires which became sorted out as they experienced emotional healing, and the experience of healing from trauma may be interpreted as a change in orientation.[129]

Some people who celebrate a transition from what they call a "homosexual lifestyle" to a "heterosexual or celibate lifestyle" have experienced a simultaneous spiritual breakthrough or conversion. The peace, purpose, and promise that comes with the acceptance of Jesus as their Lord and Savior and the presence of the Holy Spirit in their lives brings spiritual freedom and deliverance from bondage. This spiritual breakthrough is the most impactful change in their lives. The lifestyle they left behind because of this spiritual breakthrough may have been a promiscuous or otherwise unhealthy lifestyle. Since they are taught that same-sex marriage is incompatible with Christian faith, these new or newly reborn Christians are content to give up the fulfillment of their sexual and romantic desires because a life with Christ is more valuable to them than a sexual or romantic relationship. They proclaim joy and contentment in Christ because of having been delivered from homosexuality, but what they may more accurately be experiencing is the joy that comes from accepting Christ and freedom from unhealthy relationships and lifestyles. They don't realize that they didn't have to choose between having the joy of Christ *or* a same-sex marriage. Since they don't recognize the option to embrace Christ *and* same-sex marriage, and because their relationship with Christ is most important to them, they choose celibacy or a mixed-orientation marriage. Some end up finding their choice untenable in future years.

---

129. Wendy VanderWal-Gritter, *Generous Spaciousness: Responding to Gay Christians in the Church* (Grand Rapids: Baker, 2014), 61.

A non-affirming view might say:

Christians can renounce conversion therapy without affirming same-sex sexual relationships. Those who are not able to change or who are waiting for change can find spiritual fulfillment in a celibate life or relational fulfillment in a mixed-orientation marriage. If they cannot find fulfillment, that may be their "cross to bear" for Jesus in this life, and they can be reassured that they will experience fulfillment with Jesus in the afterlife. LGBTQ+ Christians should consider their identity to be in Christ rather than in their sexual orientation, and they should lean into their relationship with Jesus to sustain them.

The Physical Act of Anal Sex

Content warning: The next section discusses the physical act of anal sex which may make some people feel uncomfortable. It is included here because many have questions that they don't feel comfortable asking anyone about, and it can be hard to find information. The information provided is not a replacement for medical advice.

A non-affirming view might say:

Many people experience feelings of discomfort or disgust when they think about anal sex. Their instinctive reaction reinforces their belief that same-sex sex is against God's will and contrary to his creation purpose. They might say that anal intercourse is unsanitary, unhealthy, and painful for the receptive partner, and therefore is an inherently abusive type of sexual activity even if it is a mutually agreed upon act.

An affirming view might say:

Feelings of disgust are often related to experiencing something new or different. Certain foods or smells may be disgusting to one person but enjoyed by another. Cultural practices may seem disgusting to people from other cultures, even though there is nothing immoral about the practice. Examples can include hair length, tattoos, body piercings, language, gestures, and ways to deal with saliva, mucus, fingernails, and toenails. The point is that someone's feelings of disgust related to another person's actions does not mean that that other person has done something wrong. Any exchange of bodily fluids is unsanitary, whether between same-sex or opposite-sex partners. Monogamy can minimize the risk of sexually transmitted diseases. As with vaginal sex, the use of a condom or barrier can significantly reduce the risk of transmission of body fluids from one person to the other.

Feelings of repulsion that some straight people might have when thinking about same-sex sex can be due to homophobia or difficulty considering other peoples' perspectives.[130] Gay and lesbian people can have similar feelings of repulsion when thinking about opposite-sex sex. The thought of *anyone* having sex can cause some people to feel uncomfortable and disgusted. Teenagers often feel disgusted by the thought of their parents having sex, but that does not mean that their parents' sexual acts are morally wrong. Rather than serving as evidence that sex is against God's will, feelings of repulsion when considering the sexual acts of other people indicate that sexual activity, whether in the context of same-sex or opposite sex relationships, is meant to be a private act between spouses, and not imagined or thought about by others.

People's thoughts and imaginations about what happens in other peoples' bedrooms are not always accurate. A 1994 study of 3432 Americans aged 18-59 revealed that 20% of heterosexual women and 25% of heterosexual men had engaged in anal sex at least once in their lifetime.[131] The study also showed that about 20% of male-male sexual partners had not participated in anal sex.[132] If anal sex is the problematic behavior, then the church should teach everyone to avoid it, including heterosexual people, and it should accept same-sex marriages that do not participate in it. About 14% of men report severe and frequent pain during anal sex, which is similar in number to the 10-15% of women who report pain and discomfort during vaginal penetration. Strategies such as using adequate lubrication, adequate foreplay stimulation, and relaxation techniques can reduce pain for both vaginal and anal sex. Same-sex partners have the option of positioning themselves such that the man who experiences pain during anal sex is the penetrating partner.[133] The idea that anal sex is an inappropriate activity based on hygiene, health, or pain should not be a deciding factor in whether to affirm same-sex marriage.

The Scriptures do not give the physical design of male and female bodies fitting together as a reason for opposite-sex marriage, nor do they give it as a reason to prohibit same-sex sex. Reasons that are given

---

130. VanderWal-Gritter, *Generous Spaciousness*, 228.
131. E. Laumann et al., *The Social Organization of Sexuality: Sexual Practices in the United States* (Chicago: University of Chicago Press, 1994), 107.
132. Ibid., 320.
133. Will Damon and B. R. Simon Rosser, "Anodyspareunia in Men Who Have Sex with Men," *Journal of Sex & Marital Therapy* 31, no. 2 (2005): 139.

for marriage are kinship/companionship (Genesis 2:18), procreation (Genesis 1:28), and to satisfy sexual need (1 Corinthians 7:2-9). Procreation was obviously planned to require male and female pairings, however non-procreative opposite-sex marriages are not typically prohibited by the church. Non-procreative marriage between same-sex spouses should not be ruled out based on human anatomy and physiology because it can still meet the purposes of kinship/companionship and satisfaction of sexual needs. Same-sex sex functions on physical and physiological levels to unite couples emotionally and to provide mutual pleasure. Anal sex can be pleasurable for the penetrated man because of the way it stimulates the prostate gland. Even during male-female sex, women often experience pleasure through methods other than penile penetration and do not always experience pleasure through penile penetration.[134]

A non-affirming view might say:

The conversation on creation and the image of God can be summarized in this way: God created people to be male or female and said that they were created in the image of God. To honor God, people should accept the bodies with which they were born. Male and female bodies were designed to fit together for the purpose of procreation and mutual pleasure. Marriages or sexual relationships that are not male/female couplings are not in keeping with God's creation design. If people cannot participate in an opposite-sex marriage, they have the option to remain single and celibate.

An affirming view might say:

The conversation on creation and the image of God can be summarized in this way: considerations related to being made in God's image, the effects of the fall, and the physiology of anal sex do not necessarily rule out same-sex sex and gender affirming care as being within God's will. Important considerations that weigh in favor of affirming LGBTQ+ orientations and identities include diversity in creation, the trajectory towards new creation rather than a return to the conditions of Eden, the desire for wholeness, health and a reduction of harm, and the limited success and intense harm associated with change attempts, conversion therapy, and mandated celibacy.

---

134. Kathy Baldock, *Walking the Bridgeless Canyon: Repairing the Breach Between the Church and the LGBT Community* (Reno, NV: Canyon Walker Press, 2014), 216.

Procreation

Be Fruitful and Increase in Number

Background:
Genesis 1:28 says:

> God blessed them and said to them, "Be fruitful and increase in number; fill the earth and subdue it. Rule over the fish in the sea and the birds in the sky and over every living creature that moves on the ground."

People have different ideas about what God meant by "be fruitful and increase in number."

A non-affirming view might say:
The command to "be fruitful and increase in number" shows that God's primary purpose for designing sex and marriage is procreation. Same-sex marriages are therefore unacceptable to God because of their inability to fulfill a procreative function.[135] The design and function of the male and female reproductive systems make it clear that God designed sex and marriage to be between two people of opposite sexes.

An affirming view might say:
The phrase "be fruitful and increase in number" is more accurately interpreted as a blessing, not as a command. Genesis 1:28 says "God blessed them" as he spoke. Paul himself did not attempt to have children, so if it was a command, he clearly did not believe it to apply universally.

Procreation was essential after the time of creation (and specifically after the fall) for humanity to survive. Following the exodus from Egypt, procreation was essential for God's people to establish themselves in a new land. It was also essential during the time of the Israelites' return from captivity in Babylon, when God's people once again had to establish themselves. Some scholars believe that the Old Testament books were written during the time of the return from Babylon, to help the people remember their heritage. In this case, even though the stories in Genesis describe a time far before the Babylonian captivity, the context of the Babylonian exile has an influence over the way the stories were told and passed down.

---

135. Stephen R. Holmes, "Listening to the Past and Reflecting on the Present," in *Two Views on Homosexuality, the Bible, and the Church,* ed. Preston Sprinkle (Grand Rapids, MI: Zondervan, 2016), 175.

Our context is different. The earth is well-populated, maybe even overpopulated. Theologically speaking, God's command to "fill the earth" was fulfilled with Jesus' birth,[136] and Christians believe that the family of God is now expanded through evangelism rather than procreation. Individually speaking, Christians no longer understand procreation to be the way to extend personal existence (i.e., to live on through one's offspring after death) because Jesus gives Christians the hope of eternal life after death.[137] People can "bear fruit" in ways other than bearing children. Non-procreative couples can parent children through adoption.[138] Raising children often requires support beyond what parents themselves can provide, and many adults can fulfill supportive childcare and educational roles without having biological children themselves. People can leave a legacy through the way they impact and influence other people, not only their own children.

Marriage does not typically have to produce children to be considered valid in the Christian church today. Many couples choose not to have children, and this choice is not considered disobedient or sinful. Procreation was expected during biblical times, but infertile couples were still considered to have valid marriages, such as Abraham and Sarah as well as Zechariah and Elizabeth (prior to their respective angelic visits which bestowed children on them). In the Old Testament, the Song of Solomon celebrates sexual lovemaking without mentioning procreation, and procreation was never a focus in the New Testament. 1 Corinthians 7:8-9 says, "Now to the unmarried and the widows I say: It is good for them to stay unmarried, as I do. But if they cannot control themselves, they should marry, for it is better to marry than to burn with passion." In this verse, Paul teaches that a legitimate purpose for marriage is to manage sexual passions. The instructions for households in Ephesians 5:22-6:9, Colossians 3:18-4:1, and 1 Peter 2:13-3:7 provide teaching about marriage which does not focus on procreation as its purpose, but rather gives directions for mutual care and companionship.[139] Procreation is a blessing of marriage but is not needed to validate or justify a marriage. It is inconsistent to prohibit same-sex marriage

---

136. Meagan K. DeFranza, "Response to Stephen R. Holmes," in *Two Views on Homosexuality, the Bible, and the Church*, ed. by Preston Sprinkle (Grand Rapids, MI: Zondervan, 2016), 204.

137. Ibid., 201.

138. Robert Song, *Covenant and Calling: Towards a Theology of Same-Sex Relationships* (London: SCM Press, 2014), 35.

139 Brownson, *Bible, Gender, Sexuality*, 112.

because it is not procreative, when infertile couples are permitted to have sex, and fertile couples are permitted to use contraception.

A non-affirming view might say:

Infertile couples in biblical times longed for children and considered infertility to be a problem, rather than a choice. Some churches do consider procreation or openness to procreation to be an essential element of marriage, and they continue to reject the use of contraception. Non-procreative, opposite-sex marriages are still technically open to the possibility of procreation and are therefore acceptable to God. Same-sex marriages are not open to procreation. It was not necessary for Paul to specifically mention procreation in his instructions for households in Ephesus for it to be considered the primary purpose of marriage because having children was assumed to be the primary purpose of marriage in his Jewish society, and this was never questioned. Writers from Paul's time typically did not explicitly mention concepts that were assumed, because the scrolls they used were expensive and contained limited writing space, so it was wasteful to write what was already commonly understood.

An affirming view might say:

Philo and Josephus were Jewish writers contemporary to Paul who did emphasize procreation as essential for marriage in their writings, which is evidence that it was not so universally assumed to be so by Jewish society that it did not need to be mentioned. Also, the Ephesians and Colossians to whom Paul wrote were from a Greco-Roman culture which did not prioritize procreation to the degree that Jewish people did. If Paul thought procreation was the primary purpose of marriage, he would have said so. Therefore, his silence about it can be taken as evidence that procreation (or openness to procreation) is not essential to validate a marriage. Some teachings of the early church did emphasize the necessity of procreative marriages for Christians, however some of these early church fathers' teachings displayed a misogynistic bias against women that Christians do not accept today.[140] For example, they taught that women do not possess the full image of God, but are rather an image of the image (in other words, they are the image of man who is the image of God); that women do not possess the image of God until they are married to a

---

140 Preston Sprinkle, "Homosexuality, The Bible, and the Church," in *Two Views on Homosexuality, the Bible, and the Church,* ed. by Preston Sprinkle (Grand Rapids, MI: Zondervan, 2016), 220-221.

man; that women are twice as fallen as men; and that men are superior in body and mind to women. Since some of the early church fathers' teaching is not considered accurate today, their teaching on the necessity of procreation should not be indiscriminately accepted without further evaluation.

Many opposite-sex couples participate in non-coital sex or means of pleasure other than penile penetration of the vagina. Many use birth control, including permanent methods like vasectomy and tubal ligation. Others are infertile, including those where the woman is in menopause. They are therefore not "open to the possibility of procreation," yet they are accepted. If non-procreative coital sex and sexual acts other than penile penetration of the vagina are not prohibited within an opposite-sex marriage, it is inconsistent to prohibit same-sex marriages based on the idea that non-procreative ways of experiencing sexual pleasure are inherently wrong.

Genesis 38:8-10: Onan

Background:
Aside from Genesis 1:28's directive to be fruitful and increase in number, another place where Christians get the idea that sex must be procreative is from a story in Genesis 38:8-10. Although obscure, it has had considerable influence. In the story, a man named Onan disobediently conspires to avoid fulfilling his Israelite duty to impregnate his deceased brother's wife by withdrawing and ejaculating on the ground during intercourse. This action is said to be wicked in the Lord's sight, and the Lord puts him to death for it.

A non-affirming view might say:
The condemnation of Onan for his use of the withdrawal method of birth control teaches that engaging in sexual intercourse without the possibility of procreation is against God's will. This teaching prohibits opposite-sex intercourse that uses contraceptive methods, as well as same-sex sexual intercourse. Sex for infertile, opposite-sex married couples is within God's will, since God can miraculously make barren women conceive.

An affirming view might say:
Genesis 38:8-10 condemns Onan's deceptive refusal to complete his customary duty to give his deceased brother (and his brother's widow) a child to carry on his family line. The condemnation of Onan's withdrawal method in this passage was contextual and was

related to a specific requirement in the Old Testament law that does not apply to Christians. The directive for a man to provide a child to his deceased brother's widow was a way to care for her. Denying her the child was a form of oppression and possible abuse. The interpretation that it was the spilling of semen on the ground that was condemned may have been related to the ancient understanding that the semen contained the babies, and that it was of limited supply, which made wasting it problematic. It is now known that semen is not of a limited supply, and that it needs to join with an egg before becoming an embryo.

The passage does not condemn the use of birth control methods in and of themselves. Access to birth control is essential to reduce poverty, ensure children can be cared for, and protect women's health and well-being. It is a blessing that enables families to live well in contemporary times. The Onan passage has been interpreted by some Christians as condemning male masturbation, but this can also be seen to be a misinterpretation of the story.

Gender Complementarianism

Background:

The belief that women and men are equal but have been assigned specific gender roles by God is called Gender Complementarianism. It promotes the idea that men/husbands have authority over women/wives, and women/wives are to submit to men/husbands. It was heavily promoted in the 1980's and 1990's by some conservative churches and organizations, and it remains influential to this day.

Was Adam Originally Androgynous?

The next section gets technical and obscure, but it discusses a point that is made by both affirming and non-affirming views, so is worth addressing at the start of the conversation about complementary gender roles.

Genesis 2:18-25 says:

> The Lord God said, "It is not good for the man to be alone. I will make a helper suitable for him."
>
> Now the Lord God had formed out of the ground all the wild animals and all the birds in the sky. He brought them to the man to see what he would name them; and whatever the man called each living creature, that was its name. So the man gave names to all the livestock, the birds in the sky and all the wild animals.

But for Adam no suitable helper was found. So the Lord God caused the man to fall into a deep sleep; and while he was sleeping, he took one of the man's ribs and then closed up the place with flesh. Then the Lord God made a woman from the rib he had taken out of the man, and he brought her to the man.

The man said, "This is now bone of my bones and flesh of my flesh; she shall be called 'woman,' for she was taken out of man." That is why a man leaves his father and mother and is united to his wife, and they become one flesh. Adam and his wife were both naked, and they felt no shame.

A non-affirming view might say:

The first human described in Genesis was originally an androgynous person, being both male and female. The Hebrew word *tsela`*, translated in the NIV as "rib," is more accurately translated as "side." By removing one side, God essentially split the original person into two people, one male and one female. Prior to the split, the original created person was called *âdâm*, and after the split, in Genesis 2:23, the man is called *ish* and the woman was called *ishah*. Marriage represents a reunion of the two distinct and complementary genders (the *ish* and the *ishah*) into a one-flesh union (the *âdâm*). This reunion, and thus marriage itself, is only possible between a male and female.[141]

An affirming view might say:

The original *âdâm* was male, not androgynous. After Eve was created from Adam's rib/side in verse 22, the man was still referred to as *âdâm* in verse 23 and again in verse 25. Genesis 2:23 says that the *ishah* was taken out of the *ish*. This suggests that Adam was male (*ish*) even before the creation of Eve, and it confirms that people do not need to try to somehow recreate an androgynous entity through a one-flesh union of male and female through marriage. The theory that two sides of a split person reunite in marriage is based on a story told by a character in a philosophical discourse on love, written by Plato. Plato himself did not believe that the story he recounted was true or that it described the origin of same-sex attraction.[142] In any case, however, this is not a concept taught in the Bible.

An alternative affirming view might agree that the original *âdâm* was androgynous, or non-binary, and say that this is evidence that it

---

141. Gagnon, *The Bible and Homosexual Practice*, Part VII, chap. 1.
142. Loader, "Homosexuality and the Bible," in *Two Views on Homosexuality, the Bible, and the Church*, 29.

is not necessary to have a binary sense of gender to reflect God's image.[143]

Adam and Eve's Example

An affirming view might say:
The first married couple was male and female, but this does not set a pattern that every marriage must follow. The male/female pairing was descriptive of Adam and Eve's marriage but is not prescriptive of all subsequent marriages. That Eve was taken out of Adam is an indication that they had a shared humanity and therefore had the same worth. This was a radical and important statement to make in an ancient, patriarchal culture. It emphasizes Adam and Eve's similarities, not their differences.

A non-affirming view might say:
Genesis 2:24 says, "For this reason a man will leave his father and mother and be united to his wife and they will become one flesh." Adam did not have a father and mother, so this verse clearly speaks about future marriages, not only that of the first couple. The reason for marriage, listed in 2:23, is that the woman was taken out of man, which provides clear evidence that the Bible defines marriage as being between one man and one woman. Adam and Eve's marriage provides the foundation for all subsequent marriages, so marriage by its very nature requires opposite-sex spouses to complement each other. [144]

The complementary nature of the man and the woman is explicitly clear in Genesis 2:18-25. God observed that it was not good for the man to be alone, so he created the woman as a complement to the man, his "suitable helper." The Hebrew word translated as "suitable" is *kenegdô*, which means "like against him" or "as opposite him," emphasizing the fact that Eve was the opposite sex of Adam.

An affirming view might say:
Many Christians who affirm same-sex marriage also endorse egalitarianism, or equality between genders (as opposed to complementarianism). An egalitarian view says that since the Hebrew word *kenegdô*, or "suitable," is only used twice in the Old Testament, its meaning is not clear. According to Strong's Hebrew Dictionary, it can mean a "counterpart" or "mate," implying a similarity rather than

---

143. Justin Tanis, *Trans-gendered*, 58.
144. Sprinkle, *People to be Loved*, 32.

a difference. It was the similarity, not the difference between the man and woman that made them suitable for each other in Genesis 2. This is why God emphasized that the two are of the *same* flesh. The intention of the phrase "same flesh" was not to refer to the physical fitting together of genitalia during intercourse, but rather to emphasize the kinship bond and mutual responsibility between spouses. It also served to assert the value of women within the Israelites' highly patriarchal culture, and reminded people that women are of the same species as men—created from the same flesh and thus suitable for each other.

In ancient agricultural societies, a son did not typically leave the family home and land. Instead, a wife would join her new husband to live with or near his family in order to work and eventually inherit the farm. Therefore the word "leave" in Genesis 2:24 did not describe a physical separation between the son and his parents, but rather referred to leaving the family unit he had with his parents to start a new family unit (a kinship unit) with his wife.[145] Since leaving his family involved a relational change rather than a physical separation, it makes sense that being united to and becoming one flesh with his wife also describes a relational union. Becoming one flesh refers to the formation of a new kinship unit rather than to the physical sexual union. Sex within marriage helps strengthen the kinship unit but is not the sole or even the most important uniting factor. The Old Testament frequently uses the word *basar*, translated as "flesh," to define kinship ties with no sexual component.

Complementary Nature

Background:
The idea of the complementary nature of the relationship between a man and a woman can be understood in different ways, including the social hierarchy, social roles, our biological nature, and/or our psychological nature.

A non-affirming view might say:
Regardless of how Genesis 2 intends the complementary nature of the male-female union to be understood, it provides a clear affirmation of opposite-sex sex within marriage, saying that the man was united with his wife, and was naked but unashamed.

---

145. Brownson, *Bible, Gender, Sexuality*, 32.

Social Hierarchy

A non-affirming view might say:

The traditional complementary, hierarchical social roles for men and women are natural and necessary and were set in place in Genesis 3:16 when God said that the woman's desire would be for her husband, and that he would rule over her. Paul reinforces these roles in Ephesians 5:22 when he instructs wives to submit to their husbands. Paul says, "Wives, submit yourselves to your own husbands as you do to the Lord. For the husband is the head of the wife as Christ is the head of the church, his body, of which he is the Savior." This describes how married, opposite-sex couples function as an image of Christ's love for the church.[146] God gave husbands the responsibility to lead their wives, but this does not mean women are not equal in value and status before God. Equal value between men and women does not negate the complementary aspect of their sexes and the necessity for both sexes to unite to form a marital union. Designated leader roles and follower roles allow a marriage to function smoothly. A marriage requires one spouse to take the lead and carry the final responsibility for decision making. God has ordained that the husbands will be the ones to fulfill this role. Taking on this leadership responsibility often requires sacrifices to be made by the husband. Whether they agree with it or not, Christians are called to obey God's plan for marriage. A husband who is laying his life down for his wife, as he is biblically called to do, will consider her needs and desires and will make decisions in her best interest. This means that wives have considerable influence over decisions made, even if they don't have the final say. The Bible contains instructions for how husbands and wives should treat each other in Ephesians 5, but there are no clear instructions given for leadership and submission within a same-sex marriage. The reality that same-sex spouses cannot follow God's plan for complementary gender roles suggests that same-sex marriage is not within God's will for his people.

An affirming view might say:

God's declaration that the woman's husband would rule over her was a curse, or a consequence, resulting from Adam and Eve's fall from grace. The rest of the Bible tells the story about how God goes on to redeem people from that curse. Christians should work to bring healing from the curse and help usher in God's kingdom, rather than

---

146. Hill, "Christ, Scripture, and Spiritual Friendship," in *Two Views on Homosexuality, the Bible, and the Church*, 130.

to further entrench the effects of the curse in human society. This includes working towards equality within marriage.

Paul's primary emphasis in Ephesians 5 is mutual submission between spouses. Ephesians 5:21, "submitting to one another out of reverence for Christ," leads into verse 22, which describes the wives' call to submission. In verse 25, the husband is called to love his wife as Christ loved the church and gave himself up for her, which was a radical expectation of sacrificial love and serves as the husband's call to mutual submission to his wife. Ephesians 5:33 brings the section to a close with another call to mutual obligation, saying, "However, each one of you also must love his wife as he loves himself, and the wife must respect her husband." Grammatically, in the original Greek language, the sense is that husbands must love their wives in order that wives will respect their husbands. In Paul's culture, where wives were typically much younger than their husbands and had minimal education, influence, or opportunities within society, the direct call for husbands to give themselves up for their wives would have been shocking. It supports the idea that equality and mutual submission within marriage was God's ultimate plan.

In Ephesians 5:32, after discussing marital roles, Paul says, "This is a profound mystery—but I am talking about Christ and the church." This verse casts doubt on the exact meaning of his discussion about the nature of marital roles in Ephesians 5:21-31, but it makes a clear statement that the church needs to respect and submit to Christ, as Christ loves the church sacrificially. Contemporary marriages are not biblically mandated to align themselves within a hierarchical system. God's ultimate will is for equality between genders, which eliminates the concern about who will lead and who will follow in marriages. In same-sex marriages, both spouses would submit to Christ and would respect and love each other, as should also be the case in opposite-sex marriages.

Social Roles

A non-affirming view might say:

Some believe that the fact that the woman was created as a suitable helper for the man doesn't ordain a social hierarchy, because the word *êzer* (helper) implies a strong helper and does not require the one helping to be of an inferior status. For example, in Psalm 121:1-2, God is described as man's *êzer* (help). The complementary nature of male/female relationships can be understood to mean that men and women fulfill different social roles and functions while maintaining equal status and value. For example, males fill provider/protector roles and females fill nurturing roles. The roles are equal but different. A division of labor according to gender is necessary for societies to function well. Men as providers and protectors and women as nurturers of children and families is a logical and practical division of labour and responsibility.

An affirming view might say:
While social roles according to sex may make sense in some cultures and time periods, in contemporary Western culture, it is increasingly recognized that people of any gender can fill social roles such as provider and nurturer. Many men are wonderful nurturers, and many women are financial providers for, and protectors of, their families.

Biological Nature

A non-affirming view might say:
Men's and women's physical anatomy and physiological design work together for procreation. This is evidence that marriage is meant to be between a man and a woman.

An affirming view might say:
Not all marriages need to be procreative, and the Bible never suggests the fit of genitalia as a reason for marriage.

Psychological Nature

A non-affirming view might say:
The complementary nature of marriage can also be understood to be psychological. Since men and women tend to think differently and communicate differently, intimately partnering for life with someone who has a different perspective strengthens a marriage and family, expanding each spouse's understanding of the world and building their capacity for compassion and grace towards people who are different from themselves.

An affirming view might say:
All people have unique personalities and perspectives. The opportunity to learn and practice grace and compassion between different personalities and perspectives exists any time two people partner together, regardless of their sexes. For many gay and lesbian

people, the choice they can make is between a same-sex partner or celibacy. Celibacy denies them the opportunity to learn and practice grace and compassion for different personalities and perspectives with a life partner.

Love

A non-affirming view might say:

The English word "love" encompasses several unique concepts for which the Greeks had a variety of different terms. People who are different from each other are equipped for romantic, sexual love (*eros*), while people who are the same are equipped for deep friendship love (*philia*). Being sexually attracted to someone who is the same sex is essentially an unhealthy attraction to the self, or to an idea of the self that one would like to become.[147] It can be thought of as an admiration of someone one aspires to be like, rather than a love for someone who is different. Attraction to someone who is of the same sex is problematic because the other person is too similar. This is also why attraction to someone related by blood is problematic.[148]

An affirming view might say:

A marriage relationship should involve romantic love as well as friendship love. All people are uniquely created and are different from each other, whether they are the same sex or opposite sex. Same-sex love requires a giving of one's self to another and is not a form of self-love. Mandated celibacy denies gay and lesbian people the opportunity to selflessly give themselves away to another person in marriage.

Jesus' Quote in Mark 10:6-8

A non-affirming view might say:

Jesus quoted Genesis 1:27 in Mark 10:6-8, saying, "But at the beginning of creation God 'made them male and female.' 'For this reason a man will leave his father and mother and be united to his wife, and the two will become one flesh.' So they are no longer two, but one flesh." This quote reveals that Jesus viewed a male-female couple as necessary for marriage.

---

147. Gagnon, *Bible and Homosexual Practice*, Kindle ed., Part IV, chap. 5.
148. Ibid., Conclusion.

An affirming view might say:

Jesus was speaking about the permanence of marriage in Mark 10:6-8 when he quoted Genesis 1:27. He was not specifically teaching about the sexes of the spouses. There would have been no context for him to have made a statement for future clarification about equal-status, monogamous, covenantal same-sex relationships, because those relationships would have been rare and such a statement would have confused his audience.

Marriage

One Flesh

Background:

Genesis 2:24 describes the first marriage, between Adam and Eve, saying, "That is why a man leaves his father and mother and is united to his wife, and they become one flesh."

Since the creation of Adam and Eve and the first marriage, the understanding of the nature of marriage has undergone significant changes. During biblical times, marriage was a family arrangement, with the wives being youths. The bride joined the groom's family, as another daughter, and the groom's family would pay a bride price, primarily to compensate her father for the loss of his daughter. Weddings were family and community-based ceremonies.[149]

The first detailed record of the church performing a marriage ceremony is from the 9th century. In 1140 AD, verbal consent and consummation of marriage were formalized as necessities. Shortly after that, marriage began to be considered a sacrament, or sacred institution. Wedding vows were introduced in the Book of Common Prayer in 1549 and continue to influence weddings to this day. In 1753, England declared that all marriages had to be registered and officiated by a minister. About 80 years later, in 1836, it allowed for civil marriages to be conducted outside of the church. Around then, during the Victorian era, the idea of marrying for love became popular. Previously, marriage had been primarily a practical match, and if it were to become a loving marriage, the love would grow after the wedding. Birth control became available in the late 19th century, and was approved by the protestant church in the 1930's. This allowed married couples to choose not to procreate. The Catholic church

---

149. Hayyim Schauss, "Ancient Jewish Marriage," *My Jewish Learning*, accessed March 29, 2024, myjewishlearning.com/article/ancient-jewish-marriage.

continues to consider openness to procreation to be essential for marriage.[150] The Divorce Act was passed in Canada in 1968, making divorce easier to obtain from a legal standpoint. Legal, same-sex civil unions and marriages began to be recognized in the early 2000's.

This brief timeline shows that marriage as a result of love between spouses is a fairly recent understanding, as is marriage between people who do not intend to have babies. Marriages have not always required explicit consent from the people being married, nor has it always been controlled by the state or even by churches.

Aside from Christian marriages traditionally being assumed to be between a man and a woman, the features of a traditional marriage have differed based on which time period and location in the world the tradition originates from.

A non-affirming view might say:

"One flesh" in Genesis 2:24 refers to the union that occurs when the husband's penis fits into the wife's vagina during sexual intercourse as an act that joins two bodies into one and consummates a marriage. Paul confirms this meaning of "one flesh" in 1 Corinthians 6:15-16, where he says: "Do you not know that your bodies are members of Christ himself? Shall I then take the members of Christ and unite them with a prostitute? Never! Do you not know that he who unites himself with a prostitute is one with her in body? For it is said, 'The two will become one flesh.'"

An affirming view might say:

The phrase "one flesh" refers to a kinship bond. Elsewhere in the Old Testament, the Hebrew word *basar* (flesh) is used to refer to kinship, such as in Genesis 29:14, where Laban tells Jacob, "You are my own flesh and blood," and in Genesis 37:27, when Joseph's brothers decide not to kill him because they are one flesh (see also Judges 9:2, 1 Chronicles 11:1, 2 Samuel 5:1 and 19:12). A kinship bond can be formed between two people through a covenant promise made to each other before God. It is the promise and prayers rather than the physical sexual union that form the kinship bond. It is this kinship bond between spouses that protects against sexual promiscuity.[151] Sexual relations strengthen and support the kinship bond between

---

150. Lauren Everitt, "Ten Key Moments in the History of Marriage," *BBC News Magazine*, March 14, 2012, accessed March 29, 2024, https://www.bbc.com/news/magazine-1735113.

151 Brownson, *Bible, Gender, Sexuality*, 88.

spouses, binding them together spiritually and emotionally, but the physical act of inserting penis into vagina does not create the one-flesh union. The idea that marriage requires consummation through sexual intercourse is based on a mistaken theology and is problematic for many couples who have disabilities or other circumstances that make consummating a marriage in the traditional manner impossible. In contemporary North America, neither the church nor the state requires marriages to be consummated in order for them to be considered valid (although in some places and some churches non-consummation can be grounds for an annulment).

Ephesians 5:31-32 says, "For this reason a man will leave his father and mother and be united to his wife, and the two will become one flesh. This is a profound mystery—but I am talking about Christ and the church." In Ephesians 5, Paul compares Christ and the church to a groom and his bride. The relationship between Christ and the church is a spiritual, kinship union rather than a physical, sexual union, and its comparison to groom and bride suggests that marriage is likewise formed by a spiritual kinship union. Revelation 19:7 also uses the imagery of a marriage between Christ and the church, saying, "Let us rejoice and be glad and give him glory! For the wedding of the Lamb has come, and his bride has made herself ready." Again, this image implies a spiritual kinship bond rather than a physical sexual bond. Sex functions to bond two spouses together emotionally, and as such it is best suited in a life-long, committed relationship. This is true for both same-sex and opposite-sex marriages. In 1 Corinthians 6:15-16, Paul warns men not to unite with a prostitute because they become one body with her, not because they become "one flesh" with her. Being one body is different than being one flesh. Marriage typically includes, but is more than, sexual intercourse. Paul is saying that because a marriage is "one flesh," spouses must not become "one body" with other people. As New Testament scholar James Brownson says, Paul is warning them not to "say with their bodies what they will not say with the rest of their lives."[152] In other words, he is warning them not to have sex with people with whom they do not have a lifetime commitment, or not to have a physical sexual bond unless they have a kinship bond through marriage.

A non-affirming view might say:
In Matthew 19:4-6, Jesus references Genesis 1:27 and 2:24:

---

152. Ibid., 120.

"Haven't you read," he replied, "that at the beginning the Creator 'made them male and female,' and said, 'For this reason a man will leave his father and mother and be united to his wife, and the two will become one flesh'? So they are no longer two, but one flesh. Therefore what God has joined together, let no one separate."

Jesus references the two creation stories, fusing them in a way that shows that male and female genders are essential for marriage, and that only opposite-sex marriage is accepted. [153]

An affirming view might say:

In Matthew 19:4-6 Jesus was making a point about divorce and the permanence of marriage, not about whether marriage can only be between opposite-sex spouses. Since nobody was asking him about the possibility of same-sex marriage, it would have made no sense for him to address it or qualify his quotation of Genesis to make allowances for it. His quotation of Genesis does not indicate what he would think of same-sex marriage today, except that the marriage bond is intended to be permanent, with a few exceptions.

Jesus was also making a point about monogamy. Genesis 2:24 says "they become one flesh," but when Jesus quoted this verse, he adds the word "two," saying, 'the two will become one flesh."[154] During the time between the Old Testament and the New Testament, God's people began to view monogamy as an essential component of marriage, and Jesus, Matthew, and Mark emphasize the change from previous acceptance of polygynous practices to an expectation of monogamy and marital faithfulness for both men and women. In Ephesians 5, Paul teaches that an ideal marriage involves a mutual submission to one's spouse, which would be difficult if not impossible for more than two partners.

A non-affirming view might say:

The potential to procreate is essential for the formation of a one-flesh union, even if the union is considered to be a kinship bond rather than a sexual bond. Procreation creates a new familial, or kinship line and since same-sex unions cannot procreate and form a new familial line, they do not form a new kinship bond or one-flesh union.

---

153. Hill, "Christ, Scripture, and Spiritual Friendship," in *Two Views on Homosexuality, the Bible, and the Church*, 129-130.

154. See Matthew 19:4-6, Mark 10:6-9, 1 Corinthians 6:15-16, and Ephesians 5:31-32.

An affirming view might say:

Procreation is a benefit that results from opposite-sex marriages but is not a necessity for them to be valid. The absence of procreation should not be used to invalidate same-sex marriages. The kinship bond is described as being between adults, and there is no requirement to produce children in order to validate it.

Biblical Examples

A non-affirming view might say:

There are many positive examples of opposite-sex marriages within the Bible which confirm that opposite-sex marriages are acceptable and pleasing to God. In contrast, there are no positive examples of same-sex marriages or even same-sex sexual relationships found in Scripture. The absence of positive examples of same-sex relationships or positive statements made about same-sex sex in the Scriptures serves as evidence that Christians should not affirm same-sex marriage.

An affirming view might say:

There are some possible examples of same-sex romantic love that are presented positively in the Scriptures, including the love between David and Jonathan in 1 Samuel 18:3, and the centurion and his "highly valued servant" in Luke 7:2.

A non-affirming view might say:

There is no evidence that David and Jonathan's love was more than a strong friendship, and likewise there is no indication that the centurion and his servant were in a romantic or sexual relationship.

An affirming view might say:

Because of the extreme patriarchal views held during biblical times, having an equal-status, monogamous, covenantal same-sex relationship would have been nearly impossible. Therefore, their absence from Scripture is expected and does not preclude them from being accepted by God today. There are many practices that are not found in the Bible that many Christians accept and embrace today based on an understanding of the biblical principles of love and grace. One such example is birth control, which was generally unsupported by all Christian churches until the Church of England accepted contraception in 1930, and many other Protestant denominations followed their lead. The opportunity to use birth control is now fully endorsed by many Christians in our society today. Other examples of practices that would not have been accepted by the early church but are common today include charging interest on loans, amassing wealth, and gluttony.

There are other practices that seem to be positively affirmed in the Bible yet are not accepted by most churches. For example, Scripture condones slavery. It also contains positive depictions of polygyny[155] as well as marriages where the wife does not have to consent.[156] The way marriages are portrayed in the Bible are not the only way marriages should be formed, nor are they the way marriages should function for all time.

Jesus' Silence

A non-affirming view might say:

Jesus' silence on the matter of same-sex marriage shows that he conformed to the typical Jewish understanding of his time, which would have rejected same-sex sex of any form. He did not say or do anything to indicate that the teaching in Leviticus was directed against specific forms of male-male sex, or that the law against same-sex sex was no longer applicable for his followers.

An affirming view might say:

Jesus would not be expected to teach acceptance of same-sex marriage in the politically charged environment in which he ministered because in his highly patriarchal culture it was not deemed legally or morally possible for a marriage to be between two people of the same sex and/or equal social status. Marriage was always hierarchical, partly because women were of lower social status than their husbands. Since the concept of an equal-status same-sex marriage would have been completely foreign to his followers, it would not have been the right time for Jesus to introduce such teaching. Due to the ingrained patriarchal understanding of marriage and the cultural expressions of same-sex sex being abusive and/or excessively lustful, an endorsement of same-sex marriage by Jesus would have severely undermined the spreading of the gospel message of salvation and the inauguration of God's kingdom, which were his primary concerns. This reasoning may also explain why Jesus did not

---

155. Lamech, Jacob, King David, and King Solomon each had more than one wife.

156. See Deuteronomy 22:28.

speak more clearly against slavery or in favor of women's rights. His cultural context was not ready to accept a dramatic challenge to its patriarchal, hierarchical system. Jesus' mission was to proclaim the gospel message, and he trusted that his followers after him would go on to apply his message of love in their social and political contexts to initiate further cultural change and improve the lives of the oppressed and marginalized. Jesus could have clearly reinforced the prohibition of same-sex sex without causing any political conflict or disruptions to his ministry, since it was already Jewish practice to prohibit it. However, the Bible does not record Jesus directly addressing same-sex sex in any of his teachings. His silence on the matter shows that he was not concerned about same-sex sex unless it contravened his other teaching, such as loving one another and caring for the poor and oppressed.

The Future of Marriage

An affirming view might say:

In Matthew 22:30, Jesus teaches that "[at] the resurrection people will neither marry nor be given in marriage; they will be like the angels in heaven." Since marriage is a temporary practice that is not going to continue in heaven, the definition of marriage should not be an essential doctrine. We should not continue to let disagreements about who people can marry undermine the sharing of God's gospel of grace and salvation for all people, including those who are LGBTQ+.

A non-affirming view might say:

The future state of marriage in heaven does not affect our responsibility to serve God now on earth, either through opposite-sex marriages or through celibate lifestyles.

The Purpose of Marriage vs. the Benefits of Marriage

Background:

Genesis 2:18 says, "The LORD God said, 'It is not good for the man to be alone. I will make a helper suitable for him.'"

An affirming view might say:

The problem that God solved for Adam by creating Eve was the problem of loneliness, not the problem of how to procreate. This implies that the primary purpose of marriage is companionship, or "covenanted kinship and mutual support."[157] Friendship does not solve the loneliness problem the same way marriage does, because friends do not typically form a covenantal kinship bond, do not typically share belongings and finances, buy homes together, or plan their futures intricately together. The problem of loneliness can be solved through a same-sex spouse or an opposite-sex spouse. It is not necessary to have male and female pairings to fulfill the companionship purpose of marriage. Opposite-sex marriages are out of the question for many gay and lesbian Christians. The options they can choose from are a same-sex marriage or a celibate life, which can be a very lonely life.

Living out a marriage commitment builds character in Christlikeness, as partners make self-sacrificial actions and decisions and give their whole selves to another person, "growing into the type of love that unites Jesus to the church."[158] This sanctifying experience is a benefit of marriage that resonates just as deeply for same-sex marriages as it does for opposite-sex marriages. Withholding the opportunity for a marriage relationship from LGBTQ+ people denies them the opportunity to have this character building, or sanctifying experience.[159]

In 1 Corinthians 7:9 Paul says, "It is better to marry than to burn with passion," teaching that the satisfaction of sexual desire is a legitimate reason to get married. This benefit of marriage is true for same-sex marriages as well as for opposite sex marriages. Same-sex marriage fulfills the purpose of marriage, which is the provision of companionship and mutual support, and it offers the benefits of mutual sanctification and the stewardship of sexual desire.[160]

A non-affirming view might say:

The need for companionship, sanctification, and sexual fulfillment are better met with people who are different from each other, i.e., opposite sexes. People who cannot enter an opposite-sex

---

157. Karen Keen, "The Streckert Lecture on Christianity, Sexuality, and Gender," Wheaton College, video, April 5, 2022, accessed July 16, 2023, https://www.youtube.com/watch?v=KWPx7jJy094.

158. Mark Achtemeier, *The Bible's Yes to Same-Sex Marriage, An Evangelical's Change of Heart* (Louisville, KY: Westminster John Knox Press, 2014), 51.

159. Eugene F. Rogers Jr., "An Argument for Gay Marriage," Religion Online, https://www.religion-online.org/article/an-argument-for-gay-marriage, accessed November 16, 2024.

160. Karen Keen, "The Streckert Lecture on Christianity, Sexuality, and Gender."

marriage can stay single and celibate, and form deep, committed friendships.

An affirming view might say:

The purpose of marriage is to form a kinship bond for mutual support and societal benefits. The essential element of marriage is permanence (with allowances made to end marriages based on humanitarian need). Procreation, sanctification, and sexual satisfaction are benefits of marriage, but are not essential for a relationship to be a marriage.[161] Same-sex marriages fulfill the purpose of marriage and, with the exception of procreation, provide the same benefits as opposite-sex marriages.

Divorce

Background:

Divorce is another controversial topic for Christians. Many people have been hurt by the church's response to their marital breakdown. Although it is a heavy and significant topic, it will only be touched upon here.

Jesus' teaching about divorce in Mark 10 is relevant to the discussion regarding same-sex marriage because it gives an indication of how Jesus viewed marriage in general. Looking again at Mark 10:1-12:

> Jesus then left that place and went into the region of Judea and across the Jordan. Again crowds of people came to him, and as was his custom, he taught them. Some Pharisees came and tested him by asking, "Is it lawful for a man to divorce his wife?"
>
> "What did Moses command you?" he replied.
>
> They said, "Moses permitted a man to write a certificate of divorce and send her away."
>
> "It was because your hearts were hard that Moses wrote you this law," Jesus replied. "But at the beginning of creation God 'made them male and female.' ' For this reason a man will leave his father and mother and be united to his wife, and the two will become one flesh.' So they are no longer two, but one flesh. Therefore what God has joined together, let no one separate."
>
> When they were in the house again, the disciples asked Jesus about this. He answered, "Anyone who divorces his wife and marries another woman commits adultery against her. And if she divorces her husband and marries another man, she commits adultery."

Jesus was asked by the Pharisees (religious leaders) whether the law allowed a man to divorce his wife. Jesus quotes Genesis 2:24 in

161. Ibid.

his answer, when he says, "But at the beginning of creation God 'made them male and female.' 'For this reason a man will leave his father and mother and be united to his wife, and the two will become one flesh.' So they are no longer two, but one flesh. Therefore, what God has joined together, let no one separate" (Mark 10:6-9).

A non-affirming view might say:

By quoting Genesis 2:24, Jesus shows that he understands marriage to consist of a relationship between one man and one woman, with the couple becoming one flesh through the act of sexual intercourse. In Mark 10:9, Jesus informs his followers that God is the force that creates the marriage bond, making it sacred.

An affirming view might say:

This dialogue is best understood when studied in relation to its historical context. Near the same location where Jesus and the Pharisees are conversing, King Herod had recently beheaded John the Baptist after John had spoken out against divorce and implied that King Herod had committed adultery against his brother when he married his brother's ex-wife. When the Pharisees ask Jesus about divorce, they are hoping his answer might also be interpreted as a similar critique of King Herod's marriage, resulting in Jesus' own imprisonment or execution.[162] Jesus risks his own life by answering that the marriage bond is permanent, and divorce is not permissible. Because this question was asked as a hostile trap, Jesus could not be expected to provide comprehensive teaching on either divorce or on the definition of marriage here. When Jesus quotes Genesis 2:24, he is addressing questions about divorce, not same-sex marriage. Questions about same-sex marriage and transgender identities were far from being on the minds of Jesus, his followers, or his opponents. Jesus' emphasis was on the permanent nature of the monogamous union, not the sex of the spouses.[163]

Jesus reminds his listeners that both males and females are created in God's image, in order to assert that women are equal in status to men. He knows that his Jewish audience would have the creation story memorized and would subconsciously fill in the detail about being made in God's image as soon as they heard the words, "God created them male and female." He further supports women's rights by saying

162. Craig Blomberg, "Marriage, Divorce, Remarriage, and Celibacy: An Exegesis of Matthew 19:3-12," *Trinity Journal* 11 NS (1990): 162.

163. Ibid., 166.

that men cannot not divorce their wives without just cause, which contradicted the teaching of some Jewish leaders. Since only husbands could initiate a divorce, and divorce left women without financial support, Jesus' statement about the permanence of most marriages protected women's rights and well-being within his context. An approach that protects women's rights and well-being today might look different than it did during that time in history.

Jesus has two goals in Mark 10:6-9. First, he wants to establish God's intention for the permanency of marriage. Second, he wants to establish an equal responsibility for husbands and wives to maintain sexual fidelity within the marriage. His second point, made in Mark 10:11-12, that wives could initiate divorce and husbands could be guilty of committing adultery against their wives was so shocking that in the version of the story told in Matthew 19:10 the disciples respond, "If this is the situation between a husband and wife, it is better not to marry." Jesus was influencing a change in the way marriage roles were to be understood by Christians, ushering in more mutual and permanent commitments. He was not focused on the genders of the spouses, which were simply assumed and were not under question.

A non-affirming view might say:

A summary of a non-affirming view of the New Testament teaching on marriage might say Jesus understood and reinforced the idea that marriage is to be between one man and one woman, as was established at the time of creation. God joins the husband and wife together in a bond that should not be broken, with only a few allowable exceptions. Procreation is a primary purpose of marriage that is not fulfilled through same-sex marriage.

An affirming view might say:

A summary of an affirming view of the New Testament teaching on marriage might say that marriage is to be monogamous with a commitment to mutual fidelity. It is to be permanent but there are some exceptions allowed. The primary purpose of marriage is to solve the problem of loneliness and provide companionship and mutual support to the benefit of the individual spouses and society. Primary benefits of marriage include the opportunity for self-sacrifice, building Christian character, sanctification, stewardship of sexual desire, and procreation. These benefits are not required to be present to validate a marriage. Same-sex marriages fulfill the primary purpose and, with the exception of procreation, the primary benefits of marriage.

Sexual Immorality

Background:

The New Testament uses the Greek word *porneia* twenty-six times. It is often translated as "sexual immorality," but the word can have more specific meanings, including fornication (sex between non-covenanted persons), harlotry (prostitution), adultery, and incest. The KJV translates *porneia* as simply "fornication." Most other translations, including the NIV, consider *porneia* to be best represented by the broader term "sexual immorality."

A non-affirming view might say:

The broader term "sexual immorality" is an appropriate translation of the word *porneia*. Same-sex sex is included under the umbrella term "sexual immorality," so whenever the Bible uses the term *porneia*, same-sex sex can be assumed to be included. This means the Bible addresses same-sex sex many more times than just in the six passages that refer to it directly.

An affirming view might say:

Of the twenty-six uses of the word *porneia* in the New Testament, five refer specifically to opposite-sex sex.[164] Five verses seem to be associated with cultic worship, including three verses in Acts, which all refer to the same set of instructions, and two verses in Revelation.[165] Five verses from the book of Revelation use it to symbolize the nation falling into idolatry.[166] Matthew 15:19 and Mark 7:21 are two versions of the same teaching. This leaves only nine instances where it is possible that the intended meaning of "sexual immorality" could include same-sex sex in a broad sense, but there is nothing in the context of these verses to suggest that same-sex sex is specifically included (except that in biblical times same-sex sex nearly always happened outside of marriage and thus would have been considered fornication).

In these nine instances, sexual immorality is frequently listed alongside references to idolatry. For example, Revelation 22:15 describes people who will be outside of God's kingdom, saying, "outside are the dogs, those who practice magic arts, the sexually

---

164. See Matthew 5:32, 19:9, 1 Corinthians 5:1, 7:2, and John 8:41, which in the original Greek says, "we are not born of *porneia*."

165. See Acts 15:20, 29, 21:25 and Revelation 2:21 and 9:21.

166. See Revelation 14:8, 17:2, 17:4, 18:3, and 19:2.

immoral, the murderers, the idolaters and everyone who loves and practices falsehood." The word "dogs" was used to refer to temple prostitutes,[167] and "magic arts" is also associated with idolatry. It may be that the reference to "murder" is referring to child sacrifice (to the god Molech), that the reference to the "sexually immoral" is referring to those who make use of temple prostitutes or engage in cultic sex, and that the "falsehoods" are related to false worship. This would mean the entire vice list was related to idolatry. Same-sex sex that involves prostitution, idol worship, abuse, or is extra-covenantal, should be included in the term "sexual immorality," but same-sex sex in the context of a marriage relationship should not, because such relationships were not being considered by the New Testament authors when they used the word.

A non-affirming view might say:

Paul's teaching serves as a reminder for Christians to use their bodies in ways that are pleasing to Christ and in keeping within his will, especially when it comes to sexual practices. In 1 Corinthians 6:15, Paul says, "Do you not know that your bodies are members of Christ himself? Shall I then take the members of Christ and unite them with a prostitute? Never!"

Continuing in 1 Corinthians 6:18-20, Paul says:

Flee from sexual immorality. All other sins a person commits are outside the body, but whoever sins sexually, sins against their own body. Do you not know that your bodies are temples of the Holy Spirit, who is in you, whom you have received from God? You are not your own; you were bought at a price. Therefore honor God with your bodies.

In Ephesians 5:3, Paul says, "But among you there must not be even a hint of sexual immorality, or any kind of impurity, or of greed." These verses demonstrate the need for Christians to err on the side of caution when it comes to sexual immorality. Erring on the side of caution means that, since same-sex marriage is not endorsed in the Bible, it should be not be affirmed by Christians.

An affirming view might say:

Sexual morality is important, but sex within a same-sex marriage is no more or less immoral than sexual activity within an opposite-sex marriage. Paul's teaching applies to same-sex sex that is outside of marriage (or covenant), abusive, or excessively lustful, the same way

---

167. Gagnon, *Bible and Homosexual Practice*, Part V, chap. 1.

it applies to opposite-sex sex that is outside of marriage (or covenant), abusive, or excessively lustful.

A non-affirming view might say:

Jesus' approach to sexual sin was strict. In Matthew 5:28, he taught that looking at a woman lustfully was akin to adultery. In Matthew 19:8-9, he took the harder line related to divorce, saying that it was not permissible for any reason, except for in the case of adultery. These patterns suggest that he would have taken a strict stance against same-sex marriage as well, had he been asked about it.[168]

An affirming view might say:

Taking a strict stance against sexual sin does not include standing against same-sex marriage because the equal-status, monogamous, covenantal same-sex relationship that constitutes a same-sex marriage is not sinful. Affirming same-sex marriage does not mean endorsing actions such as adultery, prostitution, fornication, incest, sexual abuse, or lustful sex. Jesus took a stance to protect women from abuse and neglect and showed grace to a woman caught in adultery in John 8:1-11. The purpose for his strict stance against sexual immorality was to reduce harm.

Celibacy

A non-affirming view might say:

Same-sex attracted Christians who want to have a spouse have the option to enter an opposite-sex marriage even though it may be contrary to their innate desire. Bisexual people can choose an opposite-sex partner.

An affirming view might say:

Mixed-orientation marriages are marriages between people with different sexual orientations, such as when a gay person marries a straight person. While some mixed-orientation marriages are successful, others are rife with pain and problems for both spouses and their children. Not all gay and lesbian people are able to consider sex with an opposite-sex spouse as a viable option, any more than all straight people would be able to consider sex with a same sex partner as an option for themselves. People's sexual behaviors, feelings and

---

168. Sprinkle, *People to be Loved*, 73.

thoughts can fall along a spectrum, with some people being strongly and exclusively attracted to either males or females, some being predominantly but not exclusively attracted to either males or females, and some being equally attracted to males and females.[169] People with strong and exclusive attractions towards the same sex are less likely to be able to have successful mixed-orientation marriages, while people with predominant but not exclusive attractions towards the same-sex may be able to find satisfaction with an opposite-sex spouse. Although gay and lesbian people may choose to enter mixed-orientation marriages for a variety of reasons, it is a risky choice and not one that they should be advised or pressured to make by other people. Same-sex attracted people who can make mixed-orientation marriages work should not be held up as examples for others to be expected to follow.

People do not typically choose who they fall in love with, and they can't typically choose to fall out of love with someone. While hypothetically speaking, bisexual people could simply choose opposite-sex spouses, this may not be possible in actual life situations, if they fall in love with someone who is the same sex as themselves.

A non-affirming view might say:

Gay and lesbian Christians can honor God by living celibate lives. The apostle Paul was celibate and even taught that it was the preferred lifestyle choice for Christians. In 1 Corinthians 7:6-9, after teaching that spouses should be sexually faithful to one another and not deprive one another, he says:

> I say this as a concession, not as a command. I wish that all of you were as I am. But each of you has your own gift from God; one has this gift, another has that. Now to the unmarried and the widows I say: It is good for them to stay unmarried, as I do. But if they cannot control themselves, they should marry, for it is better to marry than to burn with passion.

Since Paul holds up celibacy as the ideal lifestyle, it is appropriate to suggest a celibate lifestyle for LGBTQ+ people. Celibacy is a gift which allows people freedom to serve Jesus more fully and to have a richer relationship with him.

---

169. Kinsey Institute, Indiana University, *The Kinsey Scale* (2019), accessed May 26, 2021, https://kinseyinstitute.org/research/publications/kinsey-scale.php.

An affirming view might say:

Paul refers to celibacy as a gift that only some people have been given. Prohibiting someone who does not have the gift of celibacy from seeking a spouse is unfair and contradicts the recognition made by God in Genesis 2:18 that it is not good for people to be alone. When Paul and Jesus discuss celibacy, Paul is talking about refraining from opposite-sex marriages for the sake of being able to do ministry, and Jesus is talking about refraining from remarrying after divorce. Superimposing their teaching onto all LGBTQ+ Christians is a misuse of Scripture.

For people who have the gift of celibacy, remaining celibate is not a rejection of their sexuality, but rather involves setting the sexual aspect of themselves apart for God and leaning into God to fulfill the need for intimacy in their lives, as a spiritual act of worship. On the other hand, people who lack the gift of celibacy but are not free to marry are required to reject their sexuality. Consider the difference between choosing to fast for spiritual reasons versus not eating due to poverty. It is not fair to tell a starving person that not eating is a blessing which will help them draw closer to God, even though the same statement might be true for someone who is fasting for spiritual reasons. Likewise, pressuring someone who does not have the gift of celibacy to refrain from seeking a spouse is not likely to help them draw closer to God.

If a non-affirming celibate person felt an attraction to someone of the opposite sex, their self-talk might sound something like: "My feelings are natural and healthy, but I'm choosing not to act on them because I don't believe I am called to marriage. If the church found out about my feelings, they would understand and feel empathy for me not being able to act on them. God understands my feelings and is pleased with me for staying committed to my call to celibacy despite them." If a non-affirming celibate person felt an attraction to someone of the same sex, their self-talk might sound something like: "My feelings are sinful and displeasing to God, and I may be a sinful person even for having them. I can't act on them because it would be disgraceful in the eyes of God and the church if I did. If I were a stronger person, I would be able to find a way to stop having these feelings. If the church found out how I feel, people there would think less of me." Or some non-affirming celibate people experiencing attraction to someone of the same sex might say, "My feelings are just feelings and I'm not responsible for them, but even so I can't act on them because it would be disgraceful in the eyes of God and the church if I did. It would be easier if I could find a way to stop having these feelings. If the church found out how I feel, they would likely be uncomfortable."

Requiring LGBTQ+ people to choose between celibacy and a mixed-orientation marriage can cause them psychological damage. It teaches them that their innate desires are sinful, which has a negative effect on their self-esteem and self-worth and causes emotional exhaustion and pain. The repeated rejection of something intrinsic to themselves is often emotionally traumatic.

A non-affirming view might say:

Jesus does not promise that following him will be easy. In Mark 8:34, Jesus says, "Whoever wants to be my disciple must deny themselves and take up their cross and follow me." Just because being celibate can be hard doesn't mean it is the wrong choice. It is a cross that LGBTQ+ people must bear. The church expects straight unmarried people to remain celibate as well, so this expectation is not discriminatory against LGBTQ+ people. Christians are often called to a vocation that they would not willingly choose, which they later recognize to be a "beautiful vocation."[170] It is not necessary for Christians to have their sexual needs fulfilled in order to live full and happy lives. Instead, sexual needs must be mastered and reordered as people grow into Christian maturity.[171] People can find unexpected blessing and connection to God through celibacy.

An affirming view might say:

When Jesus tells his disciples to "take up their cross and follow [him]," it is implied that they will endure suffering for the sake of God's kingdom, not simply suffer for the sake of suffering. It is not fair to tell someone what the "cross" they need to bear will look like. Jesus will ask his followers to bear specific burdens, but it is unlikely that he would ask an entire group of people to give up marriage as a way of "bearing their crosses," especially if their doing so has a neutral or negative impact on the spreading of the gospel message.

A lifelong expectation of celibacy for same-sex-attracted people is harsher than a temporary expectation for celibacy for not-yet married straight people. This is because people who are exclusively same-sex-attracted are denied any hope for a future relationship, while straight

170. Wesley Hill, "Response to William Loader," in *Two Views on Homosexuality, the Bible, and the Church*, 59.

171. Holmes, "Listening to the Past and Reflecting on the Present," in *Two Views on Homosexuality, the Bible, and the Church*, 184.

people are free to hope and pray for a spouse and pursue relationships with the intent of marriage. A straight person who falls in love is free to marry their beloved (assuming the one they love is free to marry and loves them in return), while a non-affirming, same-sex-attracted Christian who falls in love with someone would have to deny that love and suffer heartbreak, possibly even ending a friendship to avoid temptation and frustration. In Luke 11:46, Jesus says, "And you experts in the law, woe to you, because you load people down with burdens they can hardly carry, and you yourselves will not lift one finger to help them." In Acts 15:10 Peter asks, "now then, why do you try to test God by putting on the necks of Gentiles a yoke that neither we nor our ancestors have been able to bear?" Christian leaders should consider whether they themselves would be able to bear a lifetime of celibacy and the rejection of a fundamental aspect of their identity, before they burden others with such expectations.

A non-affirming view might say:

When God said, "It is not good for the man to be alone" (Gen 2:18), Adam was the only human on earth. God wasn't necessarily saying that it was not good for man to be unmarried; he was saying it was not good for Adam to have no human companionship.

An affirming view might say:

God said, "It is not good for the man to be alone" (Gen 2:18) before the fall, so Adam had God as his companion. Adam lacked a marriage relationship, not good companionship. Both Jesus and Paul taught that singleness is good for those who have the gift of celibacy and for those who "choose to live like eunuchs for the sake of the kingdom of heaven." But they also taught that those who do not have this gift should be free to seek a spouse.[172]

A non-affirming view might say:

Celibate people can enjoy deep friendships and companionship and do not have to be lonely. LGBTQ+ Christians may want to find another LGBTQ+ friend to enter a close, committed, non-sexual covenant relationship with, so that they can have something like a marriage relationship without sexual intimacy.[173] Churches and communities can intentionally include and support single people, in

---

172. See Matthew 19:12, 1 Corinthians 7:7-9.

173. Hill, "Christ, Scripture, and Spiritual Friendship," in *Two Views on Homosexuality, the Bible, and the Church*, 114.

order to make it easier for them to live celibate lifestyles without feeling lonely.

An affirming view might say:
LGBTQ+ people living a celibate life can face many relationship challenges. Fitting in with straight peers can be challenging, especially when those peers get married and have children. It can be difficult to maintain a close, bonded friendship with a same-sex peer if a sexual attraction develops and becomes a temptation in the relationship. Being LGBTQ+ in and of itself can be an isolating and lonely experience. Eliminating all hope for a romantic relationship can make it unbearable for some. Most married couples would agree that their marriages have much greater meaning than simply being a means to channel their sexual passion and/or to procreate. Both opposite-sex and same-sex marriages provide spouses with benefits which include emotional and relational security, companionship, partnership, and financial stability. They also provide the opportunity to grow in Christlikeness through giving themselves to another person in a self-sacrificial love that reflects Jesus' love for the church. All these benefits of marriage apply to same-sex as well as opposite-sex marriages. Mandated celibacy unfairly withholds these benefits from LGBTQ+ people.

Background:
In Matthew 19:10-12 Jesus taught that men who divorce their wives and then remarry are committing adultery. His disciples respond by saying that in that case it is better not to marry. Jesus replies to them by saying:

> Not everyone can accept this word, but only those to whom it has been given. For there are eunuchs who were born that way, and there are eunuchs who have been made eunuchs by others—and there are those who choose to live like eunuchs for the sake of the kingdom of heaven. The one who can accept this should accept it.

A non-affirming view might say:
Jesus seems to be referring to celibate men as eunuchs and indicating that there can be varied reasons for people to be celibate. Jesus may even have considered himself, as a single man, to be one choosing to live like a eunuch for the kingdom of God. Some believe that, like eunuchs, people can be LGBTQ+ because of genetics (being born that way), or environmental factors and/or traumatic experiences (being made that way by others). For them, as with the

eunuchs in Jesus' day, celibacy can be accepted and used to further God's kingdom.

An affirming view might say:

When Jesus taught that "the one who can accept this should" (Matt 19:12), he acknowledged that some will not be able to accept celibacy and may choose a different option (i.e., marriage). He seems to have differentiated between people who had no choice in becoming a eunuch and those who chose celibacy. People do not choose their orientations and therefore LGBTQ+ people are like the ones who did not choose to be eunuchs. Consequently, they should not be forced to live celibately, since Jesus states that only those who can accept the teaching to live celibately should do so.

A non-affirming view might say:

Paul's teaching that Christians have "crucified the flesh with its passions and desires" (Gal 5:24) suggests that Christians have the power, in Christ, to deny their passions and live celibate lives. The Holy Spirit will help Christians with exclusive same-sex attractions to overcome their passions and live holy lives if they keep their hearts focused on Christ.

An affirming view might say:

Some Christian leaders who have tried to deny their sexual passions and live celibate lives for the sake of their ministry, without having the gift of celibacy, have fallen to temptation and ended up engaging in secret promiscuous relationships or abusing vulnerable people. God gives people strong sexual passions to help them bond to another person emotionally as well as physically. Attempting to suppress these passions in unhealthy and hopeless ways can have disastrous effects.

Judgement

An affirming view might say:

The passage that many Christians believe provides the strongest support for a non-affirming view of same-sex marriage is the vice list found in Romans 1:18-32 (which was discussed in Part III). After listing a number of vices, Paul, in a surprise twist, diverts his condemnation away from people described by this vice list towards those who judge them. Romans 2:1-4 says:

You, therefore, have no excuse, you who pass judgment on someone else, for at whatever point you judge another, you are condemning yourself, because you who pass judgment do the same things. Now we know that God's judgment against those who do such things is based on truth. So when you, a mere human being, pass judgment on them and yet do the same things, do you think you will escape God's judgment? Or do you show contempt for the riches of his kindness, forbearance and patience, not realizing that God's kindness is intended to lead you to repentance?

In Luke 6:37, Jesus said something similar, "Do not judge, and you will not be judged. Do not condemn, and you will not be condemned." Considering Paul's teaching that *all* are guilty of sin, as well as Jesus' instructions to avoid judgment, Christians should not judge each other about their sexuality.

A non-affirming view might say:

Paul's point in Romans 2:1-4 is not to promote tolerance of the actions listed in his vice list but rather to encourage everyone to recognize and repent of their own sinful behaviors, including the sinful behavior of judging others. Judging others implies having an attitude of superiority over them. Christians recognize that all people are guilty of sin, which enables them to label an action as sinful without being judgmental, because they do not believe that they are in a superior position to the person committing the action. Christians do not have to affirm same-sex marriage in order to refrain from judging LGBTQ+ people. Although Christians are not to judge, they do have a responsibility to warn others that God will judge everyone for their actions. Romans 14:12 says, "So then, each of us will give an account of ourselves to God." Informing people about the types of things God will judge them for is helpful to them in the long term and is a loving approach, even if it doesn't feel loving at the time. These warnings can be shared compassionately in the context of relationship so that they are not experienced as being harsh.

An affirming view might say:

The following verse, Romans 14:13 says, "Therefore let us stop passing judgment on one another. Instead, make up your mind not to put any stumbling block or obstacle in the way of the brother or sister." The condemnation of same-sex marriage is a major obstacle not only for LGBTQ+ people, but also for their friends, families, and supporters. It may be a significant reason for declining church attendance in North America. Jesus said, "Woe to you, teachers of the law and Pharisees, you hypocrites! You shut the door of the kingdom of heaven in people's faces. You yourselves do not enter, nor will you let those enter who are trying to" (Matt 23:13). By unnecessarily prohibiting same-sex marriage in the church, non-affirming churches are proclaiming a gospel message that is stricter than is biblically called for, and which many LGBTQ+ people and their supporters are unable to accept. This has the effect of shutting the door to the kingdom of heaven in their faces, which is the very thing that Jesus warned the Pharisees against doing.

Previously, in Romans 14:1-4, Paul says:

> Accept the one whose faith is weak, without quarreling over disputable matters. One person's faith allows them to eat anything, but another, whose faith is weak, eats only vegetables. The one who eats everything must not treat with contempt the one who does not, and the one who does not eat everything must not judge the one who does, for God has accepted them. Who are you to judge someone else's servant? To their own master, servants stand or fall. And they will stand, for the Lord is able to make them stand.

While this passage is discussing food laws, the concept is transferable to other disputable matters, including same-sex marriage. Christians are accountable directly to God and should not be judged by other Christians for decisions they make related to the sex of the person they choose to marry.

A non-affirming view might say:
It is a far stretch to apply Romans 14:1-4 to same-sex marriage. The Scriptures clearly prohibit same-sex sex, so it is not a disputable matter. Teaching right from wrong is different from judging and putting up unnecessary obstacles. Christians must be able to speak out against behaviors that are clearly out of alignment with God's plan, in order to teach ethical behavior that pleases God.

Background:
James 2:12-13 says, "Speak and act as those who are going to be judged by the law that gives freedom, because judgment without mercy will be shown to anyone who has not been merciful. Mercy triumphs over judgment."

An affirming view might say:
The "law that gives freedom" that James is referencing gives Christians the freedom to love same-sex spouses. The teaching that "mercy triumphs over judgment" reinforces that Christians should not judge people for their sexual orientation or the sex of their spouse.

A non-affirming view might say:

Christians can show mercy and be non-judgmental without going so far as to affirm same-sex marriage. James is not telling Christians to disregard sin, but rather he is instructing them to offer forgiveness to those who repent of their sins. The "law that gives freedom" offers freedom from sin, not freedom to sin. James could not be offering freedom to marry same-sex partners because the prohibition against same-sex sex is carried over from the Old Testament law into the New Testament through Paul's teaching in Romans 1: 26-27, 1 Corinthians 6:9, and 1 Timothy 1:10. Even if James is saying that the Old Testament law does not apply the same way to Christians as it does to Jews, he is not dismissing the prohibition against same-sex sex and marriage.

Holiness / Obedience

Background:

As an expression of their love for the Lord, Christians are called to live holy lives in obedience to Jesus' teaching. Living a holy life often means adapting one's behavior and making personal sacrifices. Several passages of Scripture reinforce the importance of obedience. 1 John 2:4 says, "Whoever says, 'I know him,' but does not do what he commands is a liar, and the truth is not in that person." 1 John 3:4-6 says, "Everyone who sins breaks the law; in fact, sin is lawlessness. But you know that he appeared so that he might take away our sins. And in him is no sin. No one who lives in him keeps on sinning. No one who continues to sin has either seen him or known him."

Romans 6:16-18 says:

Don't you know that when you offer yourselves to someone as obedient slaves, you are slaves of the one you obey—whether you are slaves to sin, which leads to death, or to obedience, which leads to righteousness? But thanks be to God that, though you used to be slaves to sin, you have come to obey from your heart the pattern of teaching that has now claimed your allegiance. You have been set free from sin and have become slaves to righteousness.

Romans 7:4-6 says:

So, my brothers and sisters, you also died to the law through the body of Christ, that you might belong to another, to him who was raised from the dead, in order that we might bear fruit for God. For when we were in the realm of the flesh, the sinful passions aroused by the law were at work in us, so that we bore fruit for death. But now, by dying to what once bound us, we have been released from the law so that we serve in the new way of the Spirit, and not in the old way of the written code.

A non-affirming view might say:

Choosing to follow Jesus means making a commitment to obey him. This sometimes requires doing things one doesn't want to do, and it sometimes requires refraining from things one wants to do. Even though Christians are no longer bound by the law, they are called to serve one another and to serve Christ in the Spirit, which requires living holy lives. Considering the teaching in Leviticus and in Paul's letters, living a holy life requires refraining from same-sex sex. Christians who are attracted to someone of the same sex must not act on their desire, as part of their obedience to Christ and their commitment to scriptural holiness.

An affirming view might say:

It is not clear whether Jesus prohibits same-sex marriage. Being a slave to righteousness is about making sacrifices to love other people, especially people who are oppressed and marginalized. The most important commandment to obey is the one to love the Lord and to love other people, and obeying this commandment leads Christians to affirm the right of LGBTQ+ people to marry spouses whom they love and to whom they are attracted.

A non-affirming view might say:

Living a holy life includes making careful choices about who one associates with. In 1 Corinthians 5:11, Paul says, "But now I am writing to you that you must not associate with anyone who claims to be a brother or sister but is sexually immoral or greedy, an idolater or slanderer, a drunkard or swindler. Do not even eat with such people." Christians should be careful not to become complicit by associating with and becoming influenced by sexually immoral people.

An affirming view might say:

In 1 Corinthians 5:11, Paul used the term "sexual immorality" to refer to sex associated with prostitution, rape, abuse, adultery, or fornication. Equal-status, monogamous, covenantal same-sex sex was not under consideration. LGBTQ+ Christians should be welcome to participate in church fellowship whether they are single, dating, or married, to the same degree that straight Christians are welcome to participate whether they are single, dating, or married. If Christians are engaging in sexually promiscuous or abusive behavior, it should be addressed by the church in a consistent manner, whether they are LGBTQ+ or straight and cisgender. Behaviors related to sexual immorality, greed, idolatry, drunkenness, swindling, or slander should be addressed consistently.

Background:
1 Thessalonians 4:3-8 says:

> It is God's will that you should be sanctified: that you should avoid sexual immorality; that each of you should learn to control your own body in a way that is holy and honorable, not in passionate lust like the pagans, who do not know God; and that in this matter no one should wrong or take advantage of a brother or sister. The Lord will punish all those who commit such sins, as we told you and warned you before. For God did not call us to be impure, but to live a holy life. Therefore, anyone who rejects this instruction does not reject a human being but God, the very God who gives you his Holy Spirit.

A non-affirming view might say:
This passage reinforces God's call for his people to live a holy life, which involves controlling the body and not giving into lust or acting in sexually immoral ways, which includes same-sex sex.

An affirming view might say:
The sexual immorality described in this passage is lustful and abusive, involving taking advantage of another person. It is specifically said to be practiced by the pagans, which may mean it relates to cultic worship. Same-sex marriage is not being described in this verse.

Background:
Romans 16:17-19 reinforces the importance of obeying Scripture and being wary of false teaching. It says:

> I urge you, brothers and sisters, to watch out for those who cause divisions and put obstacles in your way that are contrary to the teaching you have learned. Keep away from them. For such people are not serving our Lord Christ, but their own appetites. By smooth talk and flattery they deceive the minds of naive people. Everyone has heard about your obedience, so I rejoice because of you; but I want you to be wise about what is good, and innocent about what is evil.

A non-affirming view might say:
An affirming theology serves LGBTQ+ people's own appetites, enabling them to bend or change Scripture to make it say what they want to hear, rather than accepting what Scripture says. Being obedient and innocent about what is evil requires following God's laws, such as the ones prohibiting same-sex sex, even when it is difficult to do so.

An affirming view might say:

In Romans 16:17-19, Paul addresses the divisions and obstacles that were pertinent to the original recipients of his letter. It is not clear exactly what false doctrine he refers to, but since acceptance of same-sex marriage was not a controversial issue at the time, the issue he is addressing is not same-sex marriage. Since the false teaching was related to something else, it is not appropriate to assume Paul's teaching applies to same-sex marriage.

There are examples in Scripture where a person's significant need takes priority over the holiness laws. For example, during a time of hunger, David and his men violate the law by eating consecrated bread, and later, in Matthew 12:3-4, Jesus confirms that David made the right decision. In Matthew 12:9-13, Jesus heals a man on the Sabbath, in violation of the Pharisees understanding of the law. There are contemporary examples of significant need taking priority over Scriptural teaching as well. The church has expanded its grounds for divorce to include spousal abuse, and many churches have allowed or recognized remarriage after divorce. Slavery is not tolerated by the church today, even though it is accepted in the Scriptures. Loaning money with interest goes against the holiness laws but is very commonplace today, something that is necessary to enable people to own homes and even for churches to own buildings. The significant need for LGBTQ+ people to be accepted and supported should take priority over holiness laws that do not even clearly pertain to same-sex marriage.

Biblical Authority

Background:

Jesus demonstrated that he believed the Old Testament Scriptures to be authoritative by frequently quoting them, prefacing his teaching with, "it is written." For example, he quoted Deuteronomy as authoritative during his temptation by Satan in the wilderness in Matthew 4:1-11.[174] Paul taught that the Scriptures are trustworthy, saying in 2 Timothy 3:16-17, "All Scripture is God-breathed and is useful for teaching, rebuking, correcting and training in righteousness, so that the servant of God may be thoroughly equipped for every good work." Since the New Testament canon was not yet established,

---

174. Alisa Childers, *Another Gospel? A Lifelong Christian Seeks Truth in Response to Progressive Christianity* (Carol Stream, IL: Tyndale, 2020), 167.

Paul's teaching here, like Jesus' quotations, endorses the authority of the Old Testament. Peter indicated that the New Testament is authoritative when he referred to Paul's letters as Scripture. This showed that the early church believed that Paul's letters, which formed much of the New Testament, were inspired by God and authoritative as God's word (2 Pet 3:16).

The New Testament contains repeated warnings against false teaching. 1 Timothy 4:1-5 contains another warning from Paul, saying:

> The Spirit clearly says that in later times some will abandon the faith and follow deceiving spirits and things taught by demons. Such teachings come through hypocritical liars, whose consciences have been seared as with a hot iron. They forbid people to marry and order them to abstain from certain foods, which God created to be received with thanksgiving by those who believe and who know the truth. For everything God created is good, and nothing is to be rejected if it is received with thanksgiving, because it is consecrated by the word of God and prayer.

In 2 Timothy 4:3-4, Paul says, "For the time will come when people will not put up with sound doctrine. Instead, to suit their own desires, they will gather around them a great number of teachers to say what their itching ears want to hear. They will turn their ears away from the truth and turn aside to myths." Additionally, in Galatians 1:6-10, Paul says:

> I am astonished that you are so quickly deserting the one who called you to live in the grace of Christ and are turning to a different gospel— which is really no gospel at all. Evidently some people are throwing you into confusion and are trying to pervert the gospel of Christ. But even if we or an angel from heaven should preach a gospel other than the one we preached to you, let them be under God's curse! As we have already said, so now I say again: If anybody is preaching to you a gospel other than what you accepted, let them be under God's curse! Am I now trying to win the approval of human beings, or of God? Or am I trying to please people? If I were still trying to please people, I would not be a servant of Christ.

Peter also warned against false teaching. In 2 Peter 2:1-10 he says:

> But there were also false prophets among the people, just as there will be false teachers among you. They will secretly introduce destructive heresies, even denying the sovereign Lord who bought them—bringing swift destruction on themselves. Many will follow their depraved conduct and will bring the way of truth into disrepute. In their greed these teachers will exploit you with fabricated stories. Their condemnation has long been hanging over them, and their destruction has not been sleeping. For if God did not spare angels when they sinned, but sent them to hell, putting them in chains of darkness to be held for judgment; if he did not spare the ancient world when he brought the

flood on its ungodly people, but protected Noah, a preacher of righteousness, and seven others; if he condemned the cities of Sodom and Gomorrah by burning them to ashes, and made them an example of what is going to happen to the ungodly; and if he rescued Lot, a righteous man, who was distressed by the depraved conduct of the lawless (for that righteous man, living among them day after day, was tormented in his righteous soul by the lawless deeds he saw and heard)—if this is so, then the Lord knows how to rescue the godly from trials and to hold the unrighteous for punishment on the day of judgment. This is especially true of those who follow the corrupt desire of the flesh and despise authority.

In 2 Peter 3:16, Peter observes that people were already misinterpreting Paul's letters, saying that "ignorant and unstable people distort [them], as they do the other Scriptures, to their own destruction." Jude adds his warning against false teachers in Jude 1:4, saying, "For certain men whose condemnation was written about long ago have secretly slipped in among you. They are godless men, who change the grace of our God into a license for immorality and deny Jesus Christ our only Sovereign and Lord." John also warns against false teachers in Revelation 22:18-19, saying, "I warn everyone who hears the words of the prophecy of this scroll: If anyone adds anything to them, God will add to that person the plagues described in this scroll. And if anyone takes words away from this scroll of prophecy, God will take away from that person any share in the tree of life and in the Holy City, which are described in this scroll."

A non-affirming view might say:
Affirming theology is an example of the false teaching and the different gospel that Christians have been repeatedly warned against accepting.

An affirming view might say:
As previously discussed, the false teachings that the New Testament writers warn against are not related to affirming same-sex marriage. It would be anachronistic to insert a conversation about same-sex marriage into two-thousand-year-old letters warning against false teaching, when same-sex marriage as it is understood today was an unknown practice at that time. To truly respect Scripture, Christians need to be able to approach it humbly and prayerfully, open to the possibility that traditional interpretations may need to be re-examined in light of new evidence and understanding. Blind acceptance of traditional interpretations of Scripture can put people at risk of mistreating God's word and becoming false teachers. It is

critical to guard against false teaching, as the New Testament writers emphasize, yet if new understandings are true, it is important to allow them to be heard and studied. If a traditional teaching turns out to have been based on a misinterpretation of Scripture, it is essential to allow it to be corrected, to respect the authority of the Scriptures.

A non-affirming view might say:

The Scriptures are clear about prohibiting same-sex sex. Christians who disregard this teaching are rejecting the authority of the Scriptures and are undermining the integrity of their faith. Any teaching that opposes an established doctrine that has been understood for centuries should be treated with suspicion. When Christians open their minds to affirmative teaching regarding same-sex marriage, they are at risk of being deceived in other areas of Christian doctrine, including the message of salvation through Jesus. Accepting same-sex marriage may start Christians down a path that can end with them abandoning their faith altogether.

An affirming view might say:

Changing one's view to become affirming of same-sex marriage does not require a full deconstruction of one's faith or an outright rejection of the Bible, nor does it require us to alter the traditional Christian sexual ethics of monogamy and covenant. The traditional view has not been consistent through the centuries. Martin Luther interpreted Paul's condemnation as being against the sexual abuse of boys by men, as evidenced by his translation of the word *arsenokoitai* in 1 Corinthians 6:9 and 1 Timothy 1:10 as "boy molesters."

In many ways, expanding the definition of marriage to include same-sex spouses strengthens the gospel message and the mission of the church. In current non-affirming church contexts, Christians who become affirming may find that their place in the church diminishes or even disappears. Being excluded from the church community can lead them to question or disregard other teachings of the church and give up their faith. When a non-affirming church's hard stance against same-sex marriage conflicts with people's internal conviction that affirming same-sex marriage is the ethical approach, Christians can be faced with a difficult choice. Those who trust that the church's traditional interpretation of Scripture is correct may believe that they would have to reject the authority of Scripture to affirm same-sex marriage. Some people find that their internal sense of justice and their sense of the Holy Spirit's guidance is leading them towards supporting same-sex marriage, but they can't see how to do so while upholding the Scriptures. They may feel like they are facing an unthinkable choice between their intrinsic morals, which lead them towards inclusion, and their commitment to the church. They may find themselves living in an uncomfortable tension with no clear path to resolution. Once Christians realize that they can affirm same-sex marriage while maintaining a high view of Scriptural authority, they can confidently find their place in church again without having to question other Christian doctrines or even their entire faith.

A non-affirming view might say:

LGBTQ+ people and their supporters approach the Scriptures with an agenda, searching to find acceptance of same-sex marriage. Because they have a personal stake in discovering affirming statements within Scripture, they are not able to read it objectively and are at risk of misinterpreting the Scriptures to make them say what they want to hear.

An affirming view might say:

Those who hold a non-affirming view are often motivated to find their non-affirming views justified and reinforced as they study the Scriptures. They have seen that Christians who change from a non-affirming view to an affirming view often suffer many losses. Pastors and those in vocational ministry who adopt an affirming view frequently lose their jobs, their ministries, and even their entire careers. Other Christians have lost church membership, church leadership roles, ministry opportunities, and even family and friends who disagree with them. The fact that there is so much at stake can make it difficult for those with a non-affirming view to look at the question of same-sex marriage objectively.

In the 1990's, in the United States, several conservative religious leaders and politicians gained supporters and donations by spreading fear of homosexuality. Some of their ministries required millions of dollars in weekly donations, and spreading fear about homosexuality motivated people to donate money. Gay people were stereotyped and depicted as being violent, perverted, shameless, and pederastic. Fears that gay people were recruiting and abusing young teens for sex and were out to destroy America's moral values and spiritual traditions were fanned into flames. Stories about violent incidents were made up or exaggerated and used to garner support for ministries. Disinformation spread quickly and widely throughout the United States and beyond, resulting in increased fear and hatred of LGBTQ+

people. This brought in donations to fund the ministries and votes for the political parties that would protect society from the so-called "gay agenda."[175] These leaders and politicians read and interpreted the Scriptures through their own biases, which personally benefited them, and several were unwilling to listen to an alternative understanding when one was offered to them.[176] Everyone approaches Scriptures with their own personal biases, and it takes an intentional effort to try to read the Scriptures objectively, no matter the starting perspective.

A non-affirming view might say:
The Bible is intended to be clear. The fact that an affirming argument requires complicated analysis of context, history, and language shows that the affirming view is not the view that God intended his people to uphold.

An affirming view might say:
Peter said that some of Paul's teaching was hard to understand (2 Pet 3:15-16). Jesus spoke in parables, to the point that his own disciples who knew him best had difficulty understanding what he was saying (Luke 18:34). The Bible was written in ancient languages to an audience far removed from contemporary culture. Christians should not expect the Bible to be clear in everything it says. It is essential to understand what the Scriptures meant to their original audience if we are to determine what they mean for Christians today. This requires the study of history, culture, and language. The Bible claims to be spiritually profitable (2 Tim 3:16-17), and everything that is necessary for salvation can be understood from a simple reading of the Scriptures, but not everything written in the Bible is clear, nor should we expect it to be.

History / Tradition

A non-affirming view might say:
Christian tradition has consistently interpreted the Scriptures as prohibiting same-sex marriage. It is unlikely that the truth about God's plan for Christian marriage would be dramatically different from the understanding of the disciples and church founders, as well as nearly all scholars, theologians, and pastors for the past two thousand years.

---

175. Mel White, *Stranger at the Gate: To be Gay and Christian in America* (New York, NY: Plume, 1995), Kindle ed., 317-19, 346-51.
176. Ibid., 321.

Something as fundamental as the definition of marriage would be unlikely to have been misunderstood from Old Testament times until now.

An affirming view might say:

The church has changed its understanding on various topics over the course of history in ways that are considered to be growing into God's will. For example, the church has drastically changed its views on slavery, women's rights, anti-Semitism, and even the movement of the earth in relation to the sun.[177] These changed views were significant departures from traditional theology and were experienced as very controversial in their time.

The church's understanding of history and theology have been influenced by politics throughout the course of its existence. The church has been complicit in unjust war, persecution, sexism, racism, slavery, and abuse. In Canada, awareness is growing about the residential school system which inflicted systematic abuse upon Indigenous children and families for decades. The church's significant role in the residential school system seems unfathomable to the contemporary church, but its horrific abuse of Indigenous people provides unmistakable evidence that the church is capable of severe error, even in recent history. Christians must be free to prayerfully question the traditions, interpretations, and actions of the church. Otherwise, they are at risk of blindly adopting mistaken theology and practices that were inherited from their predecessors. It is important to be able to separate theological understandings that rest on solid ground from those perched on a shakier foundation. Christians need not be afraid to examine the Scriptures with fresh perspectives. With prayer and careful study, in the context of community, the essential doctrines grow in clarity and trustworthiness while less essential doctrines (i.e., disputable matters) can be held with a more open hand.

One of the reasons the church has traditionally been adamant about all same-sex sex being sinful is because of its interpretation of the story in Genesis 19:1-29 about the town of Sodom (which was discussed previously in Part II). For many years, gay men were called "sodomites" and male-male sex was called "sodomy" due to this story's influence on how the church viewed same-sex sex. As discussed in Part II, Sodom's sin was about its hostility toward and abuse of the outsider, not homosexuality. Labelling gay men as

---

177. Vines, *God and the Gay Christian*, 40.

sodomites and male-male sex as sodomy was an error based on mistaken interpretation.

New information has recently become available which makes it necessary for the church to re-examine its response to same-sex marriage. The concept of sexual orientation, for example, is not found in ancient writings and has only begun to be studied in the late nineteenth century.[178] In Bible times, same-sex sex was understood to be driven by an excess of lust that could not be satisfied through opposite-sex marriage. The belief was that if people could learn to control their lust, they would be content within an opposite-sex marriage.

More recently, once the understanding emerged that some people are exclusively attracted to others of the same sex, it became commonly believed that this same-sex attraction was the result of relational or physical trauma, abuse, or mental illness. Same-sex sex was subject both to criminalization and attempts to treat it with medical intervention.

When the problems with the criminalization and medicalization of same-sex attraction were recognized, the focus shifted to attempts to cure people of their same-sex attraction through therapy and prayer. Conversion therapy, reparative therapy and other forms of psychological treatment were used to try to help people overcome their same-sex attraction. Some LGBTQ+ people participated willingly, while others were pressured or physically forced to participate.

It has become clear that these therapies are ineffective in changing LGBTQ+ people's orientations and identities, and they cause harm to their psyche and mental health, because the therapies directly or indirectly teach them to hate and reject an intrinsic part of themselves. They are also expensive and time-consuming.

Some churches are moving towards trying to help people embrace a life of celibacy, possibly while expressing acceptance of their orientation, or possibly while focusing on their identity in Christ to the exclusion of an LGBTQ+ identity. Some of these churches are starting to recognize that a lifetime of celibacy is not feasible for everyone and are unsure of how to proceed. As society is beginning to embrace and celebrate diversity in sexual orientation, non-affirming churches are increasingly being perceived and experienced as being less loving and less welcoming than general society. LGBTQ+ Christians are increasingly unsatisfied by the "welcoming but not

---

178. Nissinen, *Homoeroticism in the Biblical World*, 12.

affirming" approach, which welcomes LGBTQ+ people to attend their church but does not affirm their relationships and imposes restrictions on their membership and participation. Many church members within non-affirming churches are having their views questioned and challenged by friends, family, and colleagues outside of the church. Some of them in turn are asking their church leadership to re-examine their church's position on same-sex marriage.

In response to questions about why the pressure to change the non-affirming church's position on same-sex marriage is coming up now, after such a long tradition of churches prohibiting same-sex sex, pastor and author Ken Wilson asks:

> When might it have come up earlier? When Aquinas, a doctor of the church, taught that homosexual acts were worse than incest? When the church commonly conflated the horrors of the attempted gang rape of the visitors to Sodom with all homosexual acts? When the church had no understanding or even recognition of the reality of same-sex orientation? The church doesn't go looking for raging controversies. They come up when historical circumstances ripen and the issue is forced. The question of whether Christians should go along with, support or even tolerate the institution of slavery didn't arise until *nearly 18 centuries* after the gospel was announced. It didn't come up because it wasn't a real possibility. People couldn't imagine a world that worked without slavery. These things gain our attention only when the complex forces of history converge to grab our attention.[179]

The possibility of legal marriage between two people of the same sex is only a recent development. Before same-sex marriage was legalized, there was no avenue for the church to affirm same-sex relationships without affirming an extra-marital sexual relationship. Until 1969, same-sex sexual intercourse was illegal in Canada, which made it hard for churches to even engage in a conversation about whether they had been wrong about their definition of marriage. The fact that this conversation is happening now, instead of during the early years of the church, does not mean that the conversation itself is wrong. It may be that it took this long for the church and society to develop a more comprehensive understanding of gender, sex, and human rights, just as it has taken time to develop its understanding of issues surrounding racism, women's rights, children's rights, slavery, colonialism, and creation care. For the church to move forward in each of these areas, it has had to re-examine its historical

---

179. Ken Wilson, *A Letter to My Congregation: An Evangelical Pastor's Path to Embracing People Who Are Gay, Lesbian, Bisexual, and Transgender into the Company of Jesus* (Canton, MI: David Crumm Media, 2014), 153.

interpretations of Scripture and discover different insights and understandings as it engaged in that work.

A non-affirming view might say:

Tradition provides stability for the church and needs to be honored. It serves as a safeguard to protect the church from going astray. If the church disregards the clear teaching of the Scriptures about same-sex sex, other established understandings will also be vulnerable, and the church will risk having the gospel message of salvation through Jesus lost or watered down to the point where it loses its meaning.

An affirming view might say:

The inclusion of same-sex unions within the definition of marriage does not change any of the fundamentals of the Christian faith. The gospel is still the gospel. Marital faithfulness is still upheld. Family values are actually easier to affirm when same-sex couples are included within the church's definition of marriage because it allows inclusion of LGBTQ+ people into Christian fellowship without relaxing expectations that sex happen exclusively within marriage. Changing one's view about something specific like same-sex marriage, based on a careful study of the Scriptures within context, does not require one to disregard the rest of the Scriptures or the traditional creeds.

Fruitfulness

Background:

The Bible uses the image of fruit to describe the effects of people's attitudes and behavior. Attitudes and behaviors that are in keeping with God's will are understood to produce positive effects, referred to as good fruit. Straying from God's will is understood to result in negative effects, or bad fruit. In Matthew 7:16-20, Jesus describes how to discern true prophets from false prophets based on the effects of their attitudes and behavior, saying:

> By their fruit you will recognize them. Do people pick grapes from thornbushes, or figs from thistles? Likewise, every good tree bears good fruit, but a bad tree bears bad fruit. A good tree cannot bear bad fruit, and a bad tree cannot bear good fruit. Every tree that does not bear good fruit is cut down and thrown into the fire. Thus, by their fruit you will recognize them.

A non-affirming view might say:

The LGBTQ+ community is associated with a promiscuous lifestyle. Casual sex leads to sexually transmitted diseases and emotional and mental unwellness. The lifestyle associated with being LGBTQ+ and acting on same-sex attractions produces bad fruit.

An affirming view might say:

For many people, the promiscuity stereotypically associated with the LGBTQ+ community is the result of people having been forced to stay "in the closet" in many spheres of life. The lack of opportunities to have their relationships sanctioned by society created a promiscuous culture because people had extremely limited options to develop and maintain long term relationships. Many straight people endorse and participate in promiscuous behavior, and many LGBTQ+ people do not. Assumptions should not be made about a person's sexual ethic based on their orientation or gender identity. Promiscuous behaviors and sexual abuse among straight people cause people to suffer from sexually transmitted diseases, unplanned pregnancies, and emotional and mental unwellness, but this does not inspire calls for a widespread rejection of opposite-sex marriage.

LGBTQ+ people and their families and friends are significantly harmed by the teaching that same-sex sex and the desire for it is sinful. This teaching has resulted in hatred, violence, discrimination, exclusion from families, homelessness, poverty, high rates of anxiety, depression, suicide, and alienation from God and the church. These negative effects, or bad fruit suggest that the teaching that prohibits same-sex marriage does not come from God.

A non-affirming view might say:

Christians can and should maintain the traditional definition of marriage without acting in hateful and discriminatory ways towards LGBTQ+ people. Christians need to ensure that their approach towards LGBTQ+ people is loving, but this does not mean they should affirm same-sex marriages. Jesus taught that the law (which includes avoiding same-sex sex) must still be followed, but in a way that also demonstrates justice, mercy, and faithfulness. He said, "Woe to you, teachers of the law and Pharisees, you hypocrites! You give a tenth of your spices—mint, dill and cumin. But you have neglected the more important matters of the law—justice, mercy and faithfulness. You should have practiced the latter, without neglecting the former" (Matt 23:23).

Background:
James 3:17 says, "But the wisdom that comes from heaven is first of all pure; then peace-loving, considerate, submissive, full of mercy and good fruit, impartial and sincere."

An affirming view might say:
Affirming LGBTQ+ people and same-sex marriage is the best way to be peace-loving, considerate, full of mercy and good fruit, impartial and sincere.

A non-affirming view might say:
The first characteristic of wisdom that James lists is purity. This includes sexual purity, which implies celibacy or opposite-sex marriage.

An affirming view might say:
In the Old Testament, purity implied keeping oneself physically and spiritually clean, separate, and free from contamination. In the New Testament, however, Jesus shifted the meaning of purity away from external, physical characteristics to internal qualities, including motivations and attitudes.[180] For Christians, purity implies honesty, authenticity, and single-minded devotion to Christ. Asking LGBTQ+ people to disconnect themselves from their sexuality in order to hide it is asking them to compromise their integrity and live inauthentically. Such dishonesty runs contrary to James' call to purity. Colossians 3:9 says, "Do not lie to each other, since you have taken off your old self with its practices." Leviticus 19:11 says, "Do not lie. Do not deceive one another." Living deceitfully results in bad fruit, such as anxiety, mistrust, isolation, depression, and habitual dishonesty. LGBTQ+ people and their close friends and families often feel dishonest and inauthentic while the person is closeted. Many people wait until the feeling of inauthenticity becomes unbearable before coming out and finally being honest about themselves.

A non-affirming view might say:
LGBTQ+ Christians are free to be honest about their desires, just not to act on them or embrace them as their identity. Some who do not affirm same-sex marriage say that Christians are free to embrace LGBTQ+ identities if they do not engage in same-sex sex or undergo gender-affirming medical treatment. If LGBTQ+ Christians

---

180. Brownson, *Bible, Gender, Sexuality*, 195.

are honest about their same-sex attractions, these attractions can be brought into the open so that, with God's help, other Christians can help them cope with and overcome their desires.

An affirming view might say:

As long as there is a prohibition against same-sex marriage in the church, people who identify as LGBTQ+ will experience at least some degree of emotional shame and practical limitations related to fellowship and service, whether or not they are sexually active or undergo gender-affirming medical treatment. LGBTQ+ people in non-affirming churches aren't really free to be honest about their desires, because there is a high social and practical cost associated with their honesty. Non-affirming theology pressures LGBTQ+ Christians to stay in the closet, where bad fruit typically grows.

Background:

Galatians 5:19-26 says:

> The acts of the flesh are obvious: sexual immorality, impurity and debauchery; idolatry and witchcraft; hatred, discord, jealousy, fits of rage, selfish ambition, dissensions, factions and envy; drunkenness, orgies, and the like. I warn you, as I did before, that those who live like this will not inherit the kingdom of God.
>
> But the fruit of the Spirit is love, joy, peace, forbearance, kindness, goodness, faithfulness, gentleness and self-control. Against such things there is no law. Those who belong to Christ Jesus have crucified the flesh with its passions and desires. Since we live by the Spirit, let us keep in step with the Spirit. Let us not become conceited, provoking and envying each other.

A non-affirming view might say:

Since Paul was a Jew, he followed the teaching from Leviticus, which was interpreted to outlaw male-male sex and, by association, female-female sex. Paul would have considered same-sex sex to be included within the definition of "sexual immorality" in verse 19. Thus, in Galatians 5:19-26 he provides the same teaching to the Galatian church that he gives to the Corinthian church: that unless they repent, people who engage in same-sex sex will not inherit the Kingdom of God.

An affirming view might say:

Galatians 5:19-21 is yet another one of Paul's vice lists. As with the other vice lists, it is important to avoid emphasizing one vice in importance over the others. Sexual immorality, whatever that word was referring to, should be treated with the same significance as dissensions, envy, and selfish ambition—as evidence that people need God's grace, rather than as ammunition to use to condemn them.

The term *porneia*, translated as "sexual immorality," is a broad term. It refers to prostitution, incest, rape, adultery, and sex outside of a marriage/covenant commitment, whether opposite-sex or same-sex in nature. Paul would have considered the prohibitions against male-male sex in Leviticus to refer to the ways it was commonly known to be practiced in his context and which fit with the definition of *porneia*. These were extra-marital, pederastic, idolatrous, abusive, excessively lustful, and/or exploitative relationships.

The concept of being fruitful in the New Testament no longer implies procreation but rather refers to generating the fruits of the Spirit, which are, "love, joy, peace, forbearance, kindness, goodness, faithfulness, gentleness and self-control" (Gal 5:22-23). Romans 7:4 says, "So, my brothers and sisters, you also died to the law through the body of Christ, that you might belong to another, to him who was raised from the dead, in order that we might bear fruit for God." Colossians 1:9-10 says, "We continually ask God to fill you with the knowledge of his will through all the wisdom and understanding that the Spirit gives, so that you may live a life worthy of the Lord and please him in every way: bearing fruit in every good work, growing in the knowledge of God."

The fruits of the Spirit, including love, joy, peace, forbearance, kindness, goodness, faithfulness, gentleness, and self-control, are often experienced within and through same-sex marriages. Many Christians who oppose same-sex marriage have acted in ways that are not loving, peaceful, patient, or kind towards LGBTQ+ people, exhibiting bad fruit. If the acts of the flesh and the fruit of the Spirit are obvious, as Paul says they are in Galatians, then same-sex marriage is more associated with the fruit of the Spirit than it is with the acts of the flesh.

A non-affirming view might say:

There are other practices that arguably produce good fruit but are still considered sinful from a biblical standpoint, such as polyamory and certain types of idol worship. The indication that an action appears to generate good fruit is not a sufficient reason to consider a practice to be holy, especially if there is biblical evidence against it.[181]

---

181. Holmes, "Listening to the Past and Reflecting on the Present," in *Two Views on Homosexuality, the Bible, and the Church*, 185.

Love For One Another

Background:

In Matthew 22:37-40, religious leaders ask Jesus to identify the greatest commandment in the law. Jesus replies by saying, "Love the Lord your God with all your heart and with all your soul and with all your mind. This is the first and greatest commandment. And the second is like it: 'Love your neighbor as yourself.' All the Law and Prophets hang on these two commandments." To love God and others should be the primary desire and occupation of every Christian. The New Testament writers all reaffirmed this teaching of Jesus. For example, in Galatians 5:14-15, Paul says, "For the entire law is fulfilled in keeping this one command: 'Love your neighbor as yourself.' If you bite and devour each other, watch out or you will be destroyed by each other." In Romans 13:9-10, he says, "The commandments, 'You shall not commit adultery,' 'You shall not murder,' 'You shall not steal,' 'You shall not covet,' and whatever other command there may be, are summed up in this one command: 'Love your neighbor as yourself.' Love does no harm to a neighbor. Therefore love is the fulfillment of the law." In James 2:8-9, James says, "If you really keep the royal law found in Scripture, 'Love your neighbor as yourself,' you are doing right. But if you show favoritism, you sin and are convicted by the law as lawbreakers." In 1 Peter 4:8, Peter says, "Above all, love each other deeply, because love covers over a multitude of sins."

In 1 John 4:7-21, John says:

Dear friends, let us love one another, for love comes from God. Everyone who loves has been born of God and knows God. Whoever does not love does not know God, because God is love. This is how God showed his love among us: He sent his one and only Son into the world that we might live through him. This is love: not that we loved God, but that he loved us and sent his Son as an atoning sacrifice for our sins. Dear friends, since God so loved us, we also ought to love one another. No one has ever seen God; but if we love one another, God lives in us and his love is made complete in us.

This is how we know that we live in him and he in us: He has given us of his Spirit. And we have seen and testify that the Father has sent his Son to be the Savior of the world. If anyone acknowledges that Jesus is the Son of God, God lives in them and they in God. And so we know and rely on the love God has for us.

God is love. Whoever lives in love lives in God, and God in them. This is how love is made complete among us so that we will have confidence on the day of judgment: In this world we are like Jesus. There is no fear in love. But perfect love drives out fear, because fear has to do with punishment. The one who fears is not made perfect in love.

We love because he first loved us. Whoever claims to love God yet hates a brother or sister is a liar. For whoever does not love their brother and sister, whom they have seen, cannot love God, whom they have not seen. And he has given us this command: Anyone who loves God must also love their brother and sister.

A non-affirming view might say:

Christians can love people without accepting their behavior. Christians who do not affirm same-sex marriage can and do love and accept their LGBTQ+ neighbors. Encouraging people to make righteous lifestyle choices is the most loving response, and allowing people to make self-destructive choices without warning them of the consequences is not loving.

An affirming view might say:

A loving response requires acceptance of LGBTQ+ people's identities and marriages. Many people experience their sexual attractions as an integral part of themselves which cannot be separated from the rest of their identity. The teaching that same-sex sex is unacceptable inspires rejection and hatred of LGBTQ+ people which leads to violence and discrimination against them in both religious and secular circles.[182] This severely damages their self-esteem and threatens their physical and emotional safety. Those LGBTQ+ Christians who believe they are rejected by God as well as by their communities experience even more significant psychological harm than non-Christian LGBTQ+ people. Studies have shown that religious faith is protective against suicide attempts for straight and cisgender youth, but it puts LGBTQ+ youth at greater risk.[183]

1 John 4:19 says, "we love because he first loved us." Many people who feel unloved or unlovable are not able to love themselves and

---

182. LGBTQ+ youth in Ontario are 14 times higher risk for suicide and substance abuse than their heterosexual peers. 45% of trans people have attempted suicide. 20% of trans people report being physically or sexually assaulted and 34% report being victims of verbal threats or harassment due to their identity. Half of all trans people live on less than $15,000 per year. CMHA Ontario, *Lesbian, Gay, Bisexual, Tran & Queer Identified People and Mental Health*, accessed January 17, 2021, https://ontario.cmha.ca/documents/lesbian-gay-bisexual-trans-queer-identified-people-and-mental-health. 29% of youth experiencing homelessness in Canada identify as LGBTQ+. A Way Home, *Youth Homelessness in Canada*, accessed January 17, 2021, https://awayhome.ca/youth-homelessness.

183. The Trevor Project, *The Trevor Project Research Brief: Religiosity and Suicidality among LGBTQ Youth*, April, 2020, accessed July 16, 2023, https://www.thetrevorproject.org/research-briefs/religiosity-and-suicidality-among-lgbtq-youth/Online.

can struggle to love others. Vicky Beeching relates that when she was hiding her sexual orientation, "the same wall [she] built to keep part of [her] in was also, emotionally, keeping everyone out."[184] In order to love others well, people need to love themselves, and in order to love themselves, they need to accept themselves, understanding that they are made in God's image and are loved and accepted by him. When LGBTQ+ people understand themselves to be God's good creation, they are better able to honor God by loving others.

The tone Paul uses when he condemns same-sex sex is harsh, portraying a decidedly negative view of same-sex sex. Paul does not teach that there is an option for Christians to welcome and accept same-sex couples as part of the church community but with restricted membership and leadership opportunities. Paul's harshness only makes sense if the same-sex sex he is condemning is extremely sinful, such as self-serving, lustful, abusive, or idolatrous sex.[185] If Paul is condemning specific, sinful forms of same-sex sex, the possibility remains for Christians to affirm equal-status, monogamous, covenantal same-sex relationships and to fully include LGBTQ+ people in the church community.

A non-affirming view might say:

Paul's tone is harsh because same-sex sex is a serious sin. Paul would not have welcomed same-sex couples into the church, and the church is compromising itself under the influence of the culture when it does so. Hebrews 10:26-31 says:

> If we deliberately keep on sinning after we have received the knowledge of the truth, no sacrifice for sins is left, but only a fearful expectation of judgment and of raging fire that will consume the enemies of God. Anyone who rejected the law of Moses died without mercy on the testimony of two or three witnesses. How much more severely do you think someone deserves to be punished who has trampled the Son of God underfoot, who has treated as an unholy thing the blood of the covenant that sanctified them, and who has insulted the Spirit of grace? For we know him who said, "It is mine to avenge; I will repay," and again, "The Lord will judge his people." It is a dreadful thing to fall into the hands of the living God.

1 Peter 4:5 also teaches that people "will have to give account to him who is ready to judge the living and the dead." In 2 Peter 2:4-14,

---

184 Vicky Beeching, *Undivided: Coming out, Becoming Whole, and Living Free from Shame* (Broadway, NY: HarperOne, 2018), 121.

185. Meagan K. DeFranza, "Response to William Loader," in *Two Views on Homosexuality, the Bible, and the Church*, 52.

Peter warns about punishment for the unrighteous on the day of judgement. He references the destruction of Sodom and Gomorrah as examples of what will happen to the ungodly. The most loving approach is to encourage LGBTQ+ people to live their lives in a way that avoids sin and will enable them to avoid judgment and live with God for eternity after death. Encouraging LGBTQ+ Christians to remain celibate is a loving attempt to save them from the consequences of engaging in sinful behavior that can cause them spiritual, physical, and emotional harm, both now and in their eternal future. Encouraging people to engage knowingly in sinful behaviors is unloving because of the judgment they will face for their sinful behavior. Eternal life with Jesus in heaven is more important than happiness in this life.

An affirming view might say:

There is insufficient biblical evidence to label same-sex marriage as sinful. In 2 Peter 2:14, the sins that Peter says will be judged are adultery and greed. These do not describe same-sex marriage. Loving their neighbors is part of the greatest commandment for Christians, and it is this commandment to which Christians will be held most accountable. The non-affirming stance toward same-sex marriage and the resulting rejection of LGBTQ+ people cause harm to individuals and society and limit a Christian's ability to love their neighbors.

A non-affirming view might say:

Same-sex sex can be physically, emotionally, and spiritually unhealthy for the people who participate in it. Men who have sex with other men face physical health risks, as do women who do not bear children. Same-sex sex is spiritually unhealthy because engaging in sinful activities separates people from God. The widespread incidence of mental health issues among LGBTQ+ people suggests that their identity as or experience of being LGBTQ+ is a symptom of mental illness. As a symptom of mental illness, there is potential for change in orientation through healing, but for such healing to occur, the LGBTQ+ identity needs to be recognized as a problem. When LGBTQ+ identities are affirmed and accepted, they cannot be recognized as a problem, and healing is less likely to occur. The physical, mental, and spiritual health risks incurred by LGBTQ+ people serve as evidence that the prohibition against same-sex marriage is God's will, and Christians uphold the prohibition as part of their duty to love others. Prohibiting same-sex sex and encouraging celibacy is a form of tough love, done for the sake of LGBTQ+ people's overall health.

An affirming view might say:

The high incidences of mental health problems experienced by LGBTQ+ people include depression, anxiety, suicide, and suicide attempts. These are exacerbated by the increased rates of poverty, homelessness, and unreached potential associated with being LGBTQ+. These mental health and socioeconomic problems result from rejection, hatred, and discrimination, largely inspired by the non-affirming religious influence on society. LGBTQ+ youth from non-accepting families and communities suffer more mental health challenges than those whose sexual identities are accepted. This suggests that it is the community's non-affirming response that leads to the mental health problems experienced by LGBTQ+ people, rather than the idea that pre-existing mental health problems lead people to identify as LGBTQ+.[186]

Christians often take risks with their physical health without having their choices scrutinized, spiritualized, and condemned. For example, overeating and living a sedentary lifestyle poses significant health risks, having multiple pregnancies without sufficient recovery time in between is dangerous to a mother's health, and Christian ministry often involves an elevated risk of burnout and stress-related health concerns. Christians do not tend to condemn each other for making risky choices such as these with their health but rather believe that people should be free to make choices about their own personal health risks.

Most of the physical health risks associated with men having sex with men are related to sexually transmitted diseases due to having sex with multiple partners.[187] Monogamy within same-sex marriage is an answer to mitigating these health risks. Marriage, whether opposite-sex or same-sex, typically increases the health and well-being of both spouses, as it provides emotional support, physical support, and financial stability for the couple.

---

186. M. Rosario, E.W. Schrimshaw, and J. Hunter, "Disclosure of Sexual Orientation and Subsequent Substance Use and Abuse among Lesbian, Gay, and Bisexual Youths: Critical Role of Disclosure Reactions," *Psychology of Addictive Behaviors* 23, no. 1 (2009): 183.

187. Rita Lee, "Health Care Problems of Lesbian, Gay, Bisexual, and Transgender Patients," *Western Journal of Medicine* 172, no. 6 (2000 June): 403-8.

A non-affirming view might say:

Same-sex marriage is harmful to society in general for multiple reasons. It undermines the institution of family and marriage. An element of straight, cisgender people's sense of gender and sexuality is lost when LGBTQ+ identities are affirmed and normalized. The affirmation of same-sex marriage confuses children and results in straight cisgender children becoming LGBTQ+, causing them to adopt sinful lifestyles and forego the possibility of having children of their own. Children who grow up in homes with two same-sex parents suffer for not having had both a mother and a father. The response that is most loving toward society in general is to avoid these harmful effects by discouraging same-sex marriage and reducing the acceptance of transgender identities.

An affirming view might say:

Society has much to benefit from affirming same-sex marriage. LGBTQ+ people contribute a diversity of perspectives, ideas, and skills to society. Many LGBTQ+ people have exceptional gifts of creativity, artistic talent, empathy for others, introspective skills, and insights into relationships and emotions. When they are encouraged to accept themselves and fully participate in society, society benefits from their contributions. There are many children who need to be adopted into loving homes and would benefit from having parents of any gender to love and provide for them. Children thrive when loved, whether they have a mother and father, two mothers, two fathers, a single parent, or other consistent, loving adults to support them. In today's increasingly fragmented society, it can be helpful to have non-procreative couples to fill supportive roles in child-rearing, such as aunts, uncles, babysitters, and friends. Society is strengthened socially and economically by stable, long-term, committed relationships, whether they are same-sex or opposite-sex in nature.[188]

Christians who adopt an affirming view can experience emotional and spiritual healing as they release themselves from feeling obligated to reject their intrinsic inclusive instincts. In doing so, they become free to love themselves and others fully. A society that loves and accepts those who are unique is a safer and more welcoming place for people with all types of diversity, including race, ethnicity, religion, and ability.

---

188. Brownson, *Bible, Gender, Sexuality*, 84.

A non-affirming view might say:

LGBTQ+ Christians should not make their orientation or gender identity the most important thing about themselves. They should place their primary identity in Christ, rather than in their sexual orientation. If they commit themselves to Jesus, they won't need to identify as LGBTQ+ because their sexuality will fade in importance in comparison to loving and serving Christ.

An affirming view might say:

All Christians should consider their identity in Christ to be their primary identity, but that does not prevent people from also identifying as LGBTQ+ or straight or cisgender. There is more to each person's identity than being in Christ. People also identify as mothers, fathers, siblings, friends, employees, employers, athletes, musicians, artists, and so on. Straight and cisgender people have the privilege of taking their orientation for granted without declaring it to be their identity because they are assumed to be straight and cisgender unless they indicate otherwise. Straight people who participate in LGBTQ+ groups can feel like they should indicate their straight identity, both to avoid feeling inauthentic, and so as not to seem as though they are posing as an LGBTQ+ person. Allowing people to mistakenly assume one's sexual orientation, whether it be gay or straight, can feel misleading and dishonest.

Acceptance of LGBTQ+ identities can cause confusion for some cisgender/straight people because it challenges their understanding of gender roles which have been influenced by the patriarchal society passed down from biblical times. For example, when different role expectations are held for men than for women, it can be confusing to know what expectations to hold for a transgender or non-binary person. It is the hierarchical, patriarchal system that is the problem, rather than the non-conforming gender identities of LGBTQ+ people. The acceptance of LGBTQ+ people is accompanied by freedom from bondage to hierarchical patriarchy. This freedom ultimately benefits all of society.

A non-affirming view might say:

It is clearly not right to simply accept all forms of sexual activity. Pedophilia and other forms of sexual abuse are examples of sexual activities that can and should be condemned, even if they are in line with a person's innate desires. If same-sex marriage is affirmed, it will lead to an increasing openness to these types of abusive sex. It will start a slide down a slippery slope into accepting all forms of sexual immorality.

An affirming view might say:

Pedophilia and sexual abuse are the behaviors that Paul is condemning in his letters. Recognizing these are the behaviors he condemns enables Christians to hold onto the moral teaching that pedophilia and sexual abuse are sinful while affirming same-sex marriage. The assumption that acceptance of same-sex marriage will lead to an acceptance of sexual abuse is unfair and offensive to LGBTQ+ people. Sexual abuse among straight people is not used to prohibit opposite-sex marriage. Similarly, the existence of same-sex sexual abuse should not be used as the reason to prohibit same-sex marriage.

An alternate view:

Some Christians accommodate, rather than affirm, same-sex marriage. They might say that even though the biblical evidence suggests that same-sex sex is not God's plan, Jesus' command to love takes higher priority over other biblical standards. Loving LGBTQ+ people means supporting their right to be married and to fully participate in church.[189] A precedent for letting the principle of love guide Christians' decision making has been established in the church's response to slavery, women's rights, divorce, and Sabbath keeping. In each of these areas, the church has chosen to follow the principle of love rather than plain biblical teaching.

Patriarchy and Women in Ministry

Background:

The affirmation of women as teachers, pastors, preachers, and leaders in the church is, for some Christians, an example of a disputable matter. Christians can disagree about this issue while still acknowledging each other as Christians. In a similar way, some Christians believe the affirmation of same-sex marriages by the church is a disputable matter.

Because of this similarity, churches might find it helpful to consider Christians' responses to the question of whether or not to endorse women in ministry when considering how to respond to the

---

189. Loader, "Homosexuality and the Bible," in *Two Views on Homosexuality, the Bible, and the Church*, 45-46.

question of same-sex marriage. Just like there are verses in Scripture that clearly seem to prohibit same-sex sex, there are verses in Scripture that clearly seem to prohibit women from preaching, teaching or leading men.

In 1 Timothy 2:12, Paul writes, "I do not permit a woman to teach or to assume authority over a man; she must be quiet." In 1 Corinthians 14:34-35, he writes, "Women should remain silent in the churches. They are not allowed to speak, but must be in submission, as the law says. If they want to inquire about something, they should ask their own husbands at home; for it is disgraceful for a woman to speak in the church." Many churches interpret these verses as applying universally to all churches for all time and thus place restrictions on women's involvement in ministry. However, it should be noted that most of those churches do not typically require women to refrain entirely from speaking the church, and some allow them to preach or teach when they do so under submission to a male authority, so they don't follow Paul's teaching strictly to the letter. Many women who participate in churches that do not affirm them have experienced a diminished sense of self-worth, self-esteem, and self-confidence. These psychological effects, combined with the lack of opportunities to develop leadership skills, impact women beyond the sphere of the church, affecting their employment, leisure, and family life.

A view that does not affirm women in ministry, mutual submission marriage, or same-sex marriage might say:

In Ephesians 5:22-24, Paul says, "Wives, submit yourselves to your own husbands as you do to the Lord. For the husband is the head of the wife as Christ is the head of the church, his body, of which he is the Savior. Now as the church submits to Christ, so also wives should submit to their husbands in everything."

Paul compares the marriage relationship between a husband and wife to the relationship between Christ and the church. He confirms that God's plan for marriage includes male leadership. Christians don't have to understand why it is set up this way, but they do need to obey it. A few verses later, in Ephesians 5:31-32, Paul once again compares the relationship between a husband and wife to that of Christ and the church, with the husband representing Christ and the wife representing the church. He says, "For this reason a man will leave his father and mother and be united to his wife, and the two will become one flesh. This is a profound mystery—but I am talking about Christ and the church." The significant hierarchical difference between Christ and the church confirms that "difference" is an important aspect of spouses' relationship to each other, and that the marriage relationship is intended to be patriarchal in nature. Same-sex spouses are too similar to be able to reflect the relationship between Christ and the church, and they can't follow the prescribed pattern for male headship in their relationships.

The verses prohibiting women in leadership and the verses prohibiting same-sex sex should be understood literally and applied broadly. Although women have equal value to men, in keeping with biblical teaching they should not be in leadership over men in churches or in families. Some say they should not be in leadership even in secular areas of life, such as workplaces and other organizations. Churches that support women in leadership are misinterpreting or disobeying the Bible, as are churches which affirm same-sex marriage.

A view that affirms women in ministry and mutual submission marriage might say:

In Ephesians 5, Paul advocates for mutual submission in marriages, which was a shocking idea in his time. Ephesians 5:21 introduces the passage, saying, "Submit to one another out of reverence for Christ." Paul compares husbands to Christ and wives to the church to instruct husbands to love their wives sacrificially, the way Christ loves the church, and to establish that Christ is still the head of the church, even though he is now present in spirit rather than body. His call for wives to be subject to their husbands was one element of the call to mutual submission, not an indication that the patriarchal nature of marriage should endure forever.

Hierarchy is not necessary in relationships, as exemplified by the Trinity. The Father, the Son and the Holy Spirit are all God. They are three persons who are in relationship with each other, equal in authority to each other, and are together one divine entity. Although the Trinity consists of three divine persons and marriage consists of two human people, the Triune sending of the Son serves as a model for a marriage relationship, enabling distinct and separate people to be unified in mutual submission, loving one another and serving one another in a non-hierarchical union.

A view that affirms women in ministry and mutual submission marriage but does not affirm same-sex marriage might say:

In Genesis 3:16, God told Eve that because of her sin, her desire would be for her husband, and he would rule over her. This was the establishment of patriarchy, which is a direct result of the fall. Christians should work towards undoing the effects of sin and the curse of the fall, helping to bring God's kingdom into fuller realization. This involves working towards equality between the sexes and mutual submission in marriage.

The verses that prohibit women in leadership are contextual. They would have made sense within their original, patriarchal culture. Prohibiting women from teaching may have been necessary because uneducated women who were susceptible to being misled were spreading false teaching within their communities. These verses are not applicable outside their original context, as evidenced by Paul's endorsement of specific women in leadership roles elsewhere in his letters (see Rom 16:1-3,7). Such endorsements show that Paul considers his own teaching in 1 Corinthians and 1 Timothy to be only applicable within their specific contexts. Paul's teaching against same-sex sex, on the other hand, is universally relevant because there are no examples of an endorsement of same-sex sex in any of his letters to indicate that those prohibitions were contextual. The New Testament's trajectory of increasing status for women and slaves contrasts with its reinforced prohibition against same-sex sex. Paul's doubling down on the teaching against same-sex sex demonstrates that God did not intend to move towards acceptance of same-sex marriage.[190]

An affirming view might say:

Paul's doubling down and reinforced prohibition against same-sex sex in the New Testament were against the types of same-sex sex that were most commonly occurring, which were extra-marital, lustful, abusive sex that involved a dominant man increasing in status while shaming a boy, servant, slave, or prostitute. Neither Jesus nor Paul would have moved towards increasing acceptance of these types of sex. Jesus' silence about same-sex sex and Paul's condemnation of it do not reveal what they would have said about same-sex marriage.

---

190. William J. Webb, *Slaves, Women & Homosexuals: Exploring the Hermeneutics of Cultural Analysis* (Downers Grove, IL: InterVarsity Press, 2001), 260.

The verses that prohibit same-sex sex are contextual, as are the verses that prohibit women from leadership. They would have made sense within their original, patriarchal culture, partly because of the way equal-status same-sex sex would have challenged the deeply entrenched gender roles for men and women. In a culture with strict, gender-related customs, where gender defined almost all of a person's actions, it would have been unacceptable to subvert gender roles in order to have a same-sex relationship.

In biblical times, gender relations were strictly hierarchical. Women were uneducated and considerably younger than their husbands, which reinforced their inferiority and submissiveness. Women rarely received inheritances, were not allowed to initiate divorce, and were devalued in comparison to men. They were treated as a source of contamination or ritual impurity when menstruating.[191] It would be culturally inappropriate for a man to behave like a woman, or for a woman to behave like a man. In many societies today, same-sex marriage does not violate strict, cultural gender norms the way it would have in biblical times.[192] The prohibitions against same-sex sex, like the prohibitions against women in leadership, are contextual and do not apply to same-sex marriage today.

A non-affirming view might say:

The positive spiritual impact of being involved in a Bible-believing church outweighs the psychological harm that can be caused by having leadership and relational opportunities restricted due to gender or sexual orientation. People receive spiritual blessing as they humbly and obediently submit to God's word. The hope of heaven and the presence of the Holy Spirit experienced within the church are ultimately more valuable than the freedom to pursue desires for marriage or leadership roles. People such as women and LGBTQ+ people who learn to submit to God daily in practical ways, especially when it is difficult, experience rich spiritual blessings as a result of their sacrificial obedience. They have a spiritual advantage over those who are in leadership because leaders risk becoming prideful, which impairs their relationship with God.

An affirming view might say:

LGBTQ+ people should not have to choose between being involved in a Bible-believing church and being free to marry someone

---

191. Brownson, *Bible, Gender, Sexuality*, 58.
192. Ibid., 84.

of the same sex, just like women should not have to choose between being involved in a Bible-believing church and being free to pursue their calling to serve the Lord without gender-based restrictions.

Inclusion of Sexual Minorities

A non-affirming view might say:

Deuteronomy 23:1 says, "no one whose male organ is cut off shall enter the assembly of the Lord." This serves as a prohibition against genital sex-change surgeries for transgender people.

An affirming view might say:

When Deuteronomy was written, the nations neighboring Israel would castrate priests and men who served and protected royal women. Castration was also used as a punishment.[193] The prohibition was meant to prevent Israel from following these practices. These ancient practices related to altering male genitalia were nothing like the gender-affirming surgeries that transgender women may undergo.

Doctors commonly perform surgery to alter the genitalia of babies with DSD, so there is already an acceptance of medical genital alteration. People with DSD who have had genital surgeries and men whose genitals have been altered by disease or accidents are not excluded from Christian worship. Deuteronomy 23:1 should not be used to support a prohibition against gender-affirming surgery for transgender Christians.

A shift towards increased inclusion of barren women and eunuchs (including castrated men) occurred between the Old Testament and the New Testament. Some of the people classified as eunuchs or barren women in biblical times may have had DSD. Eunuchs and barren women were the sexual minorities in biblical times, similar to how LGBTQ+ people are sexual minorities today. Isaiah 56:4-5 offers hope for the inclusion of sexual minorities, when it says, "to the eunuchs who keep my Sabbaths, who choose what pleases me and hold fast to my covenant – to them I will give within my temple and its walls a memorial and a name better than sons and daughters." Women who were unable to bear children were disgraced in Old Testament times.[194] Isaiah prophesied that this would no longer be the case when he wrote to barren women in Isaiah 54:1, saying, "burst

---

193. Tanis, *Trans-gendered*, 65.

194. In Luke 1:25, after Elizabeth miraculously becomes pregnant in her old age, she says the Lord "has taken away my disgrace among the people."

into song, shout for joy, you who were never in labor; because more are the children of the desolate woman than of her who has a husband." In the New Testament, Acts 8:26-40 tells the story of an Ethiopian eunuch being one of the first converts to be baptized into the Christian family of believers, further reinforcing the shift towards the inclusion of those with diverse gender expressions. In both Isaiah and the New Testament, the criteria to be considered worthy to worship God was no longer based on external characteristics, such as gender and sexuality, but rather on the internal quality of faithfulness.[195] This trajectory for increased inclusion of eunuchs and barren women in the Bible indicates that God wants us to accept those with various sexual orientations and gender expressions.

It is helpful to recognize that the arc of both the Old and the New Testaments are bent towards inclusiveness — of women, Gentiles, foreigners, the poor, the oppressed, orphans, widows, the lame, the blind, the leprous, enemies, and sexual minorities (barren women and eunuchs). Naomi and Boaz accepted Ruth as a Moabite woman, even though it was forbidden for Israelites to allow a Moabite into their community or to promote their welfare in any way (Deut 23:4, Neh 13:1-3). Although her marriage to Boaz broke the law, it was blessed by God and ultimately led to King David and, through his descendants, to Jesus (Ruth 4:13-17). Jesus harshly condemned those who excluded others from God's kingdom or put obstacles in the way to hinder them from coming to him (Matt 23:13). Peter received a vision from God telling him "not to call impure anything that God has made clean" (Acts 11:9), and followed as God led him to radical acceptance of the Roman centurion and his household. Like Peter, the church today should be careful not to call anyone impure that God considers to be clean.

A non-affirming view might say:

The biblical trajectory of acceptance for barren women and eunuchs does not equate to acceptance of a form of sex that is prohibited by the Scriptures. Same-sex marriages are prohibited in the Bible for reasons other than their inability to procreate, which was the concern with barren women and eunuchs. Although some eunuchs were passive partners in same-sex sex, not all of them were, so the acceptance of eunuchs into the temple and into the Christian faith does not set a precedent for affirming same-sex marriage.

---

195. Tanis, *Trans-gendered*, 70.

The Gospel

Jesus Christ, who is mysteriously both divine and human, came to the earth as a baby born to a virgin. As an adult, he taught God's will through his word and example. He freed his followers from the penalty and power of sin through his death on the cross. He promised eternal life to his followers and proved his power over death through his resurrection from the dead, following which he ascended to heaven to sit at the Father's side and intercede for his people. He continues to guide and comfort his people through the Holy Spirit.

An affirming view might say:

This gospel message and the invitation to participate in it is a gift that is freely given based on faith, not by works. Ephesians 2:8-9 says, "For it is by grace you have been saved, through faith—and this is not from yourselves, it is the gift of God—not by works, so that no one can boast." Many people who are in same-sex marriages or who have changed their gender identity have strong faith in Jesus, and they have a clear conscience about the way they live their lives. Their salvation is not at stake. There will be forgiveness for Christians who may have made a mistake by affirming same-sex marriages, as there will be for those who may have made a mistake by not affirming same-sex marriages.

The gift of the gospel is one that Christians are responsible for sharing with the world. The non-affirming church's teaching against same-sex marriage does not seem like "good news" to LGBTQ+ people, and some Christians may be hesitant to extend invitations to church in case those they invite are closeted LGBTQ+ people who would end up experiencing hurt rather than hope because of the invitation. They may not want to bring people to church in case the new converts, under the influence of the church, then begin to condemn LGBTQ+ relationships and identities. Many among the younger generation, which is generally more accepting of same-sex marriage, do not to want to join a group where their LGBTQ+ friends are not, or do not feel, fully welcomed. Because of this, church attendance is steadily declining. The church is strengthened when its members feel free to fully love and accept their neighbors. It is strengthened when members feel confident that those they invite to church will hear life-giving and hope-inspiring messages rather than condemnation for something intrinsic to themselves that is outside their control. If the prohibitions against same-sex marriage are mistaken, the church is unnecessarily creating significant obstacles which are preventing people from coming to faith in Jesus.

A non-affirming view might say:

The gospel involves an invitation and a call to holy living. When someone accepts Jesus as their Lord and Savior, they commit to living their lives in obedience to him. He then helps them to eliminate sinful habits and behaviors from their lives. Trying to make the gospel message more appealing by accepting sinful habits and behaviors ends up negatively affecting people's relationship with Jesus and is spiritually damaging to Christians. Revelation 21:27 says this about God's coming kingdom: "Nothing impure will ever enter it, nor will anyone who does what is shameful or deceitful, but only those whose names are written in the Lamb's book of life." Purity requires abstaining from same-sex sex. The gospel offers forgiveness for sin, which brings freedom. When the church claims that sinful behavior is acceptable, it cannot truly offer forgiveness and therefore cannot offer freedom.

Teaching others that same-sex marriage is blessed by God when it is clearly prohibited in the Bible could cause others, especially children, to adopt LGBTQ+ identities and enter into same-sex relationships, which would lead them away from faith in God. Teachers who teach the affirmation of same-sex marriage will ultimately cause suffering to themselves and to their students.

Background:

Matthew 18:6-9 says:

If anyone causes one of these little ones—those who believe in me—to stumble, it would be better for them to have a large millstone hung around their neck and to be drowned in the depths of the sea. Woe to the world because of the things that cause people to stumble! Such things must come, but woe to the person through whom they come! If your hand or your foot causes you to stumble, cut it off and throw it away. It is better for you to enter life maimed or crippled than to have two hands or two feet and be thrown into eternal fire. And if your eye causes you to stumble, gouge it out and throw it away. It is better for you to enter life with one eye than to have two eyes and be thrown into the fire of hell.

The Greek word, *skandalizō*, translated as "to stumble" in Matthew 18:6, also means "to scandalize," which could insinuate sexual wrongdoing.

An affirming view might say:

Rather than warning against causing children to participate in sin, Jesus might have been warning adults not to sexually abuse, or scandalize, children. In his context, this would have amounted to Jesus warning men not to engage in pederasty or sexual exploitation of youth.[196]

Teaching LGBTQ+ children to deny their natural feelings about themselves can alienate them from their family, church, and support system and cause them immeasurable shame and pain which may cause them to "stumble." Doctrine that mistakenly prohibits same-sex marriage is causing many people to stumble in their faith, because their hearts do not agree with the church's teaching. The church should re-examine its doctrine about same-sex marriage to make sure it is not proliferating a misguided teaching that is causing people to stumble in their faith.

Psalm 34:18 says, "The Lord is close to the brokenhearted and saves those who are crushed in spirit." In Luke 4:16-30, Jesus reads from Isaiah 61 and claims to fulfill this Scripture, saying he has been anointed to proclaim good news to the poor and freedom for the prisoners and the oppressed. The people are pleased with his message, until it implies that the Gentiles, or non-Jewish people, will be included in this freedom, at which point they become angry enough to want to kill Jesus. Many LGBTQ+ people have been broken-hearted and crushed in spirit because they have been rejected by the church. Many LGBTQ+ people identify with the poor, oppressed, and imprisoned because society has discriminated against them. If Jesus does want LGBTQ+ people to be included within the church, those who oppose their inclusion are at risk of being like the religious leaders who opposed Jesus' inclusion of Gentiles. Jesus harshly condemned the religious leaders in his day who enforced religious rules that excluded people from the community (Matt 23:13).

A non-affirming view might say:

LGBTQ+ people are included in the invitation to respond to the gospel and to receive salvation through faith in Jesus. After they place their faith in Jesus, he will empower them through the Holy Spirit to be able to live their lives in dedication to him and for his honor. This could involve receiving a change in orientation or gender identity back

---

196. Loader, "Homosexuality and the Bible," in *Two Views on Homosexuality, the Bible, and the Church*, 32.

to straight and cisgender, or it could involve receiving the strength to live a celibate life or as their sex assigned at birth.

An affirming view might say:

Living their lives in dedication to Jesus and for his honor could involve LGBTQ+ people living as their authentic and diverse selves, whom God created them to be, and living in loving relationship with a same-sex spouse, whom God has gifted to them.

Conclusion to Part IV

Proponents of both an affirming view and a non-affirming view find support for their positions related to same-sex marriage and LGBTQ+ identities in an examination of biblical principles.

PART V: PERSONAL REFLECTIONS AND MY CONTINUED STORY

———— ❧ ⟋ ————

Following my study of the verses that address same-sex sex and the biblical principles relating to same-sex sexuality, I was not convinced of a clear answer about whether same-sex marriage and LGBTQ+ identities should be affirmed. I could see that both views had biblical support and could be arrived at by committed Christians who loved Jesus and loved the Bible. This understanding provided welcome relief from the pressure I had felt related to guiding my son. It seemed to me that it was a disputable matter which came down to personal conviction. I came to this conclusion when I was nearing the point of my final interview, prior to being approved for ordination within my denomination, as I was continuing to pray for guidance from the Holy Spirit. One evening, as I was praying for my son (who at that time I understood to be my gay daughter who wanted a partner), I was surprised to find myself praying for him to find a nice girlfriend. When I finished my prayers, it felt like a shift had happened within my heart. I believed that this prayer had come to me from the Holy Spirit rather than from myself, because I was still not ready to pray for that outcome on my own. I would have prayed that his being gay was a phase he would grow out of, if I were authoring my own prayer. I noticed that, in addition to surprise, I had peace about having prayed for him to find a girlfriend. I recognized that praying that prayer and confirming it in my heart afterwards demonstrated that I had become affirming of same-sex marriage.

I imagined myself as the one who was gay and single. I asked myself whether, considering everything I had read and studied, I would remain celibate or seek a spouse. I reflected on how much I valued my husband and our life together and how much being married has shaped me and supported me, and I concluded that, if I were gay and single, I would seek a same-sex spouse.

I considered how my conversation with Jesus might unfold at the end of my time here on earth, when I believe I will meet with him and give an account of my life. I realized that I was much more comfortable with the idea of explaining my reasons for fully affirming and including LGBTQ+ people within the church than I was with the idea of explaining reasons why I might have continued to exclude them. I remembered that this was the same thought process I had gone through when, as a woman, I began preaching and leading in the church. I had realized I would be more comfortable having to explain why I taught others about Jesus's love for them than having to explain the reasons why I might have restricted my ministry involvement.

I held my views tentatively at first, but as time has passed and I have listened to people's stories, read books, watched videos, and continued to pray, I have never once felt a conviction that my affirming view was displeasing to God. Instead, I have felt encouragement from the Holy Spirit to complete this writing project and continue the advocacy work that I have been involved in, working towards full acceptance, inclusion, and affirmation of LGBTQ+ people within their families, their communities, and their churches.

Adopting an affirming position towards same-sex marriage and LGBTQ+ identities has been life-changing. I am beyond grateful for the good fruit that has come into my life and my family because of my change of heart. The most important benefit has been that my son's emotional struggles no longer involve suicidal temptations. His journey towards mental health has not been easy, and some days are still challenging, but much progress has been made. He is finishing up his university education and looking forward to starting his career, and I couldn't be prouder of him. I will always regret that it took time for me to offer my unwavering and unqualified support, and I fear that the burden he bore while waiting for it may always impact him to some degree. But he has that support now, and I think it came just in time. Our relationship is strong now. His faith has persevered, and he has found an inclusive and affirming church where he is able to serve according to his giftings.

I have met some amazing people in Christian affirming circles. They are thoughtful, intelligent, and compassionate people, and it is a privilege to rub shoulders with them. I have come to understand God's love as being even wider and deeper than I had been previously taught to imagine it. I love God more freely and fully, no longer having to wonder or try to justify why God would reject people because of their sexual orientation or gender identity.

My experience with church has been more challenging. Because my husband is a pastor in a denomination that does not affirm same-sex marriage, I continued to attend church for a time, but in order to avoid controversy I refrained from being involved in leadership or extra activities. Many within my local church family were kind and supportive, but I did not feel free to share my whole self within the church, and I kept my distance from the people there. For a time, our denomination seemed willing to engage in conversation about this question, however strong voices prevailed, and the conversation has been shut down, leaving me with little hope that the denomination will take any steps towards more inclusion.

Eventually, I found that my spiritual health was suffering while I continued to attend my local church, in spite of my having no concerns with the preaching, worship, or people. My spiritual health suffered because my thoughts began to be consumed by the fact that, regardless of how wonderful a church service might be, LGBTQ+ people could not be fully included because of church policy and doctrine, which has been set by the denomination and is impossible to change. It got to the point where these thoughts crowded out my thoughts of worship and contemplation of the teaching while I was at church. I have recently stopped attending this church and am searching for an inclusive Christian group that I can join for worship.

As can be imagined, this situation has brought challenges in my relationship with my husband. Doing ministry together had previously brought us closer and given us shared experiences and ample opportunity for conversation. With me stepping back and then stepping out, we have had to make a conscious effort to find other ways to connect and stay close. Finding time and energy for this has been difficult, because his ministry lifestyle is busy, and I have started working full-time. I am blessed because he understands and supports my journey and the work I am doing. I think he can see that our son is healthier because of my advocacy for inclusion, and he is thankful for that. We find it helpful to respect each other's different understanding related to these questions, with neither of us feeling we need to convince the other to adopt our own views. Because we don't see it as a "salvation issue," we have been able to "table the conversation" and not let it dominate our lives. Our challenge has been finding time to be together, but we were able to take a couple of trips together over the past year and have intentionally set aside one night a week for "movie night," so we are figuring out how to navigate this new stage of our relationship. I am concerned that finding times like these may become more difficult when I do connect into a new, inclusive Christian community, but we are committed to each other and to making it work.

There have been challenges and blessings, but I am overwhelmingly thankful for my heart-change. I call it a "heart-change" rather than a "decision," because it didn't feel like a decision that I made. Rather, it felt like my heart changed first, and then, over time, I recognized, then accepted, then finally embraced this change. I am thankful that I have not lost family members because of it. I recognize that some people do and that it can be devastating for them. That recognition has further motivated me to complete this book, in the hope it might help families accept each other more easily, even when hearts and minds differ on these matters.

I share these aspects of my story, in part, to encourage people with the knowledge that, although the stakes can be high, God is present in the experience of questioning and conversing, and there are blessings for those who participate. Although I have made sacrifices, I have also experienced the blessings that come from understanding that my support of LGBTQ+ people to live and love authentically is based on an informed and theologically consistent interpretation of the Bible.

AUTHOR'S NOTE

This overview of the conversation around same-sex marriage and LGBTQ+ identities is intended to inspire readers to continue asking questions and doing research. My goal is to help readers increase awareness of alternate views and become better equipped to make their own informed decisions about whether the Bible prohibits same-sex marriage, and if not, whether the church should affirm same-sex marriage. To avoid pressuring readers to adopt a particular view, I have opted not to include personal stories and anecdotes beyond what I shared in the introduction and in Part V. Instead, I have tried to present information in an impersonal way, aiming for an objective tone that would enable readers with diverse views to engage non-defensively with the material. As a next step, I encourage readers to search out personal stories and testimonies to learn more about how this discussion relates directly to people's personal experiences. As the church processes this question, it is important to remember that real people's lives hang in the balance.

If readers reach the end of this book with an understanding that Christians who hold affirming views and Christians who hold non-affirming views can both arrive at their views out of a passion for God's word and a desire to be obedient to it, if it leads to more amicable conversations amongst Christians who hold different perspectives, and especially if it enables parents to fully accept and support their LGBTQ+ kids, and LGBTQ+ Christians to fully accept themselves, this book will have fulfilled its vision.

SCRIPTURE INDEX

BIBLIOGRAPHY

"A Way Home." *Youth Homelessness in Canada.*. https://awayhome.ca/ youth-homelessness.

Achtemeier, Mark. *The Bible's Yes to Same-Sex Marriage: An Evangelical's Change of Heart.* Louisville, KY: Westminster John Knox Press, 2014.

Baldock, Kathy. *Walking the Bridgeless Canyon: Repairing the Breach Between the Church and the LGBT Community.* Reno, NV: Canyon Walker Press, 2014.

Banister, Jamie A. "Ὁμοίως and the Use of Parallelism in Romans 1:26-27." *Journal of Biblical Literature* 128, no. 3 (2009): 569-90.

Beeching, Vicky. *Undivided: Coming Out, Becoming Whole, and Living Free from Shame.* Broadway, NY: HarperOne, 2018.

Bentz, Leslie. "The Top 10: Facebook 'vomit' button for gays and other Pat Robertson quotes." *CNN.* July 9, 2013. https://www.cnn.com/2013/07/09/us/pat-robertson-facebook-remark/index.html.

Blomberg, Craig. "Marriage, Divorce, Remarriage, and Celibacy: An Exegesis of Matthew 19:3-12." *Trinity Journal* 11 (1990), 161-96.

Brownson, James V. *Bible, Gender, Sexuality: Reframing the Church's Debate on Same-Sex Relationships.* Grand Rapids: Eerdmans, 2013.

Bustos Valeria P., et al. "Regret after Gender-affirmation Surgery: A Systematic Review and Meta-analysis of Prevalence." *Plastic and Reconstricutive Surgery Global Open* 10, no. 4 (2021): 1-12.

Butterfield, Rosaria Champagne. *The Secret Thoughts of an Unlikely Convert: An English Professor's Journey into Christian Faith.* Pittsburgh, PA: Crown & Covenant, 2012.

_____. "Rosaria's Story." https://rosariabutterfield.com/biography.

Capes, David B., Rodney Reeves, and E. Randolph Richards. *Rediscovering Paul: An Introduction to His World, Letters and Theology.* Downers Grove, IL: IVP Academic, 2007.

Canadian Mental Health Association, Ontario. *Lesbian, Gay, Bisexual, Trans & Queer identified People and Mental Health.* https://ontario. cmha.ca/documents/lesbian-gay-bisexual-trans-queer-identified-people-and-mental health.

Carmichael, Calum M. *The Laws of Deuteronomy.* Ithaca, NY: Cornell University Press, 1974.

Childers, Alisa. *Another Gospel? A Lifelong Christian Seeks Truth in Response to Progressive Christianity.* Carol Stream, IL: Tyndale, 2020.

Coderington, Graeme. "The Bible and Same Sex Relationships, Part 8: Male-Bedders – The Meaning Of 'Arsenokoitai.'" *FutureChurchNow* (August 24, 2015). https://www.futurechurch now.com/2015/08/24/the-bible-and-same-sex-relationships-part-8-male-bedders-the-meaning-of-arsenokoitai.

Cook, Beckett and Brett McCracken. "From Gay to Gospel: The Fascinating Story of Beckett Cook." *The Gospel Coalition.* https://www.thegospelcoalition.org/article/gay-gospel-becket-cook.

Cunnington, Brian D. *Open Wide the Gates: An Argument for Welcome, Affirmation, and Inclusion of Gay and Lesbian People in the Local Church.* Eugene, OR: Wipf and Stock, 2023.

Damon, Will and B. R. Simon Rosser. "Anodyspareunia in Men Who Have Sex with Men." *Journal of Sex & Marital Therapy* 31, no. 2 (2005): 129-141.

DeFranza, Megan K. "Journeying from the Bible to Christian Ethics in Search of Common Ground." In *Two Views on Homosexuality, the Bible, and the Church.* Edited by Preston Sprinkle, 69-101. Grand Rapids, MI: Zondervan, 2016.

_____. "Response to Stephen R. Holmes." In *Two Views on Homosexuality, the Bible, and the Church.* Edited by Preston Sprinkle, 200-206. Grand Rapids, MI: Zondervan, 2016.

_____. "Response to William Loader." In *Two Views on Homosexuality, the Bible, and the Church.* Edited by Preston Sprinkle, 49-54. Grand Rapids, MI: Zondervan, 2016.

di Giacomo, Ester, et al. "Estimating the Risk of Attempted Suicide Among Sexual Minority Youths: A Systematic Review and Meta-analysis." *Journal of the American Medical Association Pediatrics* 172, no. 12 (2018): 1145-52.

Everitt, Lauren. "Ten Key Moments in the History of Marriage." *BBC News Magazine.* March 14, 2012. http://bbc.com/news/magazine-1735113.

Francis. "The Married Couple is the Image of God," *Inside the Vatican: Pope Francis' General Audience on the Sacrament of Marriage.* Vatican City, 2014. https://insidethevatican.com/popeswords/married-couple-image-god.

Gagnon, Robert A. *Bible and Homosexual Practice.* Nashville: Abingdon, 2002. Kindle Edition.

Government of Canada. *LGBTQ2 Terminology: Glossary and Common Acronyms*. https://www.canada.ca/en/canadian-heritage/campaigns/free-to-be-me/lgbtq2-glossary.html.

Grant, Jaime M., Lisa A. Moffet, and Justin Tanis. "Injustice at Every Turn: A Report of the National Transgender Discrimination Survey." Washington DC: National Center for Transgender Equality and National Gay and Lesbian Task Force, 2011.

Hartke, Austen. *Transforming: The Bible and the Lives of Transgender Christians*. Louisville, KY: Westminster John Knox Press, 2018.

Hill, Wesley. "Christ, Scripture, and Spiritual Friendship." In *Two Views on Homosexuality, the Bible, and the Church*. Edited by Preston Sprinkle, 124-47. Grand Rapids, MI: Zondervan, 2016.

_____. "Response to William Loader." In *Two Views on Homosexuality, the Bible, and the Church*. Edited by Preston Sprinkle, 55-60. Grand Rapids, MI: Zondervan, 2016.

Holmes, Stephen R. "Listening to the Past and Reflecting on the Present." In *Two Views on Homosexuality, the Bible, and the Church*, ed. Preston Sprinkle, 166-93. Grand Rapids, MI: Zondervan, 2016.

Interact Advocates for Intersex Youth. "FAQ: What is Intersex?" May 18, 2020. https://interactadvocates.org/faq/#howcommon.

Jernigan, Dennis. *DJ's Testimony*. https://www.dennisjernigan.com/djs-story.

Johnson, Greg. *Still Time to Care: What We Can Learn from the Church's Failed Attempt to Cure Homosexuality*. Grand Rapids, MI: Zondervan, 2021.

Johnson, Katherine. "A Biblical Theology of Gender." Leadership Development Curriculum. The Reformation Project, 2023.

Jones, Stanton L. and Mark A. Yarhouse. "Ex Gays? An Extended Longitudinal Study of Attempted Religiously Mediated Change in Sexual Orientation." *Sexual Orientation and Faith Tradition Symposium; APA Convention* (2009), 2-12.

Kaplan-Levenson, Laine. "NPR's Embedded: All the Only Ones." *NPR*. November 2, 2023. https://www.npr.org/series/1212940848/nprs-embedded-all-the-only-ones.

Keen, Karen R. *Scripture, Ethics, and the Possibility of Same-Sex Relationships*. Grand Rapids, MI: Eerdmans, 2018.

_____. "The Streckert Lecture on Christianity, Sexuality, and Gender." Wheaton College. Video, April 5, 2022. https://www.youtube.com/watch?v=KWPx7jJy094.

Kinsey Institute. "The Kinsey Scale." Indiana University, 2019. https://kinseyinstitute.org/research/publications/kinsey-scale.php.

Laumann, Edward, et. al. *The Social Organization of Sexuality: Sexual Practices in the United States*. Chicago: University of Chicago Press, 1994.

Lawlis, Shauna. "Understanding Transgender Healthcare and Wellness: Expert Panel." May 21, 2023. https://us06web.zoom.us/rec/play/VSF_na0AVitswGfXzJVkyuNxzxLAjoHAAcgO7TWVmOli2qQzJa8DCwzvdHSh3Z9MBAnaUTvHdL55K4Yb.pcsVYqj6UW6F4hB1?autoplay=true&startTime=1684709995000.

Lee, Justin. *Torn: Rescuing the Gospel from the Gays-vs-Christians Debate*. New York: Jericho Books, 2012.

Lee, Rita. "Health Care Problems of Lesbian, Gay, Bisexual, and Transgender Patients." *Western Journal of Medicine* 172, no. 6 (June 2000): 403-8.

Loader, William. "Homosexuality and the Bible." In *Two Views on Homosexuality, the Bible, and the Church*. Edited by Preston Sprinkle, 17-48. Grand Rapids, MI: Zondervan, 2016.

Martin, Colby. *Unclobber: Rethinking Our Misuse of the Bible on Homosexuality*. Louisville, KY: Westminster John Knox Press, 2016.

Martin, Dale B. "Arsenokoites and Malakos: Meanings and Consequences." In *Biblical Ethics and Homosexuality: Listening to Scripture*. Edited by Robert L. Brawley, 117-36. Louisville, KY: Westminster John Knox Press, 1996.

Munn, G. Lacoste. "The Historical Scriptural Background of First Corinthians." *Southwestern Journal of Theology* 3 (Fall, 1960). https://preachingsource.com/journal/the-historical-Scriptural Background-of-first-corinthians.

Nissinen, Martti. *Homoeroticism in the Biblical World: A Historical Perspective*. Minneapolis, MN: Augsburg Fortress, 1998.

Oxford, Ed. "Has 'Homosexual' Always Been in the Bible?" *Forge* (March 21, 2019). https://www.forgeonline.org/blog/2019/3/8/ what-about-romans-124-27.

Pearcey, Nancy R. *Love Thy Body: Answering Hard Questions about Life and Sexuality*. Grand Rapids, MI: Baker Books, 2018.

Plato. *Laws*. Translated by Benjamin Jowett, Sue Asscher and David Widger. The Project Gutenberg E book, 2013. https://www.gutenberg.org/ files/1750/1750-h/ 1750-h.htm#link2H_4_0008.

Rice, Linda. "A Heavenly Purpose of Marriage: Image-Bearing," *Biblical Counseling for Women*. https://bc4women.org/a-heavenly-purpose-of-marriage-image-bearing.

Rogers, Eugene F. "An Argument for Gay Marriage." *Religion Online*. https://www.religion-online.org/article/an-argument-for-gay-marriage.

Roggio, Sharon, dir. *1946: The Mistranslation That Shifted Culture*. Minneapolis: Acowsay, 2022. Film.

Rosario, Margaret, Eric W. Schrimshaw, and Joyce Hunter. "Disclosure of Sexual Orientation and Subsequent Substance Use and Abuse Among Lesbian, Gay, and Bisexual Youths: Critical Role of Disclosure Reactions." *Psychology of Addictive Behaviors, 23*(1) (2009): 175–84.

Schauss, Hayyim. "Ancient Jewish Marriage," *My Jewish Learning*. https://myjewishlearning.com/article/ancient-jewish-marriage.

Scheinerman, Rachel. "Gender and Sexuality: The Eight Genders in the Talmud." *My Jewish Learning*. https://www.myjewish learning.com/article/the-eight-genders-in-the-talmud.

Simon, Lianne and Megan DeFranza. "Intersex Christians and the Image of God." Video. https://www.youtube.com/watch?v=331smwhg0gM.

Sklar, Jay. *Leviticus*. Tyndale Old Testament Commentaries. Edited by David G. Firth and Tremper Longman III. Downers Grove, IL: IVP Academic, 2014.

Snaith, N. H. "The Cult of Molech." *Vetus Testamentum* 16, no. 1 (1966): 123-4.

Snyder, Howard A. *Homosexuality and the Church: Guidance for Community Conversation*. Franklin, TN: Seedbed, 2014.

Song, Robert. *Covenant and Calling: Towards a Theology of Same-Sex Relationships*. London: SCM Press, 2014.

Sprinkle, Preston. *A People to be Loved: Why Homosexuality is not just an Issue*. Grand Rapids, MI: Zondervan, 2015.

Tanis, Justin. *Transgendered: Theology, Ministry, and Community of Faith*. Cleveland, OH: The Pilgrim Press, 2003.

The Gender Dysphoria Bible. "But the Chromosomes!!!" https://genderdysphoria.fyi/gdb/chromosomes.

The Reformation Project. "Brief Biblical Case for LGBTQ Inclusion." https://reformationproject.org/case/tradition.

The Trevor Project. "Conversion Therapy & Change Attempts," *National Survey on LGBTQ Youth Mental Health*. 2020.

https://www.thetrevorproject.org/survey2020/?section=Conve
rsion-Therapy-Change-Attempts.

_____. *The Trevor Project Research Brief: Religiosity and Suicidality among LGBTQ Youth*. April 2020. https://www.thetrevorproject.org/ research-briefs/religiosity-and-suicidality-among-lgbtq-youth/Online.

Thurston, Isabella. "The History of Two-Spirit Folks." *The Indigenous Foundation*. June 29, 2022. https://www.theindigenous foundation.org /articles/the-history-of-two-spirit-folks.

Trueman, Carl. *Strange New World: How Thinkers and Activists Redefined Identity and Sparked the Sexual Revolution*. Wheaton, Ill: Crossway, 2022.

VanderWal-Gritter, Wendy. *Generous Spaciousness: Responding to Gay Christians in the Church*. Grand Rapids: Baker, 2014.

Vines, Matthew. *God and the Gay Christian: The Biblical Case in Support of Same-Sex Relationships*. New York: Convergent, 2014.

Webb, William J. *Slaves, Women and Homosexuals: Exploring the Hermeneutics of Cultural Analysis*. Downers Grove, IL: InterVarsity Press, 2001.

Westendorf, Wolfhart, "Homosexualitat," *Lexicon der Agyptologie* 2, no. 1077: 1272-74.

White, Mel. *Stranger at the Gate: To be Gay and Christian in America*. New York, NY: Plume, 1995.

Wilson, Ken. *A Letter to my Congregation: An Evangelical Pastor's Path to Embracing People who are Gay, Lesbian, Bisexual, and Transgender into the Company of Jesus*. Canton, MI: David Crumm Media, 2014.

_____. "First, Do No Harm: Foundation for an LGBTQ-Affirming Theology." Webinar Handout. February 27, 2022.

About the Author

D. Leanne Harris lives in Ontario, Canada. She holds a Master of Divinity and served 3 years as a pastor before starting an online ministry called Clearly Love. Clearly Love was initially intended to serve parents with LGBTQ+ children but is now open to anyone interested in respectfully engaging in conversation about what the Bible does and does not say about same-sex marriage and LGBTQ+ identities. She is a loving wife and proud mother.

www.ingramcontent.com/pod-product-compliance
Lightning Source LLC
Chambersburg PA
CBHW071337090426
42738CB00012B/2925